D0098765

San Diego Christian College
2100 Greenfield Drive
El Cajon, CA 92019

the center cannot hold

my journey through madness my journey
through madness my journey through madness
my journey through madness my journey
through madness my journey through madness

THE CENTER CANNOT HOLD

through madness my journey through madness
my journey through madness my journey
through madness my journey through madness
my journey through madness my journey
through madness my journey through madness
my journey through madness my journey
through madness my journey through madness
my journey through madness my journey
through madness my journey through madness
my journey through madness my journey
through madness my journey through madness

ELYN R. SAKS

NEW YORK

Copyright © 2007 Elyn R. Saks

THE BELL JAR by Sylvia Plath Copyright © 1971
by Harper & Row, Publishers, Inc.

THE BELL JAR by Sylvia Plath reproduced by permission
of Faber and Faber Ltd. as publishers and © The Sylvia Plath Estate.

Library of Congress Cataloging-in-Publication Data has been applied for.

ISBN 978-1-4013-0138-5

Hyperion books are available for special promotions and premiums.
For details contact Michael Rentas, Assistant Director, Inventory Operations,
Hyperion, 77 West 66th Street, 12th floor, New York, New York 10023,
or call 212-456-0133.

Design by Jo Anne Metsch

FIRST EDITION

5   7   9   10   8   6

FOR
WILL AND STEVE

ή γὰρ νοῦ ἐνέργεια ζωή

For the activity of the mind is life

—ARISTOTLE, *The Metaphysics*

the center cannot hold

prologue

IT'S TEN O'CLOCK on a Friday night. I am sitting with my two classmates in the Yale Law School Library. They aren't too happy about being here; it's the weekend, after all—there are plenty of other fun things they could be doing. But I am determined that we hold our small-group meeting. We have a memo assignment; we have to do it, have to finish it, have to produce it, have to . . . Wait a minute. No, *wait*. "Memos are visitations," I announce. "They make certain points. The point is on your head. Have you ever killed anyone?"

My study partners look at me as if they—or I—have been splashed with ice water. "This is a joke, right?" asks one. "What are you talking about, Elyn?" asks the other.

"Oh, the usual. Heaven, and hell. Who's what, what's who. Hey!" I say, leaping out of my chair. "Let's go out on the roof!"

I practically sprint to the nearest large window, climb through it, and step out onto the roof, followed a few moments later by my reluctant partners in crime. "This is the real me!" I announce, my arms waving above my head. "Come to the Florida lemon tree! Come to the Florida sunshine bush! Where they make lemons. Where there are demons. Hey, what's the matter with you guys?"

"You're frightening me," one blurts out. A few uncertain moments later, "I'm going back inside," says the other. They look scared. Have they seen a ghost or something? And hey, wait a minute—they're scrambling back through the window.

"Why are you going back in?" I ask. But they're already inside, and I'm alone. A few minutes later, somewhat reluctantly, I climb back through the window, too.

Once we're all seated around the table again, I carefully stack my textbooks into a small tower, then rearrange my note pages. Then I rearrange them again. I can see the problem, but I can't see its solution. This is very worrisome. "I don't know if you're having the same experience of words jumping around the pages as I am," I say. "I think someone's infiltrated my copies of the cases. We've got to case the joint. I don't believe in joints. But they do hold your body together." I glance up from my papers to see my two colleagues staring at me. "I . . . I have to go," says one. "Me, too," says the other. They seem nervous as they hurriedly pack up their stuff and leave, with a vague promise about catching up with me later and working on the memo then.

I hide in the stacks until well after midnight, sitting on the floor muttering to myself. It grows quiet. The lights are being turned off. Frightened of being locked in, I finally scurry out, ducking through the shadowy library so as not to be seen by any security people. It's dark outside. I don't like the way it feels to walk back to my dorm. And once there, I can't sleep anyway. My head is too full of noise. Too full of lemons, and law memos, and mass murders that I will be responsible for. I have to work. I cannot work. I cannot think.

The next day, I am in a panic, and hurry to Professor M., pleading for an extension. "The memo materials have been infiltrated," I tell him. "They're jumping around. I used to be good at the broad jump, because I'm tall. I fall. People put things in and then say it's my fault. I used to be God, but I got demoted." I begin to sing my little Florida juice jingle, twirling around his office, my arms thrust out like bird wings.

Professor M. looks up at me. I can't decipher what that look on his face means. Is he scared of me, too? Can he be trusted? "I'm concerned about you, Elyn," he says. Is he really? "I have a little work to do here, then perhaps you could come and have dinner with me and my family. Could you do that?"

"Of course!" I say. "I'll just be out here on the roof until you're ready to go!" He watches as I once again clamber out onto a roof. It seems the right place to be. I find several feet of loose telephone wire out there and fashion myself a lovely belt. Then I discover a nice long nail, six inches or so, and slide it into my pocket. You never know when you might need protection.

Of course, dinner at Professor M.'s does not go well. The details are too tedious; suffice it to say that three hours later, I am in the emergency room of the Yale-New Haven Hospital, surrendering my wire belt to a very nice attendant, who claims to admire it. But no, I will not give up my special nail. I put my hand in my pocket, closing my fingers around the nail. "People are trying to kill me," I explain to him. "They've killed me many times today already. Be careful, it might spread to you." He just nods.

When The Doctor comes in, he brings backup—another attendant, this one not so nice, with no interest in cajoling me or allowing me to keep my nail. And once he's pried it from my fingers, I'm done for. Seconds later, The Doctor and his whole team of ER goons swoop down, grab me, lift me high out of the chair, and slam me down on a nearby bed with such force I see stars. Then they bind both my legs and both my arms to the metal bed with thick leather straps.

A sound comes out of me that I've never heard before—half-groan, half-scream, marginally human, and all terror. Then the sound comes out of me again, forced from somewhere deep inside my belly and scraping my throat raw. Moments later, I'm choking and gagging on some kind of bitter liquid that I try to lock my teeth against but cannot. They make me swallow it. They make me.

I've sweated through my share of nightmares, and this is not the first hospital I've been in. But this is the worst ever. Strapped down, unable to move, and doped up, I can feel myself slipping away. I am finally powerless. Oh, look there, on the other side of the door, looking at me through the window—who is that? Is that person real? I am like a bug, impaled on a pin, wriggling helplessly while someone contemplates tearing my head off.

Someone watching me. Some*thing* watching me. It's been waiting for this moment for so many years, taunting me, sending me previews of what will happen. Always before, I've been able to fight back, to push it until it recedes—not totally, but mostly, until it resembles nothing more than a malicious little speck off to the corner of my eye, camped near the edge of my peripheral vision.

But now, with my arms and legs pinioned to a metal bed, my consciousness collapsing into a puddle, and no one paying attention to the alarms I've been trying to raise, there is finally nothing further to be done. *Nothing I can do. There will be raging fires, and hundreds, maybe thousands of people lying dead in the streets. And it will all—all of it—be my fault.*

chapter one

WHEN I WAS a little girl, I woke up almost every morning to a sunny day, a wide clear sky, and the blue green waves of the Atlantic Ocean nearby. This was Miami in the fifties and the early sixties—before Disney World, before the restored Deco fabulousness of South Beach, back when the Cuban "invasion" was still a few hundred frightened people in makeshift boats, not a seismic cultural shift. Mostly, Miami was where chilled New Yorkers fled in the winter, where my East Coast parents had come (separately) after World War II, and where they met on my mother's first day of college at the University of Florida in Gainesville.

Every family has its myths, the talisman stories that weave us one to the other, husband to wife, parents to child, siblings to one another. Ethnicities, favorite foods, the scrapbooks or the wooden trunk in the attic, or that time that Grandmother said that thing, or when Uncle Fred went off to war and came back with . . . For us, my brothers and me, the first story we were told was that my parents fell in love at first sight.

My dad was tall and smart and worked to keep a trim physique. My mother was tall, too, and also smart and pretty, with dark curly hair and an outgoing personality. Soon after they met, my father went off to law school, where he excelled. Their subsequent marriage produced three children: me, my brother Warren a year-and-a-half later, then Kevin three-and-a-half years after that.

We lived in suburban North Miami, in a low-slung house with a fence around it and a yard with a kumquat tree, a mango tree, and red hibiscus. And a whole series of dogs. The first one kept burying our shoes; the second one harassed the neighbors. Finally, with the third, a fat little dachshund named Rudy, we had a keeper; he was still with my parents when I went off to college.

When my brothers and I were growing up, my parents had a weekend policy: Saturday belonged to them (for time spent together, or a night out with their friends, dancing and dining at a local nightclub); Sundays belonged to the kids. We'd often start that day all piled up in their big bed together, snuggling and tickling and laughing. Later in the day, perhaps we'd go to Greynolds Park or the Everglades, or the Miami Zoo, or roller skating. We went to the beach a lot, too; my dad loved sports and taught us all how to play the activity du jour. When I was twelve, we moved to a bigger house, this one with a swimming pool, and we all played together there, too. Sometimes we'd take the power boat out and water-ski, then have lunch on a small island not far from shore.

We mostly watched television in a bunch as well—*The Flintstones, The Jetsons, Leave It to Beaver, Rawhide,* all the other cowboy shows. Ed Sullivan and Disney on Sunday nights. When the *Perry Mason* reruns began, I saw them every day after school, amazed that Perry not only defended people but also managed to solve all the crimes. We watched *Saturday Night Live* together, gathered in the living room, eating Oreos and potato chips until my parents blew the health whistle and switched us to fruit and yogurt and salads.

There was always a lot of music around the house. My dad in particular was a jazz fan, explaining to us that when he was young, claiming a fondness for jazz had been considered fairly rebellious. My record collection overlapped with Warren's—The Beatles, Crosby, Stills & Nash, Janis Joplin. We drew the line at the Monkees (I liked them, he absolutely didn't), and he teased me mercilessly about the poster of Peter Noone from Herman's Hermits up on my bedroom wall.

And there were movies, which my parents attempted to supervise by appropriateness: *Mary Poppins* and *The Sound of Music* were OK for me, but one James Bond movie (I don't remember which one now, except it was Sean Connery) caused a battle royal with my dad: I wasn't yet seventeen, and Bond, with his martinis and his bikini-clad girlfriends, was out of bounds.

For a while in high school, I worked at a candy counter at a local movie house—"Would you also like a Coke with that?"—which meant I saw every movie I wanted to see, and many of them more than once; I think I saw *Billy Jack* more than a couple dozen times. It didn't take long, though, to decide that I didn't like movies that were scary or tension-filled—horror movies were out, and Clint Eastwood's *Play Misty for Me*, with its crazy woman stalker, freaked me out for weeks. When the theater manager was robbed after closing one night, my parents made me quit the job.

I confess to an energetic sibling rivalry with Warren. As the oldest, I did my best to stay ahead of him, working to excel at things a younger brother couldn't yet do. I learned to ride my bike first. Once he was riding one, too, I simply rode mine faster and farther. I water-skied first, and then more furiously than he did. I got good grades and made sure he knew it; he worked just as hard and made the grades, too. Dad was not a praiser (he thought it would invite the evil eye), so he never complimented anyone. But Mom did, and Warren and I competed for her attention.

As for Kevin, there were enough years between us that for a long time I thought of him as *my* child. One of my earliest, clearest memories is when he began to crawl, and how thrilled I was about that, to see him learn to make his way from one place to the other. Not only was he younger than Warren and I, he was intrinsically more sociable, too—easier to get along with and more interested in just hanging around with us rather than competing with us.

As somewhat observant Jews, we went to Temple and observed the High Holy Days. We kids were sent to Hebrew school, and we also made our Bat and Bar Mitzvahs. Although it was never spoken in so many words, I was somehow given to understand that in many places and circumstances, Jewish people were not very popular, and one needed to be both discreet and respectable in order to make one's way in life. We didn't keep kosher (although my father's parents did); another part of the mom-and-dad myth was that in order to impress her future in-laws with how observant she was, my mother—whose family had never kept kosher and didn't really know the rules—had misguidedly ordered lobster on the evening my father introduced his parents to her.

On the face of it, then, our family life was congenial—a Norman Rockwell magazine cover or a gentle fifties sitcom. Indeed, my mother was what today would be called a stay-at-home mom. She was there when we came home from school and always made sure we had a snack—to this day, cold cereal is my comfort food of choice. Our family ate its meals together, and although my mother didn't cook much (a housekeeper did, and in time, my father took it up, and excelled at it), there was always cake in the pantry (albeit store-bought), fresh fruit in the fridge, and clean laundry in our closets.

Under that pleasant surface, however, things were more complex, as family matters inevitably are. Like all parents, mine had their strengths and their weaknesses. They were profoundly close to each other; in fact, they've always enjoyed being with each other more than they like being with anyone else, including, sometimes, their children. In the style of many 1950s couples, they seemed not to exist in any way independent of each other. My mother was always very physically affectionate with my dad in public; he was less so with her, but never dismissive or rude. It was just always clear that he was the boss. For my mother, it was always "Anything you want, dear," just as it had been for her mother. If she'd had any particular professional ambition when she went off to college, I've never known what it was, although she was a central part of a successful antiques business she and my father started together. Still, nothing's changed much in their dynamic in the intervening years. Recently, my mother announced that she'd given up her own political opinions in order to share my father's.

For his part, in spite of a sense of humor that often verged on the bawdy, my father could be quite absolute in his opinions and reactions. There was also a touch of suspiciousness in his interactions with others, particularly when the subject at hand was money. In this, he was just as his own father had been.

My parents were both outspoken in their disgust for religious or racial bigotry. For example, we could swear all we wanted, but the use of racial or ethnic slurs was utterly and always forbidden. As provincial as Miami seemed back in those days (my father often said that it had all the disadvantages of a big city and none of the advantages), the tension between the city's African-Americans and Cuban immigrants, and the riots in 1970 (during which our African-American housekeeper was harassed by the police), taught us that even a familiar landscape could turn violent and unpredictable in the fog of prejudice.

Whatever their faults (or ours), there was no shortage of "I love you's" from my parents when I was a child, nor is there one now; to this day, they're openly affectionate with all of us, and even my friends are greeted with a hug and a kiss. My parents were never cruel or punitive, and never physical in the ways they disciplined us; they simply made it known from our earliest days that they had high expectations for our behavior, and when we missed the bar, they brought us up short.

Nor did we ever want for anything material. My family was solidly in the middle class, and as time went on, our means increased. My father's law practice dealt primarily with real estate, land deals, and some personal/estate planning, all of which expanded as Miami itself did. When I was thirteen, my parents opened a small antiques and collectibles shop a five-minute trip from our house. It, too, thrived, and they began to collect and sell items from Europe, which in time meant two or three trips to France each year and a lot of time spent in New York City as well.

So there were never any concerns about having a nice place to live, or good food to eat, or missing our yearly family vacation. It was expected that we would attend college; it was a given that our parents would pay for it. They were loving, hardworking, comfortably ambitious (for themselves and for their children), and more often than not, kind. To borrow a phrase from the psychological literature, they were "good enough"—and they raised three decent children, no easy feat in that or any age. My brothers grew up into fine men; Warren is a trader on Wall Street, and Kevin is a civil engineer in Miami. Both are accomplished in their professions, with wives and children they love and who love them in return. And my own penchant for hard work and my drive to succeed is traceable directly, I know, to my parents.

In short, they gave me and taught me what I needed to make the most of my talents and strengths. And (although I couldn't have predicted or understood back then how vitally important this would be to my life) they gave me what I needed to survive.

. . .

When I was about eight, I suddenly needed to do things a little differently than my parents would have wished me to do them. I developed, for loss of a better word, a few little quirks. For instance, sometimes I couldn't leave my room unless my shoes were all lined up in my closet. Or beside my bed. Some nights, I couldn't shut off my bedroom light until the books on my shelves were organized just so. Sometimes, when washing my hands, I had to wash them a second time, then a third time. None of this got in the way of whatever it was I was supposed to be doing—I made it to school, I made it to meals, I went out to play. But it all required a certain preparation, a certain . . . precaution. Because it was imperative that I do it. It simply *was*. And it taxed the patience of anybody who was standing outside the bedroom door or the bathroom door waiting for me. "Elyn, come *on*, we're going to be late!" Or "You're going to miss the bus!" Or "You were sent to bed forty minutes ago!"

"I know, I know," I replied, "but I just have to do this one more thing and then everything will all be OK."

Not long after the little quirks became part of my life, they were joined by nights filled with terror, which came in spite of all the precautionary organizing and straightening. Not every night, but often enough to make bedtime something I didn't welcome. The lights would go out and suddenly it was darker in my room then I could bear. It didn't matter (if I could just ignore the sound of my heart thudding) that I could hear my parents' voices down the hallway; it didn't help to remember that my dad was big and strong and brave and fearless. I knew there was someone just outside the window, just waiting for the right moment, when we were all sleeping, with no one left on guard. *Will the man break in? What will he do? Will he kill us all?*

After the first three or four nights of this, I finally drummed up whatever courage I had left and told my mother about it. "I think somebody has been outside my window," I said in a very small and shaky voice. "In the yard. Waiting for you and Daddy to go to sleep at night, so he can come in and get us. Or hurt us. You have to find somebody to make him go away. Do you think we should call a policeman?"

The expression on her face was so kind that it made it hard for me to look directly into her eyes. "Oh, buby"—her term of endearment for me—"there's nobody out there, there's nobody in the bushes. There's nobody who would hurt us. It's in your imagination. Hmmmm, maybe we shouldn't have so many stories before bed. Or maybe we're eating dinner too late, and it's your tummy playing tricks on your brain. Don't be silly now." As far as she was concerned, that was the end of it.

I tried to believe her, I really did. And I fessed up to my fear to my brother Warren when the two of us were at home alone, and we tried our best to reassure each other—together, we'd muster up our courage to go see if someone was indeed standing just outside the front door. And of course, no one ever was. But my feelings didn't go away, and for a long time, falling asleep felt like sliding into a place of helplessness. I fought it every night, my head under the blankets, until finally, sheer exhaustion and a tired growing body just took me under.

I am seven, or eight, standing in the cluttered living room of our comfortable house, looking out at the sunny day.

"Dad, can we go out to the cabana for a swim?"

He snaps at me, "I told you I have work to do, Elyn, and anyway it might rain. How many times do I have to tell you the same thing? Don't you ever listen?"

My heart sinks at the tone of his voice: I've disappointed him.

And then something odd happens. My awareness (of myself, of him, of the room, of the physical reality around and beyond us) instantly grows fuzzy. Or wobbly. I think I am dissolving. I feel—my mind feels—like a sand castle with all the sand sliding away in the receding surf. *What's happening to me? This is scary, please let it be over!* I think maybe if I stand very still and quiet, it will stop.

This experience is much harder, and weirder, to describe than extreme fear or terror. Most people know what it is like to be seriously afraid. If they haven't felt it themselves, they've at least seen a movie, or read a book, or talked to a frightened friend—they can at least imagine it. But explaining what I've come to call "disorganization" is a different challenge altogether. Consciousness gradually loses its coherence. One's center gives way. The center cannot hold. The "me" becomes a haze, and the solid center from which one experiences reality breaks up like a bad radio signal. There is no longer a sturdy vantage point from which to look out, take things in, assess what's happening. No core holds things together, providing the lens through which to see the world, to make judgments and comprehend risk. Random moments of time follow one another. Sights, sounds, thoughts, and feelings don't go together. No organizing principle takes successive moments in time and puts them together in a coherent way from which sense can be made. And it's all taking place in slow motion.

Of course, my dad didn't notice what had happened, since it was all happening inside me. And as frightened as I was at that moment, I intuitively knew this was something I needed to hide from him, and from anyone else as well. That intuition—that there was a secret I had to keep—as well as the other masking skills that I learned to use to manage my disease, came to be central components of my experience of schizophrenia.

One early evening, when I was about ten, everyone else was out of the house for a while, and for some reason I can't recall now, I was there all alone, waiting for them to come home. One minute it was sunset; the next, it was dark outside. Where *was* everybody? They said they'd be back by now . . . Suddenly, I was absolutely sure I heard someone breaking in. Actually, it wasn't so much a sound as a certainty, some kind of awareness. A threat.

It's that man, I said to myself. *He knows there's no grown-ups here, he knows I'm here alone. What should I do? I'll hide in this closet. Must be quiet. Breathe softly, breathe softly.*

I waited in the closet, gripped with fear and surrounded by the dark, until my parents came home. It was probably an hour, but it felt like it went on forever.

"Mom!" I gasped, opening the closet door and making them both jump. "Dad! There's someone inside the house! Did you see him? Are you both OK? Why . . . why were you gone so long?"

They just looked at each other, and then my father shook his head. "There's no one here, Elyn," he said. "Nobody's come into the house. It's your imagination."

But I insisted. "No, no, I heard him. There was someone. Go look, please." Sighing, my father walked through the house. "There's nobody there." It wasn't reassuring so much as it was dismissive. My feelings about imminent danger never stopped, but talking about it to my parents did.

Most children have these same fears, in an empty house or empty room, or even in a familiar bedroom that suddenly looks strange once the lights go out. Most grow out and away from their fears, or manage somehow to put their rational minds between themselves and the bogeyman. But I never could do that. And so, in spite of the spirited competitions I had with my brothers, or my good grades, or the powerful way I felt when I was on water skis or on a bike, I began to shrink a little inside, even as I was growing taller. I was certain people could see how scared I felt, how shy and inadequate. I was certain they were talking about me whenever I came into a room, or after I'd walked out of one.

When I was twelve years old, and painfully self-conscious about the weight that puberty was adding to my frame (and the height that had suddenly come along with it, as I headed toward six feet tall), I purposefully went on a crash diet. By then, my parents had given up bread entirely; they spoke constantly about the need to count calories, the need to maintain an attractive, healthy, and lean body. Being overweight was considered a bad thing—it was unattractive; it indicated that someone was either greedy or lacked self-control. In any case, they monitored very closely every single thing each of us ate.

This was long before it became trendy or matter-of-fact to be as conscious of what we put in our mouths (and where it came from, and what the protein count was, and the carbohydrate count, or where the item fell on the insulin scale) as people are today. And it was also long before much was known about eating disorders; anorexia and bulimia weren't on anybody's radar at the time, and certainly no one we knew went to a doctor or mental health professional for weight gains or losses—or anything else, for that matter. All I knew was I'd gotten fat and I had to get skinny again. And so I set about doing exactly that.

I cut my portions in half. I pushed food around my plate so that it looked like I was eating it. I said no to the potatoes and skipped Sunday breakfast. At school, I skipped lunch. I cut my meat into small pieces, then cut those pieces into even smaller pieces. I eliminated snacks and never ate dessert. The weight started to melt away, and for a while, nobody noticed. By the time someone did, I was five-ten and weighed barely one hundred pounds.

At the dinner table one night, my father cleared his throat in what I knew was an introduction to a serious parental discussion. "Boys, you may be excused to do your homework now," he said, and I glanced at Warren with alarm. What was *this* going to be about? "Your mother and I need to speak with your sister about a private matter." The boys left, but not without giving me that ha-ha-ha-you're-in-for-it-now look that brothers are so good at. I folded my hands in my lap and braced for whatever was coming.

"Elyn," began my mother, "your dad and I are a little concerned with—"

My father cut her off. "You're not eating enough," he said. "You're too thin. You have to start eating more."

"I'm fine," I protested. "I eat what you guys eat. I eat what everybody eats. It's just that I'm growing."

"No, you're not," said my father. "You're getting taller, but you're not growing. Your skin is pasty, you can barely stay awake at the table, you don't eat enough to keep a mouse alive. You look like a war refugee. Unless you're ill—and I'll be happy to send you to a doctor to find out—I must insist that you eat three meals a day. Because if you're not ill, you most certainly will be if this keeps up."

I protested; I argued. I defended my eating habits. "I know what I'm doing, and I feel perfectly fine," I said.

"Your attitude is very disappointing," said my mother. "This defiance, not to mention what's happening to the way you look. You've lost control. This is not what we want for you; in fact, maybe that's why you're doing this. Is it?"

Various versions of this conversation kept popping up again in the days and weeks that followed. They watched every bite that went into my mouth. They counted every bite that didn't. They woke me up earlier in the morning, made me breakfast, then sat down at the table and watched me attempt to eat it. On weekends, they took me out to lunch, then took me out to dinner. In the face of my stubbornness, they threatened to shorten my curfew and to reduce my movie quota. They would, they said, have to "take certain steps!" They pleaded; they offered bribes. I felt myself wilting under the intense pressure of their combined watchfulness and the constant lectures.

Finally, I'd had enough. "You guys are driving me crazy!" I

protested. "I'm not sick, I'm not going to die, I'm perfectly fine. I know what I'm doing. After all, I lost this weight on my own, I can put it back on if I want to."

My father got a very calculating look on his face. "OK, prove it," he said. "If you think you're so all-powerful, prove it. Put the weight back on."

I was enraged. My father had finally (and deftly) maneuvered me into exactly the position he'd been trying to get me into for weeks: He'd called my bluff. And I had no choice but to comply with what he'd demanded; otherwise, he could say I was out of control, and then he'd be justified in doing whatever (he'd never said precisely what) he felt appropriate.

So I just made up my mind to eat. Which wasn't so horrible, be-cause I'd always liked food anyway, all food, all the time—I just hadn't wanted to be fat. In three months, I was back to my normal weight. "See?" I crowed. "I *told* you I knew what I was doing! I said I could do it, and I did!" It felt like a great triumph—I'd driven myself hard in one direction, and then, once challenged, I drove myself hard in completely the opposite direction. And the whole time, I was in complete control—or so I thought.

I think of that young girl sometimes, that girl I was. Not yet a teenager, she may well have had admirable willpower; she might have been stubborn, or ferocious, or strong, or fearless—or maybe she was just plain ornery. But one thing she did not have was complete con-trol of what was going on inside her. And she was going to have to learn that the hard way.

chapter two

URING THE SUMMER between my sophomore and junior years in high school, I went, along with some other classmates, to Monterrey, Mexico, for an intensive summer-term session in Spanish language and culture at the impressively named Instituto Tecnológico de Estudios Superiores de Monterrey—or as we all quickly came to call it, Monterrey Tec. Although I'd often traveled with my parents, and had been to summer camp alone, I'd never been so far away from home by myself. And this trip was to a college campus, in a foreign country, with relatively little adult supervision.

Part of me was excited about the trip, and the opportunity to be out from under the close monitoring of my parents; another part was apprehensive, even scared. It wasn't the challenge of an accelerated language program; by then, I spoke and read passable Spanish and was genuinely curious about this country that in some long-ago way was connected to the Cubans who had come to Miami. But being in an unfamiliar place, fending for myself, being away from the predictable routine I took a certain comfort in—it made a kind of pit in my stomach.

The pit grew a little smaller as I settled into my dorm room and began to find my way around, but it never entirely dissipated.

There were students at Tec from all over the world, and although the days were filled with intensive classroom work and the occasional field trip—to Mexico City's historic areas, for example—the evenings and weekends were mostly our own. Little by little, we ventured out for meals in little cafes or large, noisy cafeterias. Mornings often began with *café con leche* and maybe a rich pastry layered with dark Mexican chocolate. At night, we deciphered the menus and ordered *tacos de pollo, empanadas,* or *burritos* washed down with tart limeade (or, for a few daring adventurers, with a cold tequila). Afterward, someone might suggest an expedition to a local club, where I mostly stood to the side; as much as I loved music, I always felt awkward on a dance floor, and I didn't like the idea of being watched, especially by people I didn't know.

Sometimes in the early evening, my friends and I would simply walk through the parts of the city we'd been told were "safe" to stroll in, near the main square, or *zócalo.* The girls eyed the Mexican boys; the Mexican boys eyed the girls. There was a lot of flirting and giggling, and every night a few kids stumbled back into the dorm many hours past whatever their curfew might have been at home.

I was one of the only people in my group of high school friends who'd never smoked marijuana. I had strong feelings that smoking was wrong, that one ought not do it, that even trying marijuana could end badly. But then the last remaining nonsmoker in our group besides me tried pot. After many nights of looking on as they lit up, I finally relented.

I watched as a friend took a lit joint from the person next to him, put it in his mouth, and inhaled. "Hold it, hold it, don't exhale yet!" someone instructed. "Wait a couple of seconds. OK, now." And my friend whooshed out a small cloud of smoke. A few seconds passed, then a few seconds more.

"Well?" I asked. "Anything?" I hadn't even tried it and already my chest felt funny; it was as though I were waiting for my friend's head to burst into flames.

"Yeah, something," said my friend. "It's . . . soft. I mean, it burns, but it's kind of soft."

Oh, what the hell, I thought. "Here, give it to me, I want to try."

I'm not sure there's a particularly graceful way to inhale one's first joint. It's on fire, after all, and there's ash, and smoke. And of course it's illegal, so the whole production is vaguely clandestine, even a little nerve-wracking—it's like you're being inducted into some kind of se-cret society, and the tape loop that lists all the dangers of marijuana keeps running through your mind while you're concentrating very hard on trying not to look stupid or, worse, uncool.

The second I brought the joint to my lips, I was dead certain that my parents were going to magically appear on the scene and—do what? *Never mind,* I thought. *It doesn't matter; they're thousands of miles away.* And then I inhaled. And, inevitably, I coughed, too, and my eyes burned and watered. Then I inhaled again, and waited. And yes, rough and soft described it perfectly. And then I heard myself laugh a little. Because mostly, it made me feel like laughing. And with that, the big marijuana question was solved. "It's all OK," I said to my friends. "I'm OK." And then I passed the joint back to the person who'd handed it to me.

Off and on for the next few days, I thought about what I'd done. I didn't *not* enjoy it, but I didn't feel like I needed to rush out and do it again anytime soon. It was OK, but oddly, that's all it was. Mostly, I was glad to have done it.

No, I was much more interested in the boys (for all the good it did me that summer), and in the dark, bittersweet chocolate, and in going days at a time without having to answer to anybody for much of anything. I made some new friends, I got some very good grades, and I saw Mexico, which was beautiful. Experimenting with a couple of joints was nothing more than a blip on an otherwise great summer.

One weekend night, a few months after I'd come home from Mexico and was well into my high school junior year (thinking nervously about SATs and ordering college catalogs), I was out with a group of friends at a drive-in movie theater. We were in someone else's car; I had my driver's license, but since I knew I was a terrible driver (I'd almost hit a cat the first time I drove with my mother), I usually preferred being someone else's passenger.

"I have some mescaline," someone announced abruptly. "Anybody want some?"

One friend giggled; another one piped up with "Yeah, sure, why not?" I just sat there for a minute, looking out through the windshield at whatever the movie was on the big screen in front of me, trying to decide what to do. Trying to decide what I *wanted* to do.

"Yes," I said finally. "I do. I want some."

I washed the little pill down with a swallow of warm Coke. There was a weird kind of silence in the car (except, of course, for the movie sounds coming through the speaker attached to the window). It seemed like we were all holding our breath. Waiting. My stomach turned upside down—from nerves? from the pill? from the prospect of the unknown? Then suddenly, my stomach felt very warm, and the warmth radiated back up into my shoulder blades. I'd been clenching my fists; now, I felt my fingers uncurl, and the palms of my hands fell open on my lap. And then, we all exhaled in a collective *"Ohhhhhhhh, looooook!"*

The images on the big screen were slowly oscillating, like runny watercolor paints. At least that's what *I* saw; everybody was reporting something different. For me, blue green was running into orange pink, yellow was slowly colliding with green and brown, and the skin on the actors' faces had started to look like stretchy Play-Doh. The car windows were all rolled down, and the night air felt liquid on my arms and face, as though I were floating in a warm swimming pool. Outside, swarms of bugs floated dreamily in the shimmery lights.

"I want something to eat!" one friend said urgently. "Let's go get something to eat!" *Hmmm,* I thought. *That seems like a good idea.* Slowly, I got out of the car and headed off in the general direction of the snack bar, my friend walking a few feet ahead of me. Suddenly, I shouted at her, "Watch out! Watch out for that fence!" She jumped a little, looked around, then laughed. "There's no fence there, Elyn— you're seeing things. I am, too, but no fences!"

When we got back to the car, we brought a second metal speaker in, then watched one movie while listening to another. No one had any idea what was actually going on in front of or inside us. It didn't matter. The dissonance was astonishing to watch.

For the rest of the night and well into the next day, I saw bright colors and changing patterns drifting in the air all around me—circles, and strings, and some kind of rubber band–looking things, crystal clear, and very intense, like shards of broken glass. The images, all pulsating, seemed to have a kind of sound to them, as though they were being heard from very far away. *Maybe this is what sound waves look like,* I thought.

At first, I was fascinated, even comfortable, with all these different sensations—everything around and inside me was so beautiful. However, as the hours passed, it all began to change, to darken somehow. Edges, where before there had been only curves. Something impending, and not at all friendly. Soon, I just wanted it gone—I couldn't turn it off, I couldn't turn it down, and it was exhausting me. It was as though there were no room inside my head to see or hear anything else.

By evening, the hallucinations seemed to have run their course and dwindled away to nothing. My parents hadn't noticed anything amiss;

my brothers didn't pay much attention to me by then anyway. Chastened, I promised myself that there'd be no more experimentation with drugs like these. Being in an altered state was no place for me. That was it.

And yet it wasn't. Even after the hallucinations stopped, I couldn't seem to get my body and brain to work right. I'd never had a hangover, but guessed that this was what one felt like. I was sluggish, almost nauseated. I was out of sorts, even a little sad and down, unable to work up much enthusiasm for school, social events, or anything else. After a few days of this, I got scared. Very scared. Had I damaged something inside me? Had something gone wrong with my brain?

And so, with equal parts paranoia and bravado, I decided to tell my parents about my drug use—just the marijuana, though; there was no way I was going to confess to the mescaline. I don't know what I hoped they'd do—reassure me, or calm me down, or maybe get me to a doctor who would prescribe an instant remedy. I just knew I couldn't manage feeling this way, and not being able to pick up a book without getting dizzy looking at the sentences marching across the page. This couldn't last; somebody had to stop it.

It was Thursday afternoon after school. On Friday, the family was supposed to go to the Bahamas for the weekend (the trip from Miami took less than an hour). My father wasn't home yet. I didn't know when he would be, but I decided I couldn't wait.

"Mom," I said, fidgeting a little as I spoke. "I need to tell you something, and you probably won't like it."

She looked appropriately apprehensive. "What's wrong?" she asked.

"I . . . I used some drugs. In Mexico. I smoked some pot. I've used it a few more times since coming home, too. I think it might have made me sick."

Her eyes got very big. "What do you mean, sick? Pot? Marijuana? Oh, dear, Elyn."

"Well, not *sick* sick. Just . . . not right, exactly. Not like I want to throw up or anything like that. Just some weird feelings."

She nodded, a very concerned look on her face. I was surprised that she didn't seem particularly angry. "This is serious," she said, "and very upsetting. We need to talk further about it. But I think we should wait until after we get back from the Bahamas to tell your father. Let's have a nice family weekend, and then we'll face this and discuss it when we all get back."

I was relieved; her plan made sense. We'd go to the beautiful white sand beaches, swim in the beautiful blue ocean, and have a nice relaxing weekend; by the time Monday came, maybe I'd feel so much better that we wouldn't have to tell Dad at all.

But of course, it wasn't going to happen like that. No sooner were we back home from our trip than my mother insisted that we had to have The Talk, and she told my father why.

"Elyn, this is very serious business," said my father with a certain urgency in his voice, the sort of urgency not unknown to come from parents in the 1960s whose children they discovered were using drugs. "Drugs are dangerous, they're nothing to fool around with. You have no idea where something like this could lead. You must promise me that you won't do it again."

By that time, the effects of the hallucinogen had completely worn off. I was no longer scared or uncomfortable; I was sunburned, clear as a bell, and in no mood for a lecture. And so I balked. "No, I won't promise. Everything's fine now, Dad, really. It was just a little pot, no big deal. I can handle myself."

He wasn't buying it. In fact, my attitude—the bravado, the casual dismissal of his concern, the lack of respect in my voice—only added fuel to the fire. "This is not acceptable!" my father said, and now he was angry. "You clearly have no idea what's good for you. If I cannot have your pledge that this will be an end to it, I will have to take steps."

For me, this had uncomfortable echoes of the diet discussion a few years before—the vague threat of "steps" my father was going to take to bend my will to his. And so instead of lying to him, or placating him (or paying any attention to the growing look of horror on my mother's face), I just stiffened my seventeen-year-old spine. "I can do whatever I want, Dad," I said. "My grades are good, I don't cause any trouble around here, and I'm smart enough to know what I'm doing. And if I want to use pot, I will. There's not much you can do about it."

Understandably, all hell broke lose. Dad raised his voice; then Mom raised her voice. Then I raised the stakes, by declaring that I didn't even care anymore about getting good grades, it was all stupid anyway.

This wasn't the sort of response that concerned parents hope to hear from their child during the big drug confrontation, but in retrospect I guess it wasn't atypical of a lot of kids—all bluff and bravado, and no apparent concern for consequences. On the other hand, it's not the kind of stance a girl with any common sense would have taken if she'd truly intended to use drugs and / or wanted to get her parents off her back. Besides, this was the late sixties; marijuana had an almost mythic power to frighten and confuse parents. The culture was imploding on so many other levels, and every magazine and newspaper was running horrifying stories every day about the effects of drug use.

Less than a week later, I was in my parents' car, sullen and nervous in the backseat, my parents tense and silent in the front, all of us headed for an open house at a place called Operation Re-Entry, a drug addiction treatment center in Miami. It was Saturday night, and Don McLean's "American Pie" was playing on the car radio. And I—well, I was on my way to rehab.

. . .

Operation Re-Entry was run by "graduates" of the Synanon program, one of the most notable "no-nonsense, tough-love" approaches to substance addiction in the country. Synanon started in California in the late 1950s, and was renowned for its success rate, although by the late 1970s the original program and its founder, Charles Dederich, had fallen into some disrepute. (Dederich had declared Synanon a religion and had even been charged with a serious crime.) But that didn't have anything to do with me, or with the place I soon learned to call "The Center."

I couldn't quite believe how quickly my world had flipped upside down. There was no bargaining, no wheedling, no reasoning with my parents. The sad truth was, my own defiance had done me in, and the subject was closed—no deals to be made, no recourse. The Center, a nonresidential program, would be my after-school destination for the next two years. I would go there every day at 3, stay until 8, and then go directly home. During the summer, I would be there all day, every day. And that was that.

By any reasonable measure, my parents' response to my confession (or my "stupid little confession," as I began to think of it) was extreme. Certainly, it was a huge stretch to claim that I was a drug addict; besides, I'd already admitted, at least to myself, that I didn't much like the effects of the drugs I'd used. But my parents were scared. And, in the face of my adolescent bravado—my refusal to give up drugs and my profession of countercultural values—they were perhaps right to be scared, and right to look for a remedy. But an actual rehabilitation center? Surrounded by people who'd actually used drugs? What had I done!

Operation Re-Entry's name came from the early days of the space program; the term described the process of a space capsule burning its way through the atmosphere in order to get back down to earth. We were told at that first meeting that most of the staff members were former junkies themselves—they knew every single tactic, every lie or con, that any of us might use to try to get away with anything. And by the time they were done with us, they pledged, we were not only going to be completely drug-free, we would never again do *any-thing* unlawful, not even jaywalk.

You'd think that being yanked out of my comfortable routine and slammed into a rehab center's restrictive regimen would have brought me up short—taught me a lesson or, at the very least, bred some caution into my tendency to resist authority. But no. After only a month in the program, in a group session, I had to confess ("cop to," in Center terminology) that I'd once again tried pot; in the same group, a boy named Matt confessed as well, and we quickly become closest friends (a case of misery loving company, I guess).

Anyone who broke Center rules (and there were *many* rules) was promptly brought up sharp with a "learning experience"—a public punishment specifically designed to humiliate and humble the offender, and edify the others. My punishment, and Matt's, was swift and painful: We each had to wear a sign around the neck that read, "I bite the hand that feeds me. Please help me." Matt also had to have his head completely shaved. Fortunately, girls were spared that indignity; instead, I was given an ugly stocking cap to wear. In those days, and in Miami, it was not a fashion statement.

My mortification wasn't limited to the sign and the ugly hat: I was also sentenced to scrub the Center's stairs—with a toothbrush—while everyone walked around and past me. "You've missed a spot," a staff member would snarl. "Go back to the bottom and start over. This place has to be clean. Every single step. I don't want to see a single speck of dirt when you're through." And, since a key component of this punishment was learning to keep my mouth shut and do what I was told, it was forbidden that I respond to staff in any way—no excuses, no defenses. Down on my hands and knees, hunched over, trying desperately not to be seen, if I could have somehow willed the floor to open up and swallow me, I would have.

Perhaps worse than any of this, I was officially shunned by the other members of my program as part of the punishment. They were told to turn away from me, to speak quietly only to one another, never to me, until such time as the staff instructed them otherwise. I'd always been happy to have friends, happy to be one; now, I was a pariah, an outcast, isolated yet on display at the same time—the sinner locked up in the stocks in the town square. And it would stay like that until the staff was convinced I'd learned my lesson. Then and only then would I have earned the right to be "restored to the community" of the Center.

This hell lasted two weeks, a nausea-producing time of going to "regular" high school during the day, trying to stay focused on my schoolwork, then abruptly changing gears to go to the Center to be humiliated, then going home at night, exhausted and tense and unspeakably angry at what my parents had sentenced me to.

Ultimately, of course, the learning experience did what it was intended to do: I never used illicit drugs again. And the underlying process (which I didn't understand then, but do now) of breaking my spirit and rebuilding it to someone else's specifications had begun.

Although I was back in good standing, I grew somewhat quiet and withdrawn—"in myself," as I came to call it when it had become much more extreme. Unless spoken to, I didn't have much to say; I wasn't sure I even deserved to be heard. I'd started to believe (or, perhaps more correctly, *feel*), that speaking was actually "bad." At one point, after I'd been asked to make a brief presentation and did so, a staff member remarked that I had spoken more in those few minutes than I had in months. Perhaps this was the beginning of my estrangement from the world, the very first inkling of my illness, something I'd never really experienced before, and a habit of mind that would intermittently mark me for the rest of my life.

It was around this time that I read Sylvia Plath's *The Bell Jar*. Even though it was fiction, Plath described the central character's gradual descent into shattering mental illness in a way that could only have come from her own struggles. I identified with it. I identified with her. "I saw myself sitting in the crotch of this fig tree, starving to death, just because I couldn't make up my mind which of the figs I would choose. I wanted each and every one of them, but choosing one meant losing all the rest, and, as I sat there, unable to decide, the figs began to wrinkle and go black, and, one by one, they plopped to the ground at my feet." *That's me,* I thought. *She's me!*

I guess Plath affects a lot of teenage girls this way, depicting as she does the sense of isolation and disengagement (and not a little fear) that typifies this time of life, especially for those who are sensitive and often lost in the world of their books. For days afterward, I couldn't stop thinking about the girl in the novel, and what she went through— for some reason it made me restless, distracted. One morning in class, with Plath on my mind, I suddenly decided that I needed to get up, leave school, and walk home. Home was three miles away.

As I walked along, I began to notice that the colors and shapes of everything around me were becoming very intense. And at some point, I began to realize that the houses I was passing were sending messages to me: *Look closely. You are special. You are especially bad. Look closely and ye shall find. There are many things you must see. See. See.*

I didn't hear these words as literal sounds, as though the houses were talking and I were hearing them; instead, the words just came into my head—they were ideas I was having. Yet I instinctively knew they were not *my* ideas. They belonged to the houses, and the houses had put them in my head.

By the time I walked through my parents' front door—one, maybe two hours later—I was tired, hot, and very frightened. Immediately, I told my mother what had happened on my long walk, and how scary it had been, to have those thoughts from the houses inside my head. Completely unnerved, she promptly called my father at work. He came right home, and after I repeated what had happened, they quickly drove me not to a doctor, but to the Center. I adamantly denied using any drugs, the counselors believed me, and although everyone tiptoed around me for a day or so, soon the incident passed with no further comment.

The Center had become the place around which we had rearranged much of our family life. I was driven there, dropped off, and picked up each day. The parents of all the Center kids met there every two weeks, for group meetings; there were occasional family picnics or other social gatherings. And, in spite of feeling a consistent low-level resentment that my parents had stuck me there until high school graduation, I had settled in and I had come to feel comfortable there.

Most of us figure out, as we grow up, that we will ultimately belong to (or struggle with) two families: the one we're born into and the one we make. For some teens, the beginning of the second family is the football team, or the drama club, or the kids we go to summer camp with every year. Gradually, those may be replaced or supplemented with friends in a college dorm, or our colleagues and friends in our first job. For me, the process of making the second family began at the Center. We all had something in common—committing to live in a world without using drugs, without, in fact, relying on anything artificial or chemical in order to get through our days. We shared a common purpose; we cared intensely about one another's well-being. How we felt, how we were, how we would cope when we moved back out into the world were *the* central topics of conversation: the fight to be strong, the determination to stay clean. Refuse to give in. Fight like hell. Succumbing is never, ever OK.

Although I was easily keeping up with my high school work (in fact, my grades were excellent, and stayed that way), I felt less and less connected to the place where I took those classes, or to the other students. My whole day, figuratively and literally, was aimed at getting to the Center, and being part of that community.

I learned to smoke cigarettes there—if the counselors (who seemed to know so much, and be so worthy of my respect and emulation) smoked, then it was cool for me, too. No one ever talked then about nicotine being a narcotic, or about this being an addiction that was as potentially dangerous as any other. It's just what people did in those days. Very soon, being without a pack of cigarettes made me very uneasy—it would be decades before I could break the habit altogether.

It was also at the Center that I had my first sexual experience.

Jack was twenty-one, I was seventeen. A big age gap, seventeen to twenty-one—that's how long it takes to go all the way through high school, to go all the way through college. Whole, massive developmental leaps happen in those four years. Given my age, the timing was probably right, but there are all kinds of legitimate reasons why the location and the relationship itself were wrong.

There was something about Jack—an addict in recovery who had traveled the world—that was incredibly attractive to a sensitive, moody girl with a vivid imagination. He may well have been seriously impaired by drug use and other life experiences, but that's not what I saw. I saw a good-looking, older, "wiser" man who listened to me and actually seemed to care what I thought. We were in some meetings together, we passed each other in the halls, we had coffee a couple of times, and when he asked me to the movies, it was a no-brainer. Holding hands with him, kissing him, being kissed by him—it was exciting. And since he'd been places I hadn't, and knew things I didn't, when it came time to decide whether or not to go further, I let him take the lead in that as well.

For me at seventeen, it was dizzying, exhilarating, as though we were getting away with something (which, in a way, we were). Still, even with all the excitement of one's "first time," I knew enough to know it was bad sex. My suspicion is that hardly anybody has a good "first time," but the whole production had loomed so large in my psyche that just getting it over with was, frankly, a relief. Just as my head didn't explode when I smoked pot, my heart didn't get broken the first time I had sex, I didn't get pregnant, and I didn't come down with a horrible disease. It could have been much worse.

My time at the Center ended when I graduated from high school, convinced (as are many eighteen-year-olds) that the most exciting part of my life was about to begin. There's no question I was stronger than I might otherwise have been, strengthened by a community that had invested a great deal in me. I'd come to love the people there—the counselors, the other "patients"—and believed they felt the same about me. I was determined never to disappoint them or let them down.

As for the Center's antidrug mission, yes, that was a success, too—but of course, I had never used drugs that much to begin with. What my experience at the Center primarily did was drill into me an unflinching attitude toward illness or weakness: *Fight it.* You can fight it, and you can win. To be weak is to fail; to let down your guard is to surrender; and to give up is to dismiss the power of your own will.

The fundamental flaw in all of this, though, is that it neglects something intrinsic to the complex real world and to complex real human beings. In fact, it is *not* necessarily true that everything can be conquered with willpower. There are forces of nature and circumstance that are beyond our control, let alone our understanding, and to insist on victory in the face of this, to accept nothing less, is just asking for a soul-pummeling. The simple truth is, not every fight can be won.

chapter three

IN SPITE OF the fact that Nashville's Vanderbilt University was a beautiful campus—old ivy-covered brick buildings, wide swaths of green lawn—my freshman-year dorm room was more than a little dilapidated and dingy. My bedroom at home had been peaceful, orderly—the housekeeper kept it clean and neat, and my mom oversaw the arcane details, like pretty curtains at the windows and a bright spread on my bed. But once at Vandy, I was on my own, dismally unprepared to think about how the furniture should be arranged, whether the linens matched, and what was the optimum position for my desk and the lamp upon it. Tall, geeky, and socially uneasy—sporting scruffy jeans most of the time (years before everybody else on this particular campus would wear them) and a nondescript hairstyle—I was suddenly back to square one in terms of fending for myself.

In the early seventies, Vandy was still happily stuck in the 1950s, or maybe even earlier; in fact, it wouldn't be a stretch to say that I'd ended up in the Old South. With rigid social mores, and hard-and-fast roles for men and women, it was a far cry from some of the other schools where I might have gone, places which might have been more welcoming to a nice Jewish girl (albeit one with more than a few moods and quirks). But those schools were in the North, my parents wanted me to stay in the South, and ultimately, Vanderbilt was it.

My very pretty roommate, Susie, was everything I wasn't—a petite, lively brunette with the requisite Southern drawl and charm to spare. She was street-smart, socially adept, and popular from her first day on campus, especially with the boys. When the phone rang, it was always for her. She was nice enough to me, but she was always on her way out, always on her way to someplace else.

One afternoon when I was studying, Susie came into our room and said that she needed to ask my advice about another girl in the dorm.

"Sure," I said, a little flattered that someone who clearly had so much on the ball would want to consult me about anything. "What's up?"

"Well," she said, "this is kind of awkward, actually. There's a girl here in the dorm who, um, kind of smells not very good. A bunch of us were talking about it the other night. We're trying to decide what's the best thing to do."

"Do about what?" I asked.

"About maybe telling her. That she really needs to take a shower once in a while." She wrinkled her little nose. "And shampoo her hair. You know? Nothing fancy or anything. Just—well, I don't know, what do *you* think? Do you think we should just tell her straight out? Might hurt her feelings, maybe. Or should we just leave little hints, or maybe a note? Not a mean one, of course. But something that might help her out."

"My gosh," I said. "That is a tough one. But how nice of you to be so concerned about her. I think you should just straight-out tell her. It's always best to be direct with people, at least in my opinion."

She nodded. "Yes, I guess so. But still, the idea of hurting somebody's feelings . . . Well, anyway, thanks for talking to me about this."

I wondered, afterward, what Susie and her friends decided to do about the unfortunate girl, and what her response to them had been.

But it never occurred to me to ask. And it certainly never occurred to me—then—that the girl in the dorm who needed to take a shower, the one they'd been talking about, was, of course, me.

Even a casual observer will agree that many college freshmen quickly become away-from-home slobs; after all, for the first time in their lives, nobody's after them to hang up their clothes or straighten out their messes. But I'll bet that even as the dirty laundry piles up to the ceiling and dorm rooms start to look like hovels, very few of those kids actually neglect to bathe or shampoo or brush their teeth regularly—because that would almost certainly guarantee an instant end to their social life. What, then, was happening to me? After all, I'd been brought up by attentive parents, in a family with means, plus two brothers who wouldn't have hesitated to tell me, "You stink!" So why was I unlearning the most basic of lessons: simple cleanliness?

Schizophrenia rolls in like a slow fog, becoming imperceptibly thicker as time goes on. At first, the day is bright enough, the sky is clear, the sunlight warms your shoulders. But soon, you notice a haze beginning to gather around you, and the air feels not quite so warm. After a while, the sun is a dim lightbulb behind a heavy cloth. The horizon has vanished into a gray mist, and you feel a thick dampness in your lungs as you stand, cold and wet, in the afternoon dark.

For me (and for many of us), the first evidence of that fog is a gradual deterioration of basic common-sense hygiene—what the mental health community calls "self-care skills" or "activities of daily living." Once away from my parents' watchful eyes, I grew inconsistent about asking myself the taken-for-granted questions. Or maybe I was muddled sometimes about what the right answers to those questions should be. Are showers really necessary? How often do I need to change clothes? Or wash them? Have I eaten anything yet today? Do I really need to sleep every night? Do I have to brush my teeth every day?

Some days, the answers were clear as a bell: Yes, of course. For heaven's sake, Elyn, clean yourself up! And so I did. But other days, the questions and the answers were just too hard to sort out. *I don't know, I don't know.* Or, simply, I just couldn't remember: Did I do that already? Did I do it yesterday? Taking care of myself meant doing more than reading a book or finishing a term paper; it meant strategizing, organizing, keeping track. And some days, there just wasn't enough room in my head to keep all that together. I'd left the Center, I'd left my parents, and everything slowly began to unravel.

Like most college freshmen, I'd gone off to school not entirely clear about what I wanted to major in or what I wanted do with my life. But I'd narrowed it down a little. Something having to do with English, maybe, because of my great love for books and for writing. Or perhaps the legal profession—I could picture myself being a lawyer, arguing passionately for or against something crucially important in a courtroom. Maybe I could even help someone. Maybe I could actually improve someone's life.

Of course, this embroidered fantasy of my bright future and the actual reality of those early days at Vanderbilt could not have been farther apart. Sororities and fraternities were at the center of campus social activities; even in the early seventies, when all kinds of anarchy were springing up at other colleges all over the country, on our sleepy Tennessee campus it was all about young Southern gentlemen and their belles. And while I may have been socially klutzy, I was not stupid—I was about as far from being a Southern belle as a girl could get. Nevertheless, it hurt to find myself so quickly on the outside looking in.

I usually ate my meals by myself in the dining hall, but eventually (weary of feeling like some kind of alien and having people staring at me), I went instead to the Campus Grill, a restaurant across the street from the university library. And there, I actually managed to meet a guy. A nice guy.

Peter was a Ph.D. student in political science. Tall (taller than I, which most guys weren't), he had jet black hair, a warm, easygoing personality, and great intelligence. And he actually liked me. We had conversations, real ones, in which he asked me about books I'd read, writers I admired, and what I thought about things. He was so open and easy to talk to, it wasn't long before he overcame my excessive shyness, and we began dating. We went to the movies, studied together, and had our meals together. Happily, Peter lived in an apartment off campus, and so we began spending our nights together there as well. I'm not sure which I loved more—being with Peter or being out of the dorm and away from Susie, who lived in a world that had little or nothing to do with me.

I don't know why I had an easier time acquiring a boyfriend than I did social friends; one would think my painful lack of social skills would have hobbled me across the board. I certainly wasn't overly sexual, and on the surface of it, I didn't really have much time to invest in a "relationship"—the rules of courtship (at least at that time, and in that particular place) were cumbersome and seemed like a foreign language to me. Besides, I was mostly absorbed in my studies. But in this case, connecting to a man came naturally. It also came as a blessing.

In addition to being a dear friend and intellectual companion, Peter taught me how to enjoy simple intimacy—time spent together not doing much, holding hands, being held, being made to feel special. Peter taught me how to enjoy sexual intimacy, something that would later become difficult for me, even frightening, during the years my illness was in full bloom. He seemed to sense a wariness in me, and he responded with great tenderness and patience.

Often when making love with Peter, I would suddenly get frightened, losing the sense of where I left off and he began. For a woman who's sure of herself, that sense of abandon, boundarylessness, ceding control, is primal and thrilling; in fact, it's at the very heart of the risk lovers take with each other. But for me, "becoming one" with a man

felt like a loss of self, and it was sometimes terrifying, as though something unspeakable lay just on the other side of it, as though I could fall
into an abyss. I wanted so much to experience what I'd read about in
books—love, passion, the kind of deep connection to another person
that would make me willing to take any risk for it. But first, I had to
learn to trust my own body and my own mind. Learning to trust Peter
was a good beginning, and he helped me to do that, but nonetheless,
in those early days, sex could be a terrifying experience.

One winter night at school, I had a guest, the daughter of a friend of
my family. I barely knew Linda, but she was interested in attending
Vanderbilt herself someday, and after her parents had spoken with
mine, courtesy dictated that she stay with me in the dorm.

A slender, very pretty girl, Linda had a drug history and (my parents had told me this) had been compelled to spend some time in a
mental hospital. As willing as I'd originally been to have the company,
her actual presence unsettled me—from the moment she arrived, I
was agitated, on edge. I don't know what ultimately set me off—the
knowledge of what had happened to her, or my own increasingly con-
voluted inner workings—but what happened next came completely
out of nowhere. I suddenly grabbed a blanket from my bed, ran outside, covered my head with the blanket, and then ran around wildly in
the ice and snow, arms stretched out, pretending to fly.

"What are you doing!?" Linda cried out, having followed me outside the dorm. "Stop that, Elyn, you're scaring me!"

Even though I heard her, even though I registered the genuine fear
in her voice, I continued to run, as though powered by some kind of
engine. "No one can get me!" I shouted. "I'm flying! I've escaped!"

Eventually, Linda's plaintive cries moved me to stop; she was genuinely frightened, and even in my odd frenzy, I knew it. Perhaps she
was scared because she recognized in me the kind of behavior she

had seen in the hospital. Or perhaps I was just out of control and might well have scared *anyone* who saw me. In fact, I'd scared myself—I had no idea what had come over me. I had no clue.

Some months later, I was in the dorm with Peter and Susie and once again felt the way I had the night Linda was visiting. Abruptly, I challenged them. "I'll do anything you ask me to!" I yelled. "Ask me *anything*, and I'll do it!"

Laughing at first, they decided to play along. "Sing a song," one of them asked.

I warbled something—a Beatles song, off-key and with all the words in the wrong places. My audience seemed delighted.

"Dance the twist!" they said. I did.

"Come on, ask me to do *anything*," I pleaded. "You want me to take my shirt off?" I did.

Glancing at each other nervously, my friends started to realize something had gone seriously haywire.

"You want me to quack like a duck? I can quack like a duck!" And I did.

"You want me to swallow this whole bottle of aspirin?" And I did.

Suddenly, the way they were looking at me sank in. They were scared to death. And suddenly, so was I—the dangers of what I'd done were staring us all in the face. I ran into the bathroom and quickly made myself vomit, then couldn't stop shaking from fear. Peter took me straight to the Vanderbilt Hospital emergency room, where the doctors thought this had been a suicide attempt.

"No, no," I said weakly, "I was just playing around. It was stupid. I'll be fine, really." They wanted to call a psychiatrist, but I assured them there was no need, that I was perfectly OK. Ultimately, and reluctantly, they allowed us to leave. Shaken and somewhat fragile (and completely mystified at myself), I left the hospital with Peter, both of us wondering what on earth had just happened. We talked about it for days afterward, and then gradually the intensity of the feelings and the experience seemed to fade. When I thought about it at all, it was with confusion and a growing sense of unease: What *was* that?

Each of these incidents was isolated and brief, lasting only an hour or so, and I was able to bring them to a close on my own. They were impulsive, even dangerous. My best guess is that my illness was beginning to poke through the shell (for lack of a better word) that helped me, indeed helps all of us, maintain a separation between what is real and what is not. For the next few years, that's where things would precariously balance—me unwittingly trying to keep the shell strong, and my illness trying equally hard to break through.

At the same time that my mind was starting to betray me, it was also becoming the source of enormous satisfaction. Beyond the narrow and disappointing world of an undergraduate social system that had no place for me, I discovered academia—great ideas, high aspirations, and people (teachers and students alike) whose own intellectual curiosity seemed to give them a real purpose in the world. In particular, I discovered philosophy. I fell in love with it. To my great delight, I found that I was actually good at it, too. My grades were excellent; my classmates sought out my opinion; and my professors welcomed me into their offices, to talk about what I was studying, or to continue conversations begun in class.

Philosophy and psychosis have more in common than many people (philosophers especially) might care to admit. The similarity is not what you might think—that philosophy and psychosis don't have rules, and you're tossed around the universe willy-nilly. On the contrary, each is governed by very strict rules. The trick is to discover what those rules are, and in both cases, that inquiry takes place almost solely inside one's head. And, while the line between creativity and madness can be razor thin (a fact that has been unfortunately romanticized), examining and experiencing the world in a different way can lead to sharp and fruitful insights.

Not only did philosophy give me a surprising joy, it also imposed a structure on both my mind and routine that I'd been unable to provide for myself. The rigor of the material, and the lively give-and-take of the students and faculty in the department, imposed a kind of order upon my days. Suddenly, I had attainable goals, a sense of productivity and purpose, and tangible results against which I could measure my progress. By the second semester of my freshman year, the department allowed me to take courses in the graduate school. I completed that year (and every year thereafter at Vanderbilt) with straight As.

The summer after that first year, I returned to Miami and my family, with a reading list, some work to do for an incomplete course grade, and some assigned research for the following semester. But once away from Vanderbilt, from the community I'd found there and the structure that academic life imposed on me, I began almost immediately to falter. I felt no enthusiasm for a summer vacation, or spending time with family or old high school friends, and in spite of the objective evidence of good grades, I couldn't summon any particular pride in what I'd accomplished. Instead, I felt gloomy, uncertain, and oddly depleted. Working in isolation, either in my room at home or in the quiet coolness of the library, I found I had a hard time concentrating. Nothing I wrote was original or good enough to turn in to my professors. When I woke up in the morning, the thought of muddling through the day filled me with dread. After a few weeks of this misery, I decided to ask my parents if I could talk to someone about it—maybe a therapist, someone who would help me straighten out my mind and put my summer to better use.

I'd never before actually asked my parents for this kind of help (the Center had been *their* idea), and it was a little awkward explaining to them that I just couldn't get my mind to work right. To their credit, however, they didn't get upset, or panic, or tell me to "shape up" on my own. Instead, they took me seriously, and arranged for me to see an acquaintance of theirs, a psychiatrist named Karen. She had a reputation for sending people home after a first meeting with the same one-size-fits-all diagnosis: there was nothing so wrong that a few and probably minor lifestyle changes couldn't fix. In addition, she was rabidly anti-medication. In fact, she was widely perceived as some kind of maverick in her profession. She'd written a book which I found and quickly read.

Even though I'd asked for this kind of help, there was nothing in my short time with Karen that calmed, reassured, or enlightened me; to the contrary, she scared the wits out of me.

"Elyn, I want you to go stand in the corner," she said at our first meeting.

Confused, I looked at the corner and then looked back at her; was I being punished for something? "I . . . I beg your pardon?"

"Yes, yes, go stand in the corner. And then, I want you to focus on the feelings you have inside right now. When you're ready, yell them out. Just yell as loud as you can."

I couldn't imagine what on earth this woman was talking about. Yelling in a corner? There was no way. I didn't know her, she didn't know me. I wasn't even sure that I trusted her; how did I know that she wasn't going to relay every single thing I said and did to my parents?

"Oh, well," I stammered. "I couldn't do that. I'm sorry, but I . . . Can't we just sit and talk about this trouble I'm having, this concentration problem? And maybe you could give me some tips or some ideas about how to get my mind to work the way I need it to?"

Patiently, Karen tried to get me to reconsider, explaining that it was a tactic she'd used before, and it often brought good results. Really, I should try it, just for a minute or two.

"No," I said adamantly. "I can't."

After I returned home from an equally disconcerting second meeting (nevertheless having scheduled a third), I underwent a sort of debriefing with my parents. Was I feeling better? Not particularly. Had she given me any exercises or new routines that might resolve the problems I was having with my schoolwork? No, she hadn't. Did I think she might be of some help soon? I didn't know. Maybe after another meeting or two, we would figure out a way for me to fix things. To fix myself. I could sense my parents' increasing anxiety that there was no clear solution to this problem.

Also, I was uncomfortably aware that this was costing my parents money, and that going further with it would cost them even more. What was the point? Besides, I felt exposed in a way I didn't enjoy— it seemed that the only thing that people wanted to talk about over coffee in the morning and at the dinner table at night was the inner workings of my mind. So I went off to my third appointment with Karen and told her it would be our last meeting.

"And why is that, exactly?" she asked.

"My parents are upset that we haven't figured this out," I said, "and that you haven't come up with some kind of plan. Besides, it costs them too much money for me to see you." I braced myself for her objection, but none came.

"All right, then," she said calmly. "We won't continue. But here's what I think: You do need help. And I just want you to know that when you decide you're ready to get it, you can and should come back to see me."

Nonplussed, I thanked her and quickly left the office. It never occurred to me back then (and if it occurred to Karen, she didn't say so), that I was taking better care of my parents than I was of myself.

At the end of the summer, I left Miami and headed back to Vanderbilt for my sophomore year. I was actually glad to be there, greeted by the few friends I'd made the year before, and once again excited at the prospect of living a life of the mind. I discovered the Saturday and Sunday open hours at the library and dove back into my books. Sadly, the relationship with Peter had come to an end. Nevertheless, I felt confident enough to date other people, more at ease with that aspect of my life than I'd been before.

Because I'd begun to take graduate-level courses, I soon made a number of friends who were graduate students—often older than I by only three or four years. They seemed a better fit, and appeared to accept me for who I was, with all my flaws and quirks. And this is when I came to know Kenny Collins, who had been my freshman English teacher and was studying for his Ph.D. in English literature.

Eight years my senior, Kenny came from a small town in Tennessee with, as he put it, "a population of one hundred eighty-four and shrinking." He was married to his college sweetheart, Margie, who was somewhat more reserved than Kenny, but sweet and welcoming. Together, they presented a picture of the kind of life I tried to imagine for myself someday—two people who obviously cared deeply for each other, an apartment filled with books and music, in a community of intellectual endeavor and excellence. Kenny had a Southerner's manners and gentility (although his Southern accent was barely detectable), but he could be tough and demanding when the situation called for it. He was the kind of teacher who expected much of his students not just because he cared deeply about them, but also because he truly loved and respected what he taught. Hardworking and incredibly smart, he demanded no less of his own scholarly work than he did of his students', and so he spent most of his waking hours in the library, as did I.

True friends help us chart our course in the world, and in my case—with the earliest mixed signals of schizophrenia beginning to fuzz my ability to think clearly—Kenny was like a guide in a forest. If you are walking on a path thick with brambles and rocks, a path that abruptly twists and turns, it's easy to get lost, or tired, or discouraged. You might be tempted to give up entirely. But if a kind and patient person comes along and takes your hand, saying, "I see you're having a hard time— here, follow me, I'll help you find your way," the path becomes manageable, the journey less frightening. For most of my college career, Kenny Collins was that person. He didn't tolerate late papers, so I was compelled to focus and finish on time. When I was stuck, he'd lead me—as opposed to pushing me—into discovering what I wanted to say. As time went on, he became more friend than teacher, often asking to read what I had written for other classes, gently showing me where I'd strayed or suggesting another direction I might go. Occasionally, he even asked me to read his work, and paid me the high compliment of listening to what I had to say and actually valuing it.

Kenny, Margie, and I often hung out together with Pat, another grad student in English, who had a wonderful sense of humor. We spent our days in the library and our weekend evenings either at Kenny and Margie's or at Pat's apartment. We had dinner parties (happily for me, the others all knew how to cook), listened to music, talked about our studies and our friends, and mostly laughed a lot. Beer and wine were easily available, but I quickly decided (as I had with my brief flirtation with drugs) that I didn't like drinking. I didn't like the taste, I didn't like the calories, and I especially didn't like the way it made me feel, either when I was doing it or the next morning. Besides, life at the time seemed much more enjoyable on a clear head.

I'd never been a giggly girl, but something about these people made me feel lighthearted much of the time. And since I thought just about everything Pat said was incredibly funny, it wasn't hard to collapse in a fit of laughing, at which point she'd crack up, too. It began to be a game, in public places, to try to embarrass our dear friend the Southern gentleman. We'd be laughing and giggling, cutting up, being anything but ladylike, while Margie looked mildly embarrassed and Kenny's face turned bright red.

"You've got to stop this now," he'd mutter in a restaurant. "People are staring at us. Elyn, Pat, quit it, this is not acceptable!" The more perturbed he was (or pretended to be), the harder we laughed, stopping only when we'd run out of breath. Being at ease and willfully silly with good friends was a wonderful kind of freedom for me, a rare lack of self-consciousness.

At the beginning of my senior year, Kenny (who by then had completed his graduate work) was offered a fine college teaching position—but not at Vanderbilt. Instead of being happy for him, I was heartbroken. Even worse, I panicked. Pat, too, had finished her graduate studies and was leaving campus. Although I had other friends, although I'd found a niche in the philosophy department, the time I'd spent with Kenny, Margie, and Pat had felt like coming home to me—they'd become like a family, and were often more accepting than my actual family. They certainly knew me better at that point. And now it was all over. How could I stay behind without their friendship, without the laughter, and without Kenny's guidance and wisdom?

Of course, he did his calm and caring best to reassure me, saying that I was more than capable of finishing my undergraduate career successfully, and besides, we'd always stay in touch. Our lives would change, but the friendship would not, and in the meantime, there were telephones, and letters, and vacations when we would visit each other.

In part of my brain, I heard what he was saying and believed it. In another, I started teetering. I was frantic during the day, sleepless during the night. Quickly, my behavior began to resemble that chaotic first year's—I got too loud again, too out-of-control, taking stupid dares, doing stupid things, with my laughter frequently accelerating into hysteria. I noticed, a time or two, people looking at me with alarm. *Let them,* I thought. *I don't care. Everything's going to hell.*

The day Kenny and Margie actually drove away from Vanderbilt, I sobbed for hours, inconsolable. For weeks afterward, I had no energy, no focus; I kept imagining I saw him on campus, just ahead of me in a crowd, or over there under the trees, in the shade. But of course I knew it was a mirage. Life went on, but not easily, and that whole last year in college, I never stopped missing him, never stopped being aware of his absence, and the absence as well of a kind of emotional order he'd brought to my life.

As my own graduation approached, I knew I had to make some decisions. For four years, I'd had a perfect academic record; in fact, I was named class valedictorian. Although I wasn't required to speak at the ceremony, I was to be called up to the podium, introduced, and applauded, which drew a mixed reaction inside me. Proud of being acknowledged for what I'd accomplished, I nevertheless didn't like sticking out, and I especially didn't like the idea of other people looking at me. Plus, I was unnerved by the whole idea of the future (and actually having to plan for it). A future meant change, and uncertainty, and I had never been comfortable with either concept. I felt a constant sense of uneasiness, as though the ground under my feet were about to shift. Something had to come next, but what?

In my philosophy studies, I'd explored the work of Aristotle, and continued to be enthralled by it—two thousand years ago, he was deftly analyzing the human character and discussing the same moral and ethical issues that we debate today. I'd taken sufficient Greek language courses to read Aristotle in the original, and decided that I wanted to do further study on him. So, after consulting with my academic advisors, I decided to apply to Oxford for graduate study. There were two scholarships that could get me there—the Rhodes and the Marshall—but the application process for each was intensely competitive and harrowing.

My interview with the Marshall committee was disastrous. The meeting was held in Atlanta, Georgia, at the British Consulate, in a large and very ornate room. We sat around a table, in old chairs with high backs—there were perhaps ten of us gathered around the table, and the other nine were looking at me. In an unfortunate side effect of my increasing inattention to myself—my periodic lapses of self-care, which always became worse during stress—my ears had become so clogged with wax I could hardly hear a word anyone spoke.

"So, Elyn, tell us, why do you want to go to Oxford?" they began.

I delivered the speech exactly as I'd rehearsed it. "Oxford is probably surpassed by none in its tradition of excellence in ancient philosophy," I said. "I love reading and thinking about Aristotle. That's one reason why I learned ancient Greek—so I could read him in the original. I couldn't get a better education in ancient philosophy than at Oxford. Also, it will be mind-opening to live in a new culture." There, I thought. Every word exactly right. But my head was buzzing with anxiety: *Am I speaking loud enough? Too loud? Did I even hear the question correctly?*

There were long silences between their questions and my responses, then more long silences after I spoke. Our voices seemed to echo. Someone coughed; someone else shifted in a chair, and the chair creaked. Was I boring them?

One question I did hear correctly was an inquiry about what I thought about my physics class. My flippant answer was an indication of my poor situational judgment: "This physics class was a gut!"

One woman on the panel asked me, "Have there been any changes in your life since the women's movement began?" Without pausing to reflect or consider the histories of the women in the room—what they might have gone through to get there, what their struggles might have been like—I quickly replied that no, I didn't notice any changes; indeed, I hadn't ever encountered any discrimination at all. And then, as though I were signing a high school yearbook, I cheerfully wished all the women "good luck in your endeavors!" Another long silence.

Evidently, we were done. There was a polite round of thank-yous and good-byes, and then I made an awkward departure, having no sense whatsoever of what they thought or what my chances were. Hapless. Hopeless. Why on earth would they want to support someone so maladept?

Happily, the interview for the Rhodes proceeded somewhat more successfully, almost as though the Marshall had provided me with a dress rehearsal. The questions were similar; my responses seemed to come more easily. *I sound fine,* I thought. *I sound fine.* However, when asked if I participated in any sports, my judgment quickly went sideways—I quipped that my primary exercise came from lifting sixty cigarettes to my mouth each day. I knew the minute I'd finished the sentence that it was precisely the wrong note—rather like a loud gong at a tea party. The interviewers later wrote that they would have approved me for the next round of interviews except for the total absence of physical recreation in my life.

Fortunately, neither my nicotine habit nor my conversational clumsiness was held against me by the panel deciding on the Marshall. To my great surprise, I was accepted to do a B.Phil., a graduate degree in philosophy. The Marshall scholarship would pay my tuition and give me a stipend, to be paid in pounds—and at that point, the pound was strong. If I planned correctly, I might even have a little left over. In August, I would go to Oxford and become a member of the University's Corpus Christi College.

As proud as I was, it was a measure of my constant tension between wanting to be acknowledged and not wanting to stand out that for the rest of the summer, whenever people thought I was talking about going off to study at Corpus Christi College in Texas, I just let them keep thinking that.

chapter four

AFTER GRADUATING FROM Vanderbilt University in June of 1977, I returned for the summer to Miami and my family.

I was completely distraught on the entire flight back to Miami—grief-stricken about leaving Vanderbilt, terrified of Oxford, and horrified about having to go home. Transitions were always hard for me—I was happiest with a predictable routine that I devised and controlled—but this seemed overwhelming. The Vanderbilt libraries, the Campus Grill, the buildings and sidewalks and trees, the places I'd walked each day, the friends I'd finally made, the schedule that prescribed almost every minute of my day—it all gave a precise order and manageability to my life, and now it was over. And so, as the summer days went by, with Miami simmering in the heat and humidity, and the members of my family coming and going in routines of their own, I began to unravel.

I re-created the regularity of my college life as best I could, by heading for the public library right after coffee in the morning, and spending the day there reading Aristotle and other philosophers;

there were some gaps in my philosophy training, and I needed to get caught up. For lunch, I went to a local drugstore for a grilled cheese sandwich and coffee; for dinner, I usually joined my parents and brothers around the table, and struggled with the bare minimum of social niceties: "How did your day go, fine, how was yours, fine." In the evening, I listened to music in my bedroom, smoked endlessly, and read some more. No one bothered me. The weekend family outings had long since ended; my brothers were living their own lives, my parents were equally involved in theirs. If anyone noticed that in effect I'd taken my leave of them even while being physically present, they said nothing. No one looking at me would have known there was a storm going on inside. But there was a storm, and it was horrible.

With the routine of my academic curriculum gone, however, I began to be regularly invaded by the strangest fantasies, very intense and hard to escape—they weren't exactly hallucinations or waking dreams, but they were extremely vivid and, for me, not entirely distinguishable from reality. They'd come out of the blue, with no warning, and no reason that I could understand. It was as though in the absence of the familiar Vanderbilt routine, the fantasies had come to fill the void, and I couldn't shut them off. Whole hours would go by at night when I was stuck in this alternative universe, struggling to decipher what was going on inside my head. Scenarios came and went of their own accord—it was like being unable to get out of the theater while demented movies ran endlessly through the night. *I have been falsely accused of using drugs and put into a residential drug treatment program. Staff from Operation Re-Entry work there. At the program I spend time with no one. I speak hardly at all. I carry my Aristotle book everywhere. Staff call me in and tell me I must start socializing more. I can't. I am called in again and staff order me to start talking. They say my Aristotle is a crutch and that I must stop carrying it around with me. "No," I cry. "I will not give up my Aristotle!" Staff take my Aristotle away by force. I lose control, tearing the office up in a wild frenzy, shouting at the top of my lungs. Staff restrain me. Several hold me down and they call 911. The ambulance takes me to the emergency room.*

I became convinced that I was not supposed to talk, particularly about myself. I was not supposed to ask for anything, not even so much as a coffee refill at the drugstore counter. Those houses that told me I was bad on that long-ago day—maybe those houses had been right.

And that man I'd believed had been looking in my window at night when I was a girl . . . I began to think that he was back, that I'd just heard something outside . . . Every single night, when the house was quiet and everyone else was long asleep, there came a moment when my heart would begin to race. I'd break into a cold sweat, and my breathing would become shallow and very rapid. I didn't know these events were panic attacks; I only knew my heart was about to burst out of my chest, and it terrified me. *That's it,* I thought: *Something is wrong with my heart.*

When I told my parents, they took me to a cardiologist immediately; he performed a number of tests, none of which indicated any heart problems. The doctor said he thought I was simply anxious, and he advised against tranquilizers, concerned that they'd make it even more difficult for me to concentrate. I wouldn't have taken them anyway—if there was one thing I took away from Operation Re-Entry, it was an absolute determination never to take any drug that altered my mental state. So instead, the doctor prescribed Inderal, a beta blocker which I believed was supposed to quiet my heart (it's also prescribed for panic attacks, anxiety, and nervous tension). I didn't know that the side effects of Inderal could include depression; indeed, I felt both sad and sleepy fairly soon after taking it. But I stopped feeling like I was about to jump out of my skin. The nights grew mostly quiet, and I was able to complete my work.

.   .   .

At the end of the summer, I boarded a plane to Washington, D.C. There I would meet the other Marshall scholars at the British Embassy, and then we would continue on our way to Oxford. I didn't really know how to act in this situation—what *is* the proper behavior before a consul general, anyway? My anxiety began to ratchet up: I had no idea how I was going to manage this, and then Oxford, and my studies.

My mother had helped me find clothes, which was one of my least favorite tasks; there were too many choices, I could never make up my mind, and whenever I tried to picture circumstances in which I would wear these new clothes, the thought alone made me anxious. Mostly, we ordered sweaters and good pants from the L.L.Bean catalog, and bought a couple of suits with blouses for dress-up occasions. I'd need a coat, and a jacket. I'd need shoes that weren't sneakers. Perhaps I'd need an umbrella—I was, after all, going to England. Somehow, having the right kind of things seemed the armor one might need when embarking on graduate studies in England.

The initial meeting-and-greeting in D.C. went past me in some kind of haze. I forgot everyone's name as soon as we were introduced, although I was gratified to see that almost everyone seemed as nervous as I was. Of course there was protocol; to my great relief, I didn't violate any of it, at least as far as I could tell. And then we were off to Oxford.

Despite our common language, it's no secret that England and America are vastly different countries, with perhaps the biggest difference being the fabled British reserve. Many aspects of casual conversation that feel quite natural to Americans are totally off-limits in England, and it didn't take me long to learn that in my new environment. One day, I asked a British friend where he planned to spend his holiday, and he looked quite taken aback. I later learned that such a question should never be asked, because the answer could reveal someone's class background. The sunny, open, Latin-tinged mores of

Miami, combined with the Old South graciousness of Vanderbilt, seemed a world away in the far older and more courtly enclaves of Oxford. For example, cashiers never said, "Y'all come back soon now!" or "Have a good day!" whenever we exchanged money for goods. I often left a shop, food or package tucked under my arm, wondering what I'd done wrong to be dismissed so coolly. Didn't it *matter* to them what kind of a day I had?

The weather turned cool, the sunlight dimmed a little, the days became shorter. Adding to my general disorientation was an educational system vastly different from the one in which I'd done my undergraduate work. Oxford's program consists of optional, university-wide lectures and seminars, plus meeting alone with a tutor or supervisor once a week for an hour or less. Exams come at the end of two or three years. For the weekly tutorial, a student reads a number of articles and then presents a paper, upon which the tutor then comments. I was accustomed to writing two or three long papers over a four-month period, not one short paper a week. I couldn't imagine being able to do it.

I made one new friend from America, a woman named Jean, who was studying in London; we met on a cigarette break in the bathroom at the British Embassy. Tall—as tall as I—and very thin and pretty, Jean had studied to be a nurse until she met her doctor-fiancé, Richard, who encouraged her to go back to school and finish her college degree. She did well, and ultimately won a Marshall Scholarship to study linguistics at University College in London. She was warm and approachable. I liked her, and she seemed to like me, too. But she was in London and I was in Oxford; although we spoke by phone maybe once a week, she was an hour away.

From time to time I got together with another woman in the dorms. She was from Canada, and initially our friendship looked quite promising. But something was happening to me—something that had begun the summer before—that short-circuited our budding friendship: I was finding it difficult to speak. Literally, the words in my head would not come out of my mouth. Our dinner conversations grew increasingly one-sided, and I was reduced almost totally to nodding in agreement, feigning a full mouth and trying to express whatever I was thinking with my face. The friendship trickled away.

And I couldn't speak on the phone with my family or friends in America, either—I'd decided that it cost too much, that it was therefore "forbidden." By whom, I couldn't have said; there just seemed to be some kind of vague but absolute rule against it. Of course, my family would have gladly paid the phone bill, but my distorted judgment told me I did not deserve to spend money on myself, or to have others spend money on me. Besides, nothing I had to say was worth hearing, or so said my mind. *It's wrong to talk. Talking means you have something to say. I have nothing to say. I am nobody, a nothing. Talking takes up space and time. You don't deserve to talk. Keep quiet.* Within weeks after my arrival in Oxford, almost everything I said came out in monosyllables.

As I grew steadily more isolated, I began to mutter and gesticulate to myself while walking down the street, something I had never done on my worst days at Vanderbilt or in Miami the summer before. When I heard the sounds I was making, I felt neither disturbed nor surprised; for some reason, it helped me feel calmer. It seemed to provide an arm's-length distance between me and the people who were walking past me. Oddly, it was soothing, much like clutching a well-worn blanket might have been to a frightened child. And so, with no reference point outside my head (friends, familiarity, being able to accomplish anything at school), I began to live entirely inside it.

And the vivid fantasies had followed me across the ocean. *My doctor finds me huddled in a corner. He wants me to socialize with other people in the program. I don't want to. They force me into a room where there are other people. I am supposed to talk to them. A man introduces himself, "Hi, my name is Jonathan." I do not respond. "What's your name?" Again I do not respond. "Are you a student here?" I mutter something to myself. My doctor comes over and encourages me to talk to this young man. I start screaming and run wildly about the room. Some of the attendants restrain me by force.*

What was real, what was not? I couldn't decipher the difference, and it was exhausting. I could not concentrate on my academic work. I could not understand what I was reading, nor was I able to follow the lectures. And I certainly couldn't write anything intelligible. So I would write something unintelligible, just to have a paper to hand to my tutor each time we met. Understandably, my tutor was flummoxed.

"This is not acceptable, Miss Saks," he said. He was neither angry nor cold, but he was somewhat disbelieving. "Surely you can agree?" he asked. "Because, you see, the work here is hard to make any sense of."

Dumbly, I nodded, sensing the hard wooden chair beneath and around me. I barely squeezed out a couple of syllables. "Yes," I said. "Yes, I know." I just didn't know what to do about it.

Jean, my London friend who'd been a nurse, sensed from our telephone conversations that something was going very wrong. I told her I was just having a hard time doing the required work, but evidently something else I said, or the way that I'd said it, let her know I was struggling with thoughts of wanting to hurt myself. During one phone call, Jean gently suggested that I talk to a doctor about seeing a psychiatrist.

"Oh, no," I said, trying to force some levity into my voice. "I'm not crazy or anything. I'm just kind of . . . stuck." Inside, another dialogue was going on: *I am bad, not mad. Even if I were sick, which I'm not, I don't deserve to get help. I am unworthy.*

A few weeks later Jean's fiancé, Richard, came to town. A neurologist, Richard was somewhat older than Jean and I, and had an air of casual authority. He intrinsically seemed to understand that for some people, it was harder to be a student than to be a professional working in the world. His presence was reassuring, not at all threatening; in fact, his looming height and excess poundage gave him the appearance of a large and generous teddy bear.

"Jean and I are very concerned about you," he said quietly. "We think you may be quite sick. Would you mind if I asked you some questions?"

"I'm not sick," I responded. "I'm just not smart enough. But questions, yes. Ask me questions."

"Are you feeling down?"

"Yes."

"Loss of pleasure in daily activities?"

"Yes."

"Difficulty sleeping?"

"Yes."

"Loss of appetite?"

"Yes."

"How much weight have you lost in the last month?"

"About fifteen pounds."

"Do you feel like a bad person?"

"Yes."

"Tell me about it."

"Nothing to tell. I'm just a piece of shit."

"Are you thinking of hurting yourself?"

I waited a moment before answering. "Yes."

Richard asked still more questions; I answered yes to each one. As dim as I was, it wasn't difficult to see the alarm on his face.

"You need to consult a psychiatrist right away," he said in a measured tone. "You need to be on antidepressant medicine. You're in danger, Elyn." This was serious business, he explained. I couldn't afford to wait.

I thanked Richard and Jean for their concern, and told them I would think about everything they'd said. But I was not persuaded.

Pills? Something chemical to go into my body and muck about with it? No, that would be wrong. That's what I'd been taught at Operation Re-Entry, that's what I believed. My father's voice: *Pull yourself together, Elyn.* There could be no drugs—everything was all up to me. And me wasn't worth much. *I'm not sick. I'm just a bad, defective, stupid, and evil person. Maybe if I'd talk less I wouldn't spread my evil around.*

I needed to present another paper in my weekly seminar, but could not write. A feverish all-nighter produced three or four pages of pure drivel. Gobbledygook. Junk. Nevertheless, I read it aloud. Eyebrows rose. But there was no laughter, only silence. I had thoroughly humiliated myself in front of my Oxford colleagues. *I have come to Oxford and I have failed. I am a bad person. I deserve to die.*

I suddenly knew, as sure as I'd ever known anything in my life, that if I tried to kill myself, I would succeed. Richard's words came back to me, and this time I really heard them: I *was* in danger. This was serious. I could die. And so many others—my parents, my brothers, my friends, the ones I'd allowed myself to actually care for—they would be badly hurt. However much pain I was in, however dimly attractive an ending to this might be—I could not bring that kind of pain to the people I loved and who loved me.

There was no time left to think, or consider, or strategize my way out of this. I called Dr. Johnson, a doctor I'd been assigned as my general practitioner when I first arrived, and urgently requested an appointment for that very day.

Once at Dr. Johnson's office, I said I was feeling depressed. He asked me why, and to my monosyllabic answers he reassured me that I could come and talk to him from time to time, as I felt the need. He'd no doubt seen his share of stressed-out students; perhaps I was simply another.

"I think I need to see a psychiatrist," I said.

"I think I can help you, if you allow me," he said. I hadn't slept in days, or bathed, or changed clothes—even I knew that I looked like hell, why couldn't he? Why wasn't he more alarmed? Couldn't he see? Didn't he know?

Dr. Johnson started to ask the same questions Richard had asked. Was I sad? Had I lost pleasure in usually pleasurable things? How were my sleeping and eating? Even though my answers were as they had been to Richard's questions, Johnson didn't yet seem much concerned. And then he asked if I'd thought about hurting myself.

"Yes," I said.

"Have you actually done anything?"

"Yes." And I showed him a quarter-sized burn on my hand, which had come from deliberately touching an electric heater.

The expression on his face underwent a subtle change. "What about killing yourself?" he asked. "Have you thought about that as well?"

"Yes."

He leaned in closer. "How might you do that?" he asked.

"I have a full bottle of Inderal. A friend said it would kill me," I said. Although I'd stopped taking the drug, I'd never thrown it out. I'd also given some thought to touching the bars of the electric heater in my dorm room and electrocuting myself, I told him. "Or maybe douse myself with gasoline, set myself on fire. That might be best, because I am bad and deserve to suffer." Then I started muttering gibberish, something which I hadn't yet done in front of anyone I knew.

Dr. Johnson asked me to wait outside for a few moments, then called me back into his office to say he had made an appointment for one o'clock that afternoon at the Warneford, the psychiatric division of Oxford's medical school.

"Will you be able to get there?" he asked.

"Yes."

"Will you go?"

"Yes." I was desperate. I held my own life in my hands, and it was suddenly too heavy to be left there.

I called for a taxi from my dormitory telephone. One of the

"scouts" (as Oxford cleaning people were called) overheard me mention the Warneford. I cringed under her squinty gaze. *Yes, yes, you are right, I am a piece of shit, and I am going to the place for bad people.*

When I arrived at the Warneford, I was quickly ushered into a small, windowless room with beige walls. There, a young woman with sandy-colored hair and a hint of freckles introduced herself as Dr. Smythe. She was not at all forbidding or official in her manner, and I tried to calm down sufficiently to pay respectful attention to the questions she was asking. But my head kept jerking in the direction of the door, as though it wanted to lead me and my body out of the room.

Our talk went on for what seemed two or three hours. There were many questions about my childhood, and even more questions about my life right then. I remember thinking she seemed not to like me. At that point, though, I was quite certain no one liked me. *There is nothing about me to like.*

Finally, Dr. Smythe asked me to step out into the waiting room, where I sat nervously for about twenty minutes, wondering what was going to happen next. When she called me back into her office, there were five or six other doctors present, mostly middle-aged to older men. Suddenly, I was frightened, as though I were in the center of a bull's-eye.

Dr. Smythe introduced me to Dr. Russell, the one speaking for the treatment team. As he proceeded to ask questions (much the same as Dr. Smythe had asked earlier), I grew increasingly uncomfortable with his stern demeanor. There was a deliberate tone in his voice—of judgment, of disdain. His language was formal and yet somehow not respectful, as though to say, "I will make the decisions here, and you will do as I say."

Finally, Dr. Russell said, "We'd like you to become a patient in our day hospital."

Terrified (and angry, both at the suggestion and his manner of speaking to me), I refused outright. I wanted help, not incarceration. I looked at the door behind him; it led out. Out.

"It's a day hospital, Miss Saks. You would be able to go home and sleep in your own bed at night."

"No," I said flatly. "I don't belong in a hospital. I'm not crazy. This isn't the right place for me."

He was undeterred. "It is our opinion that you need the support and help of a day hospital." The other doctors were looking at me as though I were a specimen in a jar.

"I'll be fine," I insisted, "as long as I can see a psychiatrist once or twice a week."

"That would not be enough," Russell said firmly. "You really need to come into the day hospital."

"No way!" I said, springing out of my chair and running as fast as I could out of the room, and out of the hospital. I kept waiting to hear the sound of footsteps behind me, their angry voices, someone yelling, "Stop that woman!" But it didn't happen. I'd left them behind.

When I hit the street, I couldn't figure out at first which direction to walk in, and didn't see any phone booths to call a taxi. So I just kept walking. My breath was coming hard and fast, my heart was pounding so hard I was certain passersby could see it.

I walked another nearly two miles to get back to my dorm. Once there, I called Jean and Richard and told them what had happened. Immediately, they insisted that I needed to follow the doctor's recommendation. "No!" I said, and hung up, defiant and scared and completely at a loss for what to do next.

That night was terrible. I lay awake in a pool of sweat, unable to sleep, a mantra running through my head: *I am a piece of shit and I deserve to die. I am a piece of shit and I deserve to die. I am a piece of shit and I deserve to die.* Time stopped. By the middle of the night, I was convinced day would never come again. The thoughts of death were all around me; I realized then that they had begun the summer before, like a small trickle in a creek where I had gone wading. Since then, the water had been steadily rising. Now it was deep and fast and slowly threatening to cover my head.

The next morning, haggard and beaten, I managed to call the hospital and reach Dr. Smythe. "I'm glad you called," she said. "Please, come in as soon as you can."

That lonely night had served its purpose. No one had locked me up against my will. I entered the hospital voluntarily. If I were going to be a mental patient, at least it would be by my choice and no one else's.

chapter five

SET AMONG THE green and gently rolling hills of Oxfordshire, the Warneford Hospital could easily have been mistaken for the sprawling estate of a British country gentleman—as nervous and distracted as I was in the backseat of the taxi that was taking me there, I would not have been surprised to see horses and hounds charging across the lawns in pursuit of a frightened fox.

Built in the early 1800s (and once called the Warneford Lunatic Asylum), the hospital was originally established "for the accommodation of lunatics selected from the higher classes of society." In those days, they used to routinely "bleed" the patients, believing that the bad blood coming to the surface and leaving the body would cool the overheated brain. If it were only that simple.

The day hospital was apart from the main building in an old, tree-shaded house. At first, I expected a program like Operation Re-Entry—intense, confrontational groups and a staff prepared to sniff out and expose any duplicity among the patients. Within an hour of arriving, however, I knew I was in the middle of something very different. The daily routine consisted of a number of activities—group therapy, one-to-one meetings with a psychiatrist, reading plays aloud, board games (mostly Scrabble, which I played but could never win, because I couldn't think straight). But much of our time was spent sitting in a dayroom, furnished somewhat like a living room, where we could talk, smoke, or just stare quietly off into space. But it was not a living room. Anyone would have known in a heartbeat that this was a place for mental patients.

Sitting in one corner was a young man rocking back and forth on the chair, talking gibberish to himself, with a blank stare, hair that hadn't been washed in weeks, and the remnants of his last meal on and around him. I was told he was from an upper-class, wealthy, accomplished family. All of his siblings had gone to Oxford; he'd ended up here instead.

This was the first seriously ill psychiatric patient I'd ever seen. He scared me to death. It was the first time I imagined that I could be *that* sick. *Will I end up like him?*

The days at the Warneford turned into a week, then a second week. I canceled my appointments with my tutor, using what no doubt sounded like completely lame excuses (on the other hand, he was probably quite familiar with the sporadically unpredictable comings and goings of moody graduate students). There was no attendance taken at lectures, so my absence there went unremarked. As for the work itself, I was convinced I would be able to keep up with my reading and somehow catch up . . . After all, this was temporary. This was like a bad cold, or a bout of the flu. Something had gone wrong; it was simply a matter of finding out what that something was and fixing it.

I slept each night in my own bed, tried to read before shutting out the light, then rose the next day and trudged back to the Warneford. It was at this point, I think, that my life truly began to operate as though it were being lived on two trains, their tracks side by side. On

one track, the train held the things of the "real world"—my academic schedule and responsibilities, my books, my connection to my
family (whom so far I'd managed to convince, on a series of blessedly
brief long-distance phone calls, that everything at Oxford was going
just fine, thanks). On the other track: the increasingly confusing and
even frightening inner workings of my mind. The struggle was to
keep the trains parallel on their tracks, and not have them suddenly
and violently collide with each other.

Daily, my thoughts grew more disorganized. I'd start a sentence,
then be unable to remember where I was going with it. I began to
stammer severely, to the point where I could barely finish a thought.
No one could stand to listen to me talk; some of the patients made
fun of me. Disengaged from my surroundings, I sat in the dayroom
for hours at a time, jiggling my legs (I couldn't sit still, no matter how
I tried), not noticing who came in or out, not speaking at all. I was
convinced I was evil. Or maybe I *was* crazy—after all, I was sitting in
a mental hospital, wasn't I? Evil, crazy; evil, crazy. Which was it? Or
was it both?

One by one, each member of the staff tried to talk me into using
antidepressant medication. Their recommendation surprised me. I
thought they would encourage me to take something that would calm
my body or organize my speech. Either way, antianxiety or antidepressant, I was adamant in my refusal. *All mind-altering drugs are bad. I
am weak, I simply need to get stronger, try a little harder, and all will be well.*
Was that the sentient part of my mind speaking, or the fractured
part? I could not tell.

I spent most of one desperate weekend walking alone near the university, in a beautiful place called Christ Church Meadows. But the
beauty of my surroundings made no impact on me at all; for all I
knew I could have been walking in an underground cave. I felt only
desperation, and a profound isolation that every day seemed to bur-
row more deeply into me. What a waste of oxygen it was for me to

draw breath. Suddenly, the solution presented itself: killing myself. There it was again. And it seemed the best option. *I'll douse myself with gasoline and light a match. A fitting end for a person as evil as I.*

When I trudged back to the Warneford and reported to the staff what my weekend stroll had consisted of, they upped the ante. "You need to come into the inpatient unit now, Elyn. You need to come in, and stay in. You're in serious danger if you don't." I didn't need much convincing. Terrified of what I might do if left to my own devices, I went back to my dormitory room, packed up my belongings, and boarded the bus that would deliver me to a mental hospital.

I boarded the wrong bus. Confused about where I was, where I needed to go, and how exactly to get there, I finally arrived at the Warneford several hours late.

I had all the makings of an excellent mental patient.

When I'd first gone to the day hospital, I at least went back to my Oxford dorm at night, and so could continue to tell myself I was a student. Throughout each day, I often felt caught somewhere in between. Was I a mental patient or a student? Where did I really belong, at Oxford or at the Warneford? Should I spend my days in the library or in group therapy? The choice always seemed to be mine.

But the minute I checked into the inpatient unit, the pretense of being a student no longer held: I was a psychiatric patient, in a hospital for the mentally ill. The in-sane. Unlike inpatient units in the States, however, this one had no locked doors. *I can leave anytime I want,* I told myself, trying for reassurance. After all, if I stayed, it was because *I* decided to.

As part of my admission to the inpatient unit, it was necessary for Dr. Smythe to give me a complete physical exam. At first, it was comforting to feel her gentle touch, hear her voice soothing me, telling me everything would be okay. Her entire manner was pure kindness; when was the last time I'd even experienced kindness? When was the last time another human being had even touched me, let alone gently and with the kind of care that might be seen as a kind of affection?

But then my mind abruptly corkscrewed: *I'm vulnerable, I'm open to attack, I'm exposed in front of her and she's going to hurt me.* Once the exam was over, I sat up quickly and covered myself, staring straight ahead as she completed her intake notes. *Only the craziest of the crazies come to a mental hospital. I am lazy. I have not fought hard enough. If I had really tried, I wouldn't need to be here.*

Most patients, including me, slept in a large dormitory, with ten or so beds in a single large room, although there were a few single rooms in each ward. The people I met, and ate with, and was in group with, were not all that different from those I'd met at the day hospital. One of them, a pleasant young woman named Lynn, was a nurse who believed that people were sending her coded messages by the way they parked their cars. She was typically British in appearance—fair skin, fair hair, medium height, a bit plump. She had an approachable manner, and I was so lonely. We became friends.

Lynn and I often took long walks around the Warneford grounds, sometimes talking for hours. One of her favorite topics of conversation was the many meds she was taking. "They're giving me placebos for medication," she said, laughing, "not the real thing!" She then shared with me her amazement and delight that they actually worked! Months later, long after we'd both gone back into the world, I saw her walking around Oxford in a daze, grown obese from the drugs.

Another patient, an older woman back at the Warneford for the second time, relayed the information about her repeat status in a matter-of-fact manner, as if it were not uncommon and might even be a good thing. Simply, she had been "in" last year, left for a while, and now here she was, back again. It gradually dawned me that many other patients were here not for the first time, but for the second, or the third. *No*, I thought. *Not me. This is my first. My last. My only.*

Dr. Smythe, along with the other staff, kept arguing on behalf of antidepressants. I resisted; they kept the pressure on. "What you have is not a fault of will, Elyn," the doctor explained. "It's biochemical. Untreated depressions can last a year or more—do you truly wish to wait that long? The meds will have you feeling better in a few weeks. These are not street drugs, they're a way to get better."

I refused. "People ought to get better because they work at it, not because they take some pill," I said. "Taking pills is cheating." The words of the counselors at Operation Re-Entry rang in my head like a big brass bell: *Take responsibility for yourself.* The idea of putting a pill in my mouth disgusted me. Just as disgusting was the idea that I'd somehow become so weak of character that I needed a drug to get better. "I'm not sick," I protested. "I'm bad."

Then one day something happened that changed my way of thinking—that changed everything.

I looked into a mirror.

It was the first time I'd actually seen myself in weeks. And it felt as if someone had punched me in the stomach. *Holy shit*, I thought. *Who is that?* I was emaciated, and hunched over like someone three or even four times my age. My face was gaunt. My eyes were vacant and full of terror. My hair was wild and filthy, my clothes wrinkled and stained. It was the visage of a crazy person on the long-forgotten back ward of a hospital for lunatics.

I was scared of dying, but even more scared of what I saw in the mirror. The woman looking back at me was in some kind of terrible,

terrible trouble. I vowed that I'd do whatever I needed to do to get her out of this place in any way I possibly could.

The choice seemed clear: drugs or death. I went off immediately to find Dr. Smythe. "OK, yes, I'll take your drugs," I said to her, the words all running together in a panicky, clumsy mess that fortunately she understood. She smiled at me in return.

"Oh, Elyn, I am so glad," she said. "This is best for you, you'll see."

Then she told me that she was going to be out of the country for some time, and that Dr. Edwin Hamilton would be my new doctor. The following day, I met with Dr. Hamilton for the first time. And for the first time I finally took a prescribed psychiatric medication— amitriptyline, an antidepressant. Three times a day, the hospital gong would ring; three times a day, I queued up with the rest of the patients for my pills.

Amitriptyline's most prominent side effect is sedation—immediately, my speech slowed down, my agitation decreased, and the world seemed to be operating in slow motion. And my mouth was always dry and I was constantly dizzy. As uncomfortable as I was (and as annoyed with how slowly my mind seemed to be working), I was determined to finish what I'd started. The good news was that I immediately began sleeping through the night, and I couldn't even remember the last time that had been the case—the summer before?

In our first therapy session after the drug started to kick in, Dr. Hamilton asked me how I felt. I mentioned the side effects, then thought about it for another moment. "Strangely, I feel less angry," I told him.

"That's very interesting," he said. "Indeed."

Not until that moment had I realized how much rage I felt, directed mostly at myself. It was as though I had been carrying a large sandbag on my back, and now some of the sand—just a little, but some—had been let out. And with my load just a bit lighter, maybe another kind of hard work could begin.

I trusted Dr. Hamilton immediately, and he was so easy to like, not to mention easy on the eyes as well. His mother was foreign, so he didn't look or act in a way I'd come to think of as classically British; he seemed more open and approachable than anyone I'd met in Oxford. He effortlessly made jokes; he spoke to me as though we were friends; he seemed to care about me. I looked forward to our appointments, no matter how difficult the conversations were. It was human contact, and I craved that.

While he listened to my negative thoughts and feelings, Dr. Hamilton showed little interest in knowing what they were about; instead, he focused solely on how I might make them go away. Rather than delving into my past or my unconscious, he focused entirely on my present—what we could do to make things better "right now" and how I might begin digging out of my depression. He offered some simple, concrete suggestions, like making written lists and a schedule, to keep me on track and not overwhelmed by what I had to do (and things I kept forgetting to do, like washing my clothes).

His approach meshed well with the daily activity groups I was attending, where I was encouraged to accomplish small things; for instance, coming up with a good word in Scrabble or helping set the table for a meal—simple achievements that I'd always taken for granted before, but which now allowed me to feel some sense of mastery and even pride.

I adored Dr. Hamilton, and I would have done anything to get better *for* him. Freud had picked up on this phenomenon in the early 1900s; he labeled it the "transference cure." Like a schoolgirl with an apple, I was eager to polish up my mental health and give it to my wonderful doctor.

After just a week, I told Dr. Hamilton I wanted to get out of the hospital, soon. And a week after that, I firmly announced that I was officially ready to leave.

"Elyn, are you sure?" he asked. I could hear the skepticism mixed with genuine concern. "There's no shame in being in a hospital while you're being treated for an illness, you know."

Yes, yes, I was sure. "I want to get back to my studies," I said. "But once I leave here, will you continue to see me on an outpatient basis?"

I was grateful when he finally said he'd not only respect my wish to go, but would continue to see me as an outpatient. The rest of the staff, however, was visibly and vocally alarmed. The nursing staff quizzed me about my plans and cautioned me about my expectations for life back in the world. "Don't feel bad if you have to come back," they said. "That sometimes happens." No, not to me it wouldn't.

Just two weeks after arriving, I left the hospital, back to the dorm and my academic work. I told anyone who asked that I'd been on vacation and was eagerly looking forward to the new term. My old tutor had gone on a sabbatical; happily, my new tutor seemed amenable to working more closely with me. In my handbag, I carried Dr. Hamilton's card with the time of our appointment the following week. Everything was going to be just fine.

By my second outpatient appointment with Dr. Hamilton—four weeks after I'd begun taking amitriptyline—it was clear to both of us that the drug was doing what I'd agreed to take it for. I was brighter, less sad. In spite of not having the kind of physical energy I'd have preferred, I did feel more mentally alert, more focused, and the suicidal thoughts had all but faded completely. I started to take pleasure in daily life—food tasted good to me, outside air and even England's rainy weather felt good to me, and, what's more, I could concentrate.

I was thrilled one night to realize that I'd been reading a complicated textbook for three hours and hadn't once had to stop and begin again, to try and unscramble text and meaning and hold my head in my hands and weep from frustration. No, I was *getting* it. Slowly, I began to speak to people in the dormitory and on the campus as I walked here and there. I went to a few college events, and even out to dinner. It was all falling into place again; I got up, I went out, I learned, I spoke with people, they spoke with me. I ate, I worked, I slept. Simple pleasures and goals, all seemingly possible. Despite my "training" at Operation Re-Entry, I was beginning to have second thoughts—could it be that drugs might have something to offer me after all?

Surprisingly, that whole academic term went very well. I did catch up with the required reading, and ultimately wrote seven papers, which impressed my tutor—at the end of that term, he wrote a very positive evaluation for my records. The outpatient sessions with Dr. Hamilton were proceeding nicely as well. I had no trouble accomplishing the simple "homework" assignments he gave me, such as preparing a daily schedule each morning and sticking to it; in the evenings I was reading Aristotle's *Metaphysics* in the original Greek. I was both the mental patient and the student, and was competently balancing both, pacing myself, managing things.

And then, as the term was about to come to an end, I suddenly stumbled. Mysteriously, I had trouble completing the final paper of the semester. I'd read all the assignments, but couldn't come up with anything to say. I made one false start after another, then crumpled the paper and tossed it to the floor. A third sentence, a second paragraph, a fourth page—nothing. I could not connect the dots. A setback that might have been only simple frustration for someone else—a slight case of writer's block, a change of plan that might have meant taking a day or two off, going to a movie, having a beer—made me wild with fear. Am I going backward again? Didn't Dr. Hamilton and I solve this, didn't the amitriptyline fix it? Had it all been some kind of chemical trick? I wanted to hit my head with something hard. The very thought of meeting with my tutor to discuss the paper reduced me to uncontrollable sobs. *I don't have anything to say. I am a failure. It is only a matter of time before people see I am stupid. And crazy.*

The Warneford staff had tried to caution me that I wasn't ready to leave the hospital yet, but I hadn't listened to them—and now, it seemed, all I could do was watch helplessly as once more, everything began to slip out of my grasp. I started to lose weight again; in just a few weeks, I was down to ninety-five pounds. I looked like a torture victim.

Dr. Hamilton, however, did not want to focus on my weight loss. "It's a red herring," he said calmly. "It's not what's really going on with you."

I was disconsolate. "But what's wrong with me, that I can't eat? Is this anorexia? Am I going to die?"

He said anorexia was a grab bag term. "We're not going to focus on symptoms and labels, Elyn. Let's focus instead on you getting your work done. And for now, just eat more, OK?"

His simple-sounding approach to my weight loss didn't help much, but it didn't dampen my feelings for him, either. He was so smart, so sensitive, so kind. *He knows me like no other,* I thought, *and he knows what's best.* I would leave his office temporarily reassured—well, if this is what he thinks, it must be true—but once outside, I'd slam into the wall of the truth: It was all going badly wrong. I started muttering again—*I am a bad person, I deserve to suffer. People are talking about me. Look at them; they're staring at me. They're talking about me.* In all likelihood, that part, at least, wasn't paranoia. Given my appearance, it seems quite likely that people *were* talking about me.

In all this time, I'd never told my parents about my illness or hospitalization. I didn't want them to worry; even more important, I didn't want them to think less of me, that I was somehow a weak or crazy failure. I wanted to fix myself, and not have my problems in any way leak into their lives. But the time for keeping the secret was coming to an end. They'd let me know that they were traveling to Paris—quite naturally, they expected that I would come join them there and we would spend some time together.

In spite of the fact that I was thin as a rail, jumped at my own shadow, refused to speak to virtually anyone, and went around talking to myself, I hoped they wouldn't notice. Indeed, it was a mark of my impaired judgment that I believed I'd actually be able to pull it off. But as soon as we met, the stunned looks on their faces told me I wasn't going to get away with it.

Nevertheless, it was four or five days of phony joie de vivre before my father finally knocked on the door of my room and said he needed to speak with me about something.

"Your mother and I are extremely worried about you," he said. I could hear the intensity in his voice and see the effort he was making to keep his face relatively calm looking. "We've tried to give you a number of chances to tell us what's happened, but you're not saying. We're so worried, Elyn, we're not sleeping at all. Please tell me what's going on."

I took a deep breath and then plunged in. "I'm sorry I didn't tell you," I said. "I got depressed during the year."

Was that relief on his face? It made me wonder what he and my mother had been imagining the past few days. Had they been discussing me each night in their room? "You're so thin," he said. "We were convinced you had cancer."

"No," I said. "Just depression."

"How did they treat you for it?" he asked. "Because you are being treated, aren't you?"

Here it comes. "I was in a mental hospital."

He paused a moment. "Did they give you any medicine or anything? Don't they have medication now for depression?"

"Yes, they do," I told him. "I didn't want to take it, but finally I did, and it has helped."

Yes, there it was—definitely, it was relief I saw. "Let's go and tell your mother."

We walked without speaking to their room.

My mother was sitting on the edge of a chair, clearly waiting for some kind of dire news that would no doubt involve my impending death. When I told her what was actually going on with me (albeit the same shortened, tidier version of the truth that I'd given my dad), she initially flinched at the news, but relaxed when she heard about the medication. It was a problem, there was a solution, and now it was fixed. End of discussion. Each person's privacy and dignity was still reasonably intact. And so, where shall we go for dinner? "Elyn, you simply must eat more."

What transpired among us didn't much comfort or reassure me, but at least my worst fantasies had not come true. They didn't disown me, or tell me I was a failure, or accuse of me being weak by having to take medication. In fact, they were kind, concerned, supportive. But I was such a horrible disappointment to myself. How could I not be a disappointment to them as well?

For the remaining days of our Paris trip, my parents pressed me to eat. Have a bite of this, try a taste of that. And, as pleasantly as I could, I took a tiny taste, faked a little bite, but in truth I continued to resist. *I am bad. Only good people get food. I deserve to starve. I deserve to be tortured. Starvation is a fitting torture for me.*

When I returned to Oxford from Paris, it got worse. I felt compelled to go back to my first tutor, because he was the top person in ancient philosophy at Oxford, and I wanted to study with the best. But it was a complete disaster. His manner was distant, even dismissive; in my view, he had a very low opinion of me. I felt doomed. I could not concentrate. I did not write. I did not sleep, I did not eat. I did not bathe.

I spent more and more time gibbering to myself, restlessly pacing through the streets of Oxford, imagining what people were saying about me. I narrated events to myself as I walked: *Now she's walking down the street. She's ugly. People are looking at her. People are not to be trusted. Be careful. Be vigilant. They will hurt you That man's face just turned into a monster face. Be inconspicuous. Don't let them see you.*

There were fantasies as well.

Dr. Hamilton finds me in my bed, emaciated and confused. I have not been able to get out of bed for weeks. He is gentle and reassures me that he can help. I want to believe he can help me. He helps me get out of bed, but even with his help I can barely walk. I am too weak. I am weak.

Thoughts of suicide came rushing back in, along with intense fantasies of exactly how I'd do it. Throw myself into the river. Set myself on fire. I was particularly drawn to the latter. I was, after all, a witch; being burned at the stake seemed especially fitting. It was only what I deserved.

Meanwhile, I was telling Dr. Hamilton some, but not nearly all, of what was going on inside my head. He'd made it clear he didn't want to delve into my darker self—and since I was still desperately trying to please him, how could I tell him something so ugly? *Please like me; please want to help me. Please don't be disgusted with me.* He constantly urged me to eat more—and then suggested (or maybe went along with my request, I can't remember now which it was) that perhaps the medication needed review. Maybe it was the medicine that was failing me, rather than me failing myself.

I'd barely had time to digest this possibility when he announced that I shouldn't become too dependent upon him, since it was time that we change the schedule of our meetings—to once every *other* week.

I was horrified. I needed more therapy, not less—even in the midst of my worsening state, I knew this was true. I was also baffled; in effect, he'd cut our time together in half. Was this rejection? Was I such a disappointment to him? Finally, Dr. Hamilton explained that he was being rotated. As of the next month, he would be transferring to another unit in the hospital. So the news was even worse than I'd thought: He would no longer be able to treat me at all.

I tried to cling to the logic of his explanation, but it only felt like loss. It was Dr. Hamilton who'd led me out of the dark woods the last time—how would I ever get out of the woods now? By the time I arrived for my next appointment, I had deteriorated badly; I could barely speak, I could not meet his eyes.

Years later, after I received my records from the Warneford, I read the note Dr. Hamilton wrote upon seeing me that day: "Looks ghastly."

He asked if I was thinking of killing myself.

"Yes." Hunched over again, eyes to the floor. *Don't look at me, don't look at me.*

"You have to come back into the hospital, Elyn. Right now."

And so, eight months after my first hospitalization—where I had had the vain hope for a quick fix and had begun to experience the "am I a student/am I a crazy person?" two-trains-running conundrum—I wearily checked back into the Warneford for my second hospitalization, officially one of those patients who had "come back." The admission note summed things up pretty well: "Thin, tall, chain-smoking, sad, inappropriate laughter at times, seems physically and mentally retarded."

I hated myself.

chapter six

ALL THROUGHOUT THOSE first long hours of my second stay at the Warneford, I stood alone in the dayroom and rocked back and forth, my own arms wrapped around me like a straitjacket, rocking myself much as a mother will quiet a distraught baby. The even regularity of the movement comforted me. Skeletal, dirty, and gibbering disjointed syllables under my breath—and unceasingly rocking—I slid deeper and deeper into my head with each passing moment. Doctors, hospital staff, and other patients moved in and out of the room and along the corridor outside it: I could barely see or hear any of them, and I cared even less.

Finally, a nurse carefully walked up to me and positioned herself directly in front of my face. "You seem so agitated, Elyn," she said, in that deliberately moderated tone of voice one might use to approach an animal chewing its own foot. "I would like you to see the doctor on call."

I shook my head, and the room spun around me. "No. That's not necessary," I muttered. "I'm fine. Thanks anyway."

As she quickly left the room to search for a doctor (evidently, she didn't think my self-diagnosis very credible), I just as quickly headed in the other direction, to go outside and wander about in the hospital courtyard. It was January—cold and damp and raw, with light patches of hoarfrost on the ground. I was wearing only jeans, a T-shirt, and sneakers, and I was cold to my bones; given the circumstances, however, I might have been just as cold if I'd been wearing a down jacket, wool hat, and heavy winter boots.

My legs gave way beneath me, and I slowly crumpled to the ground in a heap. There I stayed, curled up in a ball, for at least an hour. What was happening to me? Why had it happened? And who would help me? But no one came. *No one will ever come,* I thought. *I am worthless, I cannot even control my own mind. Why would anyone want to save me?* Eventually, I pulled myself up and wearily went back inside, stumbling around until someone directed me to the place where I was to sleep. I never did see a doctor that night.

The following day, I met with a group of half a dozen doctors for what they told me would be an intake evaluation. The meeting was held in a very large and intimidating office. I was relieved to see Dr. Smythe, who smiled and acknowledged me in a reassuring way. Then the inquisition began.

"You're very thin, Elyn. Can you tell us why you've lost so much weight?"

"I think it's wrong to eat," I told them. "So I do not eat."

"But why?" they asked.

"Food is evil," I said. "And anyway, I don't deserve to have any. I am evil, too, and food would only nourish me. Does it make any sense to you to nourish evil? No. It does not."

After a few more rounds of questions, the doctors carefully explained their recommendations to me. In England, treatment recommendations were always just that—recommendations. To leave a hospital, to stay in it, to take medications, to participate in group activities or not—they never forced any of it on me, and each time the decision was mine. Even at my craziest, I interpreted this as a demonstration of respect. When you're really crazy, respect is like a lifeline someone's throwing you. Catch this and maybe you won't drown.

First, they wanted me to go back on the amitriptyline; I agreed. Second, they wanted me to stay in the hospital for a while—how long, they weren't yet certain. This, too, was fine with me; as befuddled as I was, I knew I couldn't be away from the hospital now. But when they suggested that I drop out of Oxford altogether after my hospital stay—and then questioned whether it might be best to call my parents and let them know what was going on with me—they had crossed a line.

I came back in full force.

"I *will* remain enrolled at Oxford University. I *will* receive my degree in ancient philosophy. I will *not* return to the United States before I have completed my academic work. And under no circumstances shall you contact my parents." This was more linear speech than I'd been capable of in weeks; I wasn't quite sure where it came from, but it was exhausting. And, surprisingly, the doctors acquiesced to my conditions.

Perhaps I should have wanted or even needed my parents to know what kind of shape I was in. Maybe I should have been hurt that they hadn't seemed to pay much attention to my health after our last visit together in Paris, after I'd "confessed" my struggles. And yet it's not as though I'd been entirely forthcoming with them, either. My brother Warren, who was living in Paris at the time, came to visit me at Oxford, but I made him swear he'd not tell my parents how badly I was doing. Once a week or so, I walked to a phone booth a few minutes down the road from the hospital, and from there called them in Florida, collect. The conversations were always brief, even skimpy, but evidently sufficient not to raise any alarm bells. The basic script from my end: "I'm fine, my studies are going well here at Oxford, and how are all of you?" Aside from that, my parents usually did most of the talking and I just leaned on the booth for the duration, responding where appropriate, mostly in single syllables. As I watched everything I valued disintegrate, I nevertheless fought to somehow hang onto my autonomy—my *self*. Whatever this was I was fighting, it was my problem; I would have to find a way to solve it without either asking for my parents' help or incurring their disapproval.

My readmission to the Warneford coincided with Dr. Hamilton's rotation and departure to another ward. Although I'd known it was coming, I could not control the anxiety and sadness during our last meeting, when he introduced me to Dr. Barnes, the young woman who would now be treating me. "I'll come back and say good-bye before I leave, Elyn," Dr. Hamilton promised. "Just to check in with you and see how you're doing."

Being passed along to his replacement made it real—he was leaving me. And even though he'd be just a few rooms away, he might as well have been going across the ocean, since his move precluded our having any further relationship. To make things even worse, the good-bye visit he'd promised me never happened. He never came back. When I thought of him, I thought my heart would crack in my chest.

Unlike during my first hospitalization, this time around I was completely unable to participate in anything that was going on in the ward; the group activities that had seemed at least mildly helpful before, such as ensuring that the table was properly set, were useless now. I was in such terrible pain, physical as well as emotional. My head ached, my arms and legs ached, my back ached; there was nothing in or on me that didn't hurt. My sleeping patterns were so erratic again that I was exhausted all the time and couldn't concentrate—what earthly difference could it have made to me if spoons and forks went on the right or left side of the plate? Instead, I gravitated to the music room, where I passed hours on end listening to classical music. Sometimes I was joined there by a somewhat overweight woman ten years or so my senior. Like me, she barely spoke, other than an occasional word or two about her mother, who had died many years before. When she did speak, the content was slim—she had what psychiatrists call "poverty of speech." Still, we shared a kind of companionship; listening to Mozart or Brahms seemed to calm and comfort us both. At particularly stirring passages, our eyes would meet, and we would nod in a kind of recognition.

The other patients seemed afraid of me—or maybe, seeing me every day with my face buried in my hands, they just thought it best to leave me be. The disheveled young man from Oxford whom I had first seen at the day hospital was now on this ward as well, in much worse shape than before; he believed he was a baby, and would vomit after meals and babble nonsensical syllables. *That's going to be me,* I thought. *That's where I'm going.*

One day, a good looking, middle-aged man was admitted to the ward, but then quickly disappeared. I later learned in an offhand comment from staff that my appearance especially had unnerved him. Thereafter, he refused to spend the night at the hospital, agreeing to be a patient on the day unit only and refusing to be with patients as sick as I. There was, it seemed, a hierarchy of fear at the Warneford: sicker patients unsettled me; I, in turn, unsettled less sick patients.

For a time, I was friends with a woman named Lucinda. She was my age and was battling anorexia. The hospital had put her on a behavioral system whereby, if she hadn't gained a certain amount by designated days, she had to spend that day in bed. I, too, was very thin, but my doctors had decided that the weight loss was due to my primary diagnosis (severe depression) and not simple anorexia. Lucinda had been treated by Dr. Hamilton at one point and told me she'd taken a great dislike to him. This amazed me. How could someone *not* like Dr. Hamilton?

A month after I'd been admitted, the staff moved me from a private room to a dormitory with more than a dozen other patients, explaining with classic British understatement that I "kept myself to myself " too much, and that perhaps being with other patients would resocialize me. The move did not have the desired effect—I simply retreated to the bathroom, where I spent hours sitting on the floor, smoking, rocking back and forth, and moaning softly to myself. The bathrooms were filthy, as bathrooms can be in psychiatric hospitals, but I didn't care. All I wanted was to be alone. If I needed to sit on floors and lean against walls spotted with human feces in order to do that, so be it.

Once, there'd been a time in my life when thoughts were something to be welcomed, and pored over, like pages in a favorite book. Just to idly *think* about things—the weather, the future, the subject of a paper I needed to write for a class, the friend I was going to meet for a cup of coffee—these things felt so simple, so taken-for-granted. But now thoughts crashed into my mind like a fusillade of rocks someone (or something) was hurtling at me—fierce, angry, jagged around the edges, and uncontrollable. I could not bear them, I did not know how to defend myself against them, and I could not bear to be near anyone when I was experiencing them. *You are a piece of shit. You don't deserve to be around people. You are nothing. Other people will see this. They will hate you. They will hate you and they will want to hurt you. They can hurt you. They are powerful. You are weak. You are nothing.*

Dr. Barnes seemed to be working very hard on my behalf. At our meetings, her manner was earnest and dogged, as though we were archaeologists together digging for truth. But we simply could not connect. She was so formal in her personal manner, somewhat distant, even unsympathetic, and apparently I made her anxious as well—she was obviously uncomfortable when we were the only two in a room together. I didn't trust her, and I certainly didn't believe she had any idea of what to do with me. *Useless, useless.*

Of course, it wouldn't have mattered how competent Dr. Barnes truly was, given how harshly I compared her to Dr. Hamilton and found her wanting. I was actively pining for him, and would stand in the doorway of my ward for hours, mute and rocking, hoping to catch a glimpse of him in the hall, walking to or from a meeting.

I was surprised to find that I had a partner in this obsession, another patient, in her twenties or early thirties. Dr. Hamilton had treated her for a long time, and like me, she had developed a strong positive transference toward him—in fact, she'd clearly fallen in love with him. A day patient on the ward from eight in the morning to eight in the evening, she was considered one of the most disturbed patients there. One night, at home, she abruptly shaved her head for no reason anyone could ascertain. Although she did not speak (at least to me), we had more than our Dr. Hamilton obsession in common; she, too, spent most of her day rocking in place.

Sometime after Dr. Hamilton had left the ward for good, my companion-in-thought seemed even more agitated than usual. All day long, I watched her frantically pace the corridors. The next morning, my friend from the music room offhandedly informed me that the woman had hanged herself the night before. I was stunned, as much by my friend's tone as by the news she'd so calmly passed along to me. This patient had killed herself, I thought, over Dr. Hamilton. Why hadn't staff noticed what was driving her and done something about it? Why hadn't *I* done something? Didn't anyone realize that *she* could have been *me?*

In my fog of isolation and silence, I began to feel I was receiving commands to do things—such as walk all by myself through the old abandoned tunnels that lay underneath the hospital. The origin of the commands was unclear. In my mind, they were issued by some sort of beings. Not real people with names or faces, but shapeless, powerful beings that controlled me with thoughts (*not* voices) that had been placed in my head. *Walk through the tunnels and repent. Now lie down and don't move. You must be still. You are evil.* The effect of those commands on me during those nights and days was powerful. It never occurred to me that disobedience was an option, although it was never clear what might happen if I disobeyed. *I do not make the rules. I just follow them.*

It was quiet and dark down in the old tunnels, with just enough ambient light that I could find my way around corners. The air was musty and damp, and although I couldn't hear any of the sounds from the busy hospital above my head, I was aware of the building; it often seemed to groan above me. I wondered how many hundreds, maybe thousands, of patients had been here. I wondered what had happened to them.

Another command (or thought, or message) I continually received was to hurt myself. To inflict pain on myself, because that was all I was worthy of. So I burned myself—with cigarettes, lighters (easily come by—everyone smoked then, as I did), electric heaters, boiling water. I burned my flesh in places on my body that I thought people would never see. I'd do it in the bathroom when no one was there, or down in the tunnels, or out on the grounds. Once in the music room, when I was trying my best to set my sock on fire, an attendant went by, saw what I was doing, and tsk-tsked in a mild tone, "Elyn, really, you mustn't do that, it's simply not on, you know."

In fact, many staff members knew what was happening; after all, they dressed my wounds, putting salve on the burns, noting the when and where in their charts. "Aren't you concerned," one said to me during a repair session, "that in summer, when you wear a bathing suit, these scars will show?"

"I don't think you understand," I said patiently. "I'm not going to survive the year. I have no concerns about future swims, or what I will look like in a bathing suit."

Although the staff and Dr. Barnes knew what I was doing, no one seemed to know or understand why, and there was no way I could tell any of them that the impetus for my behavior, the commanding impulse, came from inside my head but was not mine. It was someone else commanding me. I was afraid the staff would laugh at me—and as frightened as I was, the thought of derision frightened me even more. In retrospect, it was a life-threatening deception, somewhat along the lines of hiding recurrent chest pains from one's cardiologist from embarrassment.

Nearly four months in the hospital passed like this, and I did not get better; in fact, I only got worse. At twenty-one, I was convinced that I would die soon, so much so that I refused to discuss anything about the future. I spent most of my time alone in the music room or the bathroom, burning my body, or moaning and rocking, holding myself as protection from unseen forces that might harm me. When I was able to stir at all, I roamed the hospital tunnels.

Although they were aware that my health was not improving, the doctors at the Warneford began suggesting that it was time I leave the hospital. Maybe they were fearful that if I didn't go soon, I never would. With this in mind, they referred me to Dr. Anthony Storr, a well-known psychiatrist and psychoanalyst who consulted to the Warneford.

Initially, Dr. Storr and I went through the usual question-and-answer session, but there was something a bit different about this conversation and, indeed, about the doctor himself—he seemed more alert than I was used to, and genuinely interested in hearing everything that was on my mind. I had a palpable sense of actually being *heard*, but not judged. And so, instead of keeping my darkest thoughts to myself, as I'd done with Dr. Hamilton, I told Dr. Storr everything, and edited nothing in the telling. His eyes didn't widen in surprise or horror; he didn't tsk-tsk, he didn't shake his head in dismay. He simply leaned forward, kept eye contact with me, and listened intently, without flinching, to every word.

Dr. Storr's subsequent recommendations were not only simple, they were in direct contradiction to those made by the doctors who four months before had suggested I leave school and be hospitalized. "Your mind is very sick," he said calmly, "and just as I'd advise with a sick body, it needs a specific kind of exercise to help it heal. That means resuming the work you love. It makes you happy, it gives you purpose, it challenges you. And so you need to stay at Oxford, in your program."

I was overjoyed, and relieved. In addition to hearing me, he'd somehow *seen* me as well.

"But there's a slight catch to this," he said, and I held my breath. "You need to be in intensive talk therapy. Intensive, Elyn. Rigorous, often difficult, and, if we can arrange it, every single day. And not short-term, either, but for a long time. For the foreseeable future. Do you understand what I'm telling you?"

Yes, yes, yes, whatever you say. I'm sure I was nodding like a string puppet. In fact, at that point, if he'd said, "I recommend that you walk barefoot on broken glass for an hour each day," I'd have happily done it.

Dr. Storr quickly compiled a list of five psychoanalysts who might be able to treat me, but a certain Elizabeth Jones was the only person on his list who had time immediately available.

I repeated her name to myself. *Elizabeth Jones, Elizabeth Jones.* I desperately hoped that this Elizabeth Jones might be someone who would help me reclaim whatever was left of my life.

I had come to Oxford an ambitious and even idealistic young woman. I'd wanted to make new friends; I'd wanted people to like me. I'd wanted to study what I loved, do well, earn my degree, and move full-fledged into the community of scholars I so respected. But none of that had happened. For all my efforts, I had earned only the stigma of a mental patient. Many years later, the words in Dr. Storr's report seem prescient: *"For a person like this, it is analysis or nothing."*

Elizabeth Jones's office was actually a room on the second floor of her home, a typical old and somewhat fusty Oxford house, more than a century old. Mrs. Jones herself—who greeted me at her front door—was, tall, large-boned, and stately, wearing a long flowered dress that touched the tops of her shoes. She was, without question, the ugliest woman I'd ever seen.

"Hello, Dr. Jones. My name is Elyn Saks." I heard myself as one might hear a voice echoing back from the bottom of a well. My hands were damp and shaking; I was halfway between hoping she could help me and fearing that she wouldn't be able to. Or even want to.

"Please come in," she said kindly. "Let's sit down and talk. By the way, I'm a psychoanalyst, Elyn, I'm not a doctor. Please call me Mrs. Jones."

Not a doctor? This was a little alarming; did the woman know what she was doing? And if she didn't, what were my other choices? I wasn't sure I had any.

Mrs. Jones led me up into a small sitting room that was all browns and greens. It wasn't messy, but wasn't precisely neat and tidy, either. I learned later that she had a second office (within a second home) in London; this one, in Oxford, was modest and obviously well lived in. I felt as though she'd welcomed me into a private place, which made me think I could trust her.

As Mrs. Jones and I sat down, she explained how the psychoanalysis would work. After my discharge from the hospital (in a few weeks), we would meet three times a week. When two additional openings became available in her schedule, I would then see her five times a week, paying eight pounds per session—roughly the equivalent of twelve dollars in the late seventies. An analyst of equal stature in the States would have charged many times as much. She made only one rule for our working together: I was to say everything that came to my mind, no matter how embarrassing, trivial, or inappropriate it might seem. In the years we would spend together, I'd break this rule only once: I never told Mrs. Jones how ugly I thought she was.

Three weeks later I was officially discharged from the Warneford. My official prognosis: "Very poor." I returned to my college house and my courses after four months away. Not one person inquired as to my whereabouts.

chapter seven

I STUMBLED INTO Elizabeth Jones's office in a desperate lunge for salvation, and in the process began one of the most extraordinary experiences of my life. At the time it was often unmitigated hell. The work I was beginning with Mrs. Jones was not "counseling" or "therapy" as many Americans think of it or experience it themselves. No, this was talk therapy of the densest, most intellectually rigorous, challenging, and unsettling sort: Kleinian analysis, a treatment method that found its origins in the work of Sigmund Freud.

Freud built his theory of mind and method of treatment upon the concept of the human "unconscious"—the idea that we all think, feel, and do what we do for reasons that we are not entirely aware of. He believed that the unconscious was a "seething cauldron," filled with primitive forces at war with one another, forces that literally drove us to act. Central to Freud's thinking about psychoanalysis was the powerful relationship between the analyst and the patient, or analysand. From that relationship developed the "transference"—the name Freud gave to the intense feelings, beliefs, and attitudes the patient unconsciously recalls from early life and then directs toward the analyst. It was the transference itself that was the thing to be analyzed; it provided the raw material that would then be mined by the analyst and analysand for many years.

Freud had many reservations, however, about what could be accomplished with a psychotic analysand. He believed that psychosis was too narcissistic, too inward-looking, to allow the patient to develop a transference relationship with the analyst, and without that transference, there would be no grist for the psychoanalytic mill. Now, no one had diagnosed me as schizophrenic; indeed, even the word "psychosis" hadn't yet been mentioned. Still, I was depressed, I was behaving oddly, and people had a strong suspicion that I was delusional. I'd read enough Freud at this point to know that with this new psychoanalytic relationship, I was about to launch into uncharted and potentially troubling waters.

Elizabeth Jones, however, was a "Kleinian"—she practiced an offshoot of Freudian analysis developed by Melanie Klein, an Austrian psychoanalyst who immigrated to London in the late 1920s. Unlike Freud (and later, his daughter Anna), Klein believed that people with psychosis *could* benefit from analysis and that the necessary transference would develop. It was her theory that psychotic individuals are filled with (even driven by) great anxiety, and that the way to provide relief is to focus directly on the deepest sources of that anxiety.

Because most human anxiety stems from very primitive (read: infantile) fantasies about bodily parts and bodily functions, the direct nature of Kleinian interpretation calls for using the same kind of language that the patient's fantasies are couched in. To do this, Kleinian analysts employ the same words and images that the analysand uses—and as a consequence, Kleinian analysts can sometimes sound just as crazy as their patients do. These simple yet often startling exchanges between doctor and patient operate something like arrows shot directly at whatever it is that's upsetting the person being analyzed.

If the arrow hits, it punctures the target; what results is something like a valve opening and long-pent-up steam being released.

A central tenet of both classical and Kleinian analysis is that the treater must remain fairly anonymous to her patient—she does not answer questions about herself, have pictures of her family on the wall, tell you where she went to school or where she is going on vacation. Indeed, you don't even see your analyst during your sessions—how she looks as she reacts to you and what you are saying. You're on the couch. There is a simple reason for this: If the analyst is a so-called blank slate, the traits the patient attributes to her come primarily from the patient rather than the analyst. That's where transference develops, and the patient becomes better able to see how her mind works. And it was that process—and, ideally, reaping the fruit of it—that Elizabeth Jones and I embarked upon.

Though I never knew much about Mrs. Jones's life, I came to know her well from the way she reacted to me in the consulting room: with tolerance, patience, and understanding. Her voice was calm and soothing; she clearly didn't frighten easily. At the same time she was both extremely empathic and rigorously honest. She was also the first accomplished professional woman I had come to know.

During my sessions with Mrs. Jones, I whispered—because I was convinced that people in the house next door or across the street were able to hear what I was saying. Soon, some of the beliefs that had begun at the Warneford (for example, that beings in the sky controlled my thoughts and were poised to hurt me) took center stage in my thinking again. I would mutter complete nonsense, disconnected words and rhymes, which even as I whispered them out loud gave me great shame. I didn't want Mrs. Jones to hear them, in spite of her absolute "tell everything" rule.

Me: "They're messing with fetuses. They think it's us whereas the truth is God. Voices went, tabernacle, out to the edge of time. Time. Time is too low. Lower the boom. The TV is making fun of me. The characters are laughing at me. They think I am a failure and deserve to suffer. Everyone watching knows. The TV is telling the story of my life."

The doctors in the hospital had been stiff and formal when they dealt with me, seemingly more interested in giving me advice—"Eat more, Elyn!"—than in figuring out what was going on inside my head. Mrs. Jones was different. Her training had prepared her well for me, and she went directly to the heart of the matter, in the process sparing neither my feelings nor my assumptions about how a proper British matron should speak.

Mrs. Jones: "Tell me about your difficulties at university."

Me: "I'm not smart enough. I can't do the work."

Mrs. Jones: "You were first in your class at Vanderbilt. Now you're upset about Oxford because you want to be the best and are afraid you can't be. You feel like you are a piece of shit from your mother's bottom."

Me: "I'm closing the curtains from now on because people across the street are looking at me. They can hear what I'm saying. They are angry. They want to hurt me."

Mrs. Jones: "You are evacuating your angry and hostile feelings onto those people. It is you who are angry and critical. And you want to control what goes on in here."

Me: "I *am* in control. I control the world. The world is at my whim. I control the world and everything in it."

Mrs. Jones: "You want to feel in control because in fact you feel so helpless."

Me: "I had a dream. I was making golf balls out of fetuses."

Mrs. Jones: "You want to kill babies, you see, and then make a game out of it. You are jealous of the other babies. Jealous of your brothers, jealous of my other patients. You want to kill them. And then you want to turn them into a little ball so you can smack them again. You want your mother and me to love only you."

While the content of what Mrs. Jones said to me was not always a comfort (more often than not, it was startling, and had the effect of catching me up short), her presence in the room was. So calm, so reasonable, no matter what bizarre words and images she or I used. No matter what I said to her, no matter how disgusting or horrible, she never recoiled from what I said. To her, my thoughts and feelings were not right or wrong, good or bad; they just were.

I must have looked an odd sight around the Oxford campus, making my appointed rounds in solitude, still occasionally muttering to myself, still lapsing (badly) in self-care, forgetting to eat, thin enough for a good strong wind to blow me away, and always, always, burdened with a large bag of books. In the bag were the texts I needed for my academic studies, of course, but others as well: psychiatry books; abnormal psychology books; a book on suicide that Dr. Hamilton had recommended months before; a book by Dr. Storr on the personality types that often were the underpinnings of actual mental illness ("depressive" and "paranoid" were two that particularly resonated with me).

Because the odd thing was, I didn't think I was particularly crazy, or that what I often thought or felt was unique to me. Instead, I had come to believe that everyone had these thoughts or feelings, this sense of a force or evil energy pushing on them to do evil or be destructive. The difference was, they all knew how to manage it, how to hide it, how to control it, because that was the socially appropriate thing to do. They had stronger wills, and better coping skills, than I did. They knew how to keep their demons in check; I did not. But perhaps I could learn.

As my sessions with Mrs. Jones increased, and I became accustomed to spooling out the strange products of my mind, my paranoia began to shift. Although the nameless, faceless creatures from the sky had no less power over my fears and thoughts, the actual human people in my daily comings and goings seemed less scary and more approachable. No longer a faceless, threatening mass, existing only to judge or possibly harm me (or be targets for *me* to harm), they were becoming individual persons—human beings, as I was—vulnerable, and interesting, perhaps with something in common with me, possibly even friendship. Slowly, I made one friend, and then two. One evening, I had a companion for a lecture; a few days later, I went to a small dinner party. Blinking and shaky (as though I'd been in a cave, and the light, as welcome as it was, was something I'd have to get used to), I began to move back into the world again.

In time, I found myself involved in actual friendships, in particular with three other students: Dinah and Patrick, both Brits, and Sam, a fellow American. Dinah was tall and very thin, like me, although she was often dressed more like a hip undergraduate than the Oxford scholar she was. She had been hospitalized briefly after college for depression; that made me feel closer to her, and less weird. Patrick, on the other hand, was charming, at ease, and apparently very well adjusted and comfortable with himself.

Sam—also quite tall, and handsome as well, with huge, expressive eyes—was often anxious about money and even more neurotic than I was about the workload. In spite of long, slogging hours, he wasn't convinced he would be able to do the work and finish out his degree program in time. Although he had a girlfriend in London, he seemed more like a loner than I was; he played the guitar (he wrote music), and often spoke to himself as he walked through our college house, behavior which (like Dinah's earlier treatment) reassured me that I wasn't the only nutty one.

The four of us were soon inseparable. We would cook our meals together, or go to Brown's, a north Oxford restaurant that served passable American and British food. We didn't see movies, or watch any television; in an effort to be culturally responsible, I did go off to the opera a couple of times, but didn't like it much. Instead, we spent endless hours talking late into the night, sitting together in our college house or, when the weather permitted, up on the house roof, near the chimney.

As friends will do once the newness of friendship becomes something more comfortable, I finally told them more about myself, confessing my history, even the more difficult part—it was only fair, after all, as they'd done the same with me. Learning to trust, learning which secrets were safe to tell—this was all part of the difficult terrain I was learning to navigate.

So they knew I had intermittently been hospitalized, and was now struggling through psychoanalysis. Nevertheless, there were whole parts of myself I tried desperately to keep hidden. I knew, for instance, not to share my ongoing delusions of evil, in particular the part about my being evil and my total certainty that I was capable of horrible acts of violence. Not that these thoughts were wrong; I believed everyone thought this way, but just knew better than to talk about it, much as everyone passes gas, but not in company. But as hard as I tried, I'd sometimes find the wrong words coming unbidden to my lips—for example, the memorable night we all sat on the roof and I casually mentioned having killed many children.

"It's a joke!" I quipped as fast as I could, noting with alarm the expressions on their faces—uncertainty at first, and then, slowly, a hint of horror. "A stupid joke! Oh, come on, everybody wants to kill kids once in a while, don't they? Except of course they don't—hey, it's not like I actually did that! Or would do that, you know that, right? Don't you?" Yes, they all said, they certainly did, don't be ridiculous, Elyn. They knew I'd been kidding around with them, they weren't worried about me, I hadn't frightened them. But of course, I had, and I knew it. *Got to keep control,* I thought. *Get a grip. Keep a grip.*

In spite of my occasional lapse, these three dear friends made me happy, when for so long, nothing much had. They filled a place in my heart that needed filling; it was just like Kenny and Margie and Pat all over again—a small group of friends, laughing together, studying together, sharing a life that was focused on (indeed, held together by) our books, and our deadlines, and an emphasis on intellectual rigor. If I could make friends like these, I thought, then I could find a way to save myself.

Despite sometimes being too sick to work, I was making progress on my degree. Some days, it was so slow and difficult that it felt like I was carving rocks, and there were times I lost faith that I'd ever be happy with my work, or produce enough of it to finish in an acceptable manner. But the daily routine kept forcing me to concentrate my mind and push the evil presences to the side. I had no required classes at this point—my only fixed appointments were with Mrs. Jones—so I had large chunks of time to write. I switched my program to a thesis degree, so I was required to write one long paper instead of many short ones and I wouldn't have to take an exam. I decided to write about Aristotle's philosophy of mind, and taught myself French so that I could read an important medieval commentator on the subject. I wasn't always up to the task, but each time I slipped backward a step, I'd simply resolve to move forward two more. *Work harder, work longer, keep working.*

As helpful as my relationship with Mrs. Jones was proving to be, the intensity of what I was feeling for her opened some kind of door, and the psychotic thoughts marched right through it, growing more and more violent every session.

Me: "I had a dream. My mother and I are standing outside. We hear an explosion and look off into the distance. We see a mushroom cloud. My mother and I embrace, crying, telling each other that we love each other. Then we are both killed."

Mrs. Jones: "Your rage is so great that you destroy the planet. And your mother—and I—we do not protect you. You hate us for that. Your hateful feelings cause the world to explode. You tell your mother that you love her, and you want to make contact with her and with me. But then your rage kills everyone off."

Soon, Mrs. Jones herself became the overt object of my fantasies. Notwithstanding Freud, my psychosis had not gotten in the way of my developing an intense transference to her, and that transference was not pretty. "I know you say you are my analyst," I snarled at her one afternoon. "But I also know the truth. You are an evil monster, perhaps the devil. I won't let you kill me. You are evil, a witch. I'll fight."

She never even stirred in her chair, and her reply was measured in tone. "You have hateful feelings toward me, Elyn. You hate that I know things that you don't know. You hate that you feel you need me. You put your hateful feelings in me and that's why you think I am dangerous. You fear that bad part of yourself."

"Are you trying to kill me?" I hissed. "I know about the bombs. I can make a bomb, too. You are the devil. You are trying to kill me. I am evil. I've killed you three times today. I can do it again. Don't cross me. I've killed hundreds of thousands of people with my thoughts."

Psychotic people who are paranoid do scary things *because they are scared.* And when you're both psychotic and paranoid, it's like that sweaty midnight moment when you sit bolt upright in your bed from a nightmare that you don't yet know isn't real. But this nightmare went on all through the daylight as well. The closer I felt to Mrs. Jones, the more terrified I became: She was going to hurt me. Maybe she was even going to attempt to kill me. I needed to take steps to prevent that from happening.

Walking by kitchen stores, I stared through the display windows at the knives, thinking that I should buy one and take it to my next session. Once, I even went into a hardware store to look at the axes, wondering which one, if any, might protect me. For a while, I carried a serrated kitchen knife and a box cutter in my purse to my sessions— just in case. *She is evil and she is dangerous. She keeps killing me. She is a monster. I must kill her, or threaten her, to stop her from doing evil things to me. It will be a blessing for all the other people she is hurting.*

At the very same time I was terrified of Mrs. Jones, I was equally terrified I was going to lose her, so much so that I could barely tolerate weekends when I would not see her for two days. I'd start to unravel on Thursday and be nearly inconsolable until Tuesday. In the intervening time, it took everything I had to protect myself—and my friends—from what was going on in my head: "Yes, of course, let's get a hamburger, OK, let's discuss that book we both read," all the while plotting ways to keep Mrs. Jones from abandoning me: *I will kidnap her and keep her tied up in my closet. I will take good care of her. I will give her food and clothes. She will always be there when I need her to give me psychoanalysis.*

And then, once back in her office again, I'd tell her every single evil thing.

Me: "I will not let you go on vacation this year. I have a weapon. I will take you to my room and put you in my closet. You will stay with me. You will not have a choice. I won't let you go. Throw. So."

Her: "You feel absolutely dependent on me, like a baby, and that makes you angry. You imagine ways to keep me near you, and some of these ways have violence in them, so that you will show me that you are stronger than I am."

Her tolerance and understanding seemed endless, and her steady and calm presence contained me, as if she were the glue that held me together. I was falling apart, flying apart, exploding—and she gathered my pieces and held them for me.

Psychosis is like an insidious infection that nevertheless leaves some of your faculties intact; in a psychiatric hospital, for example, even the most debilitated schizophrenic patients show up on time for meals, and they evacuate the ward when the fire alarm goes off. So it was for me. Completely delusional, I still understood essential aspects of how the world worked. For example, I was getting my schoolwork done, and I vaguely understood the rule that in a social setting, even with the people I most trusted, I could not ramble on about my psychotic thoughts. To talk about killing children, or burning whole worlds, or being able to destroy cities with my mind was not part of polite conversation.

At times, though, I was so psychotic that I could barely contain myself. The delusions expanded into full-blown hallucinations, in which I could clearly hear people whispering. I could hear my name being called when no one was physically around—in a corner of the library, or late at night, in my bedroom where I slept alone. Sometimes, the noise I heard was so overwhelming it drowned out almost all other sound. *Stop, stop, stop. No. Stop.* Days went by when I simply could not bear to be around anyone; unless I was with Mrs. Jones, I stayed alone in my room, with the door locked and my lights out.

"Elyn, are you angry with me?" asked Sam one afternoon.

"No," I said. "Why?"

"Because you're avoiding me. You didn't come out to dinner with us, you didn't answer your door last night or the night before, and right now, you're scowling at me."

It's because I can't hear you, I wanted to tell him. *It's louder than you, and if my energy goes to you, I won't have any left to fight it. I will not be able to keep it at bay. You will be in danger. We will all be in terrible danger.* I was just enough in the real world to know that what I was thinking much of the time wasn't real—or at least it wouldn't be real to him.

Think about having a bad flu, on a day when you can't stay home huddled under the covers. You have business, you have responsibilities. And so, summoning up reserves you didn't know you had, you somehow make it through the day, sweating, shaking, nodding politely to colleagues while barely controlling the nausea—because you know that if you can just pull it off, then you can go home, where your couch (or your bed, or a hot bath, or whatever you define as comfort and safety) is waiting. You hold it together, and then, once you're home, you collapse. For two straight years, I did my work, met my obligations, made it through the day as best I could, and then fled to Mrs. Jones, where I promptly took the chains off my mind and fell apart.

chapter eight

FOUR YEARS AFTER coming to Oxford, I finally completed my graduate degree in 1981. The whole endeavor had taken twice as long as I'd thought it would, on that long-ago day when I first walked around the ancient campus. I'd lost two full years to my illness.

Although (to me at least) the jury still seemed to be out as to whether or not I was sane, there seemed to be some consensus that I was reasonably intelligent: The examiners' response to my thesis was, by Oxford standards, excellent, much more than I could've hoped for. Their report said that while the extent of my thesis was appropriate to the degree I would receive (a Master of Letters, or M.Litt.), the quality of it was equal to that of a Doctor of Philosophy, or D.Phil., the highest degree that the university offers.

Happily, I had enough presence of mind to be proud of myself and what I'd accomplished. I hadn't given up. I'd managed to stay out of the hospital for two years, and the academic work I did during that time had been judged better than good, by objective critics who had no reason to be kind to me in their criticism. And there was no denying that Mrs. Jones had been the determining factor in all of that.

And so, after giving the matter careful thought, I decided it would be best for me at this point to stay on in England for one more year, so that I could continue my sessions with her. I had the financial means to do so—my parents gave each of us gifts each year, and how I spent that money was up to me. At that point, I couldn't imagine a better investment than my own mental health. In addition, the rate for my treatment was so much cheaper in England than in America—$12 an hour vs. $60, at that time—that it just made sense to stay right where I was, to continue with an analyst who knew me, knew my history, and had earned my trust.

However, since I was not a student anymore, I had to move out of my college house and find someplace else to live. Through a friend, I heard about a young, divorced mother, Janet, who lived in an old house with her four-year-old daughter, Olivia, and was looking for a tenant. I met with Janet and liked her immediately. The house was warm and comfortable, and the part of it in which I would live was exactly what I'd hoped it would be. We agreed—I would move in. In an unlikely gesture of bravura at the time, I'd bought a moped a couple of years earlier, so now I had friends, some measure of freedom, and a lovely, peaceful room of my own—there had been a time, not too long before, when I could not have imagined having any of it.

In fact, as I began that third year of working with Mrs. Jones, it was encouraging to me to see that some areas of my life improved a little each day. Dating was out of the question, of course—I wasn't sure if or when I'd ever be able to think about a romantic relationship. But I had friends, good ones. I had a nice place to live, with the occasional added bonus of an endearing little blond girl named Olivia—Livy— who brightened up every hour of every day I spent at Janet's house. And I was beginning to make an actual plan for my future.

Even though I was no longer taking classes at Oxford, I often went to lectures there, and drew up my own self-imposed reading list as well. I'd decided that going any further with philosophy was out of the question—too many bad memories from the previous four years, struggling through the densest of that literature while in the grip of psychosis. Instead, I was increasingly drawn to the study of psychology and law. I was fascinated by the insanity defense, for example, and the complicated civil issues in mental health law, such as involuntary commitment. As I paged through psychology, psychiatry, and law texts, the case histories on the pages often seemed eerily familiar to me—how easily I could have been any one of them. How easily I could have slipped beneath the waves and simply never come back up again. I wondered if there were a role I could play in the lives of people who suffered in a way that I understood only too well.

My living circumstances created an environment in which it was both easy to think and easy to heal. I hadn't spent anything remotely approaching "quality time" with my own family in a very long time, and Janet went out of her way to include me at mealtimes and holidays. Sometimes in the evening, we'd sit together in the living room and watch television—good British TV, something I'd not taken much advantage of until then. Often, her artist mother, Katherine, would join us.

Janet was soft-spoken and kind, with wonderful natural instincts as a mother. Although she didn't talk much about herself, I learned enough about her life to know that things hadn't always been easy. Olivia's father was not in the picture at all, and Janet's own father had died when she was young. She was very close to Katherine, who'd struggled with bouts of depression. It was two or three months before I told Janet about my own hospitalizations, but when I finally did, I characterized them as being for depression; I never hinted at the psychosis or the terrifying fantasies. I was too ashamed of what she might think, and afraid that she might see me as some kind of threat to her daughter. I know now I could have trusted Janet with anything, and on that day, when I sat nervously in her living room and risked telling her as much truth as I could, she was understanding and compassionate, with no judgment whatsoever in her response.

And of course, every day, there was sweet Livy. Affectionate and bright, she loved to draw and color, or play in make-believe scenarios where I was the teacher and she was the student. She couldn't wait to learn to read, and go off to school like the bigger kids in the neighborhood. She was quite content to snuggle in my lap while I read to her, but was just as happy if I was being the Wicked Witch of the West—she'd insist that I do the witch's cackle-laugh while chasing her around the room, and then she'd fall down on the carpet in a giggling heap. Unscheduled silliness, with no goal except to enjoy the moment and the little girl who was sharing it with me—it felt exactly like the sun coming out after a long, long rainy season.

Even with my daily appointments with Mrs. Jones, and the research and reading I was doing to prepare for the next phase of my life, I still had way too much free time on my hands, something that I knew had never been good for me. I needed to find a way to fill the empty hours.

I decided I wanted to make some sort of contribution, to repay my debt to the professionals who'd taken such good care of me, hoping that in the process I might be able to help others. I believed that I understood the experience of being in a hospital for the mentally ill in a way that the staff (or at least most of the staff) might not—which logically, I thought, would make me a good volunteer.

I'd been away from the Warneford long enough that I believed I could go there without being recognized. And so, one morning after I'd taken great pains with my appearance and rehearsed my best in-

terview behavior, I met with the Warneford's head of volunteers, and
we began what seemed like a very promising conversation.

"Thanks so much for meeting with me today," I said.

She nodded and smiled. "My pleasure," she said. "Now, tell me all
about yourself, Miss Saks, and why you want to volunteer here."

"Well, I'm an Oxford graduate trying to decide whether to go on
in psychology or law when I go back to the States," I said. "Whatever
I ultimately do, I would like it to be something about helping people
with mental illness. So I thought that volunteering here might be a
good place to explore this, and also get some valuable experience."

With a kind of understated enthusiasm—she seemed to convey the
idea that she thought I was a good catch—the woman began to discuss some possibilities at the Warneford where I might be of use. As
we talked, I felt encouraged, even optimistic; it would be my first experience in any kind of "professional" capacity, and it just seemed
right that it would take place at this particular hospital.

And then she mentioned the hospital unit where I'd actually been
a patient. At a momentary loss for words, I sat up straighter in my
chair.

"Well, I'm not certain that would be the best place for me," I finally said. "I was a patient there myself, not so very long ago. First I
was in the day hospital, and then later I stayed for a while, as an inpatient, hmmm, well, I just don't know how staff would feel about
that. I mean, maybe it would work out, but on the other hand I suspect that another unit would perhaps be better, at least in the beginning." *Stop talking now, Elyn. It's not going at all well.*

An expression flitted across the woman's face, and then it was
gone, replaced by a tight attempt at a smile. "I see," she said, moving
some papers on her desk from one stack to another. Then she folded
her hands. In my experience, this was rarely a good sign. "You know,
Miss Saks, I'll have to look into this further," she said. "It's not entirely clear to me at this point that there are any *actual* volunteer

vacancies right now, you understand, I'm sure. In any case, thank you for coming in, I'll be in touch just as soon as I know more."

I tried to hold on to my original optimism as I left the building. I replayed the conversation in my head—that went well, didn't it?—then got on my little moped and motored home. And I waited.

When she hadn't called in a couple of days, I called her, and left a message. The following day, I called again, leaving another message. Still nothing. After I called a third time, and once again heard nothing in response, it finally sank in what my revelation had done. It was a painful way to learn a lesson, but it's one that I've carried with me for the past twenty-five years. *Never tell them anything you don't have to tell them. Never volunteer any information they don't ask for.*

I licked my wounds for another day or two, raging and muttering about my disappointment to Mrs. Jones. Then I applied again for a volunteer position, this time at Littlemore Hospital, another psychiatric institution in Oxford. Littlemore, too, was built in the mid-1800s, but for poor people, and the buildings had a similar sense of gloom and doom. During the interview and on my application, I said nothing whatsoever about my own psychiatric history. They accepted me immediately, and scheduled me to be there five to ten hours each week.

At Littlemore, I worked primarily on the Activities Unit, where the patients, most of them chronically ill, came to spend time every day. I led exercise groups and art groups, and sometimes I just sat in the dayroom and chatted quietly with the patients. From the very first, I had no nervousness or anxiety whatsoever about being with them; it seemed completely natural to me to be there, to do whatever I could to make someone's burden of illness even a little bit lighter.

One of my favorite patients was Tom, a tall, nice-looking man, somewhat overweight (probably from the meds he was taking, which were notorious for this side effect). He'd come from a fine family and was a former patient of R. D. Laing, the prominent "antipsychiatry" psychiatrist of the sixties. Intelligent and articulate, Tom regaled me with stories of the LSD parties Laing used to stage in the woods for his patients. I wondered exactly why he was in this unit, but I presumed that he needed this kind of structure to remain as intact and coherent as he seemed to be.

There was another patient, Robert, a short, muscular man, who initially didn't seem ill at all to me. Then I learned that before he came to the Littlemore, he'd been a patient at the fabled Broadmoor in London, one of the British hospitals for the criminally insane. One day, as I was rounding up patients to go on a day outing into town, Robert walked up to me, his fists clenched, his face quite red and angry, and he muttered something unintelligible in a way I can only characterize as a threatening snarl. What on earth? Somewhat alarmed, I asked the staff what was going on.

"Oh, Robert killed his first wife," they said casually. "That's why he was in Broadmoor in the first place. And now he's just gotten engaged, so he's probably a bit wound up."

Oh, so it wasn't just that the man was crazy—he'd actually *killed somebody*. I wondered if maybe I'd momentarily reminded Robert of his wife. And the next day, when he was the only one who wanted to go into town with me, I felt a sinking sensation in my stomach. Was he angry at me? Was I in some kind of danger from this man who'd killed one woman, and perhaps could be provoked by unseen forces to kill another?

He was just fine on the trip, both going and coming. That was when I learned that for all my good intentions, I could be simultaneously on the receiving and the giving end of the stigma that goes along with mental illness.

One afternoon on the unit, one of the patients, Henry—suddenly and without apparent provocation—jumped full-body on another patient, screaming wildly as he did so. Staff and some other patients pulled him off and away, taking him to a different part of the unit, where he sat and calmed himself. An hour or so later, a doctor came in and sat with Henry, quietly telling him that what he'd done wasn't appropriate and couldn't happen again. There was no punishment for Henry's infraction, no beefy orderlies standing ready to mete out some kind of response, and no physical restraints. No straitjacket, no leather straps to hold Henry in his bed or on a chair. In fact (and in sharp contrast to most American hospitals, even now), British hospitals rarely use any kind of mechanical restraint, and have not for over two hundred years. Save for a small percentage of extreme cases, there was rarely anything dramatic that happened after the kind of scene Henry had just created other than a simple, humane, and clear response, with the basic message addressing the inappropriateness of the behavior, instead of the damaged mental capacity of the patient.

In spite of being perceived by the patients as some sort of authority figure—"on the other side of the medication counter," so to speak—I usually empathized more with them than with the hospital staff. In truth, I sometimes felt oddly competitive with the patients, weighing in my mind which of us was sicker, they or I. After all, I was seeing Mrs. Jones every day, and I was having ongoing psychotic thoughts. Yet here I was, operating autonomously, seemingly in perfect control and perfectly qualified to operate in the "outside"—that is, sane—world. Yes, part of me was proud of being a caregiver, but another part of me wanted to be taken care of, as the patients were. Their moods and emotions were all over the place, all the time, and the hospital accommodated that. I, on the other hand, was expected to stay focused, disciplined, and measured in my behavior, in spite of the soundtrack in my head that told me I was evil and potentially catastrophic. It occurred to me each time I left the hospital that I was something of a serious fraud.

And yet I did my job there conscientiously and well, and took a lot of satisfaction from it. After all these years of being buried in books, or being enmeshed inside my own head, connecting like this to other people gave me a purpose. I was doing something worthwhile, and I knew it. It wasn't arrogance I felt, it was pride, as much pride as I'd ever had bringing home a report card of As to my parents. And when, inevitably, it was time for me to leave Littlemore, the patients there made a farewell card for me, which each of them signed. Many wrote small notes thanking me for spending time with them. In my room later that night, I turned the card over and over in my hand, reading their words and marveling that it was me they were writing to, and not the other way around.

Partway into that third year of analysis with Mrs. Jones, I noticed, somewhat to my dismay, that I was becoming something of a hypochondriac. Nearly everything that happened to me physically—a cold, a paper cut, a headache, a stubbed toe—became an immediate cause for serious concern, a reason to go see the doctor, a potentially fatal illness. One day, I was riding along on my moped when a car cut me off sharply, and I fell to the street, hitting my head. I was knocked unconscious, and the hospital where I was later examined insisted on keeping me overnight for observation. I was nervous about all the bad scenarios that a head injury presented (death, amnesia, blindness, brain damage, seizures . . .) but also, oddly, exhilarated that I'd survived at all. Overall, the hospital environment—the smells, the sounds, the overhead lights that never go out, the faceless, uniformed people walking around and talking to one another in a code only they could understand—completely unnerved me. All I could think of was that I had to get out of there, before something else happened.

Well, now, this is pretty interesting, I thought. *If I fear dying so much, maybe that means that I don't want to die anymore. Maybe it means that I actually want to stay alive, and find out what happens next.*

Near the end of my third year with Mrs. Jones, my former college housemate, Patrick, was to be married, in Manchester. A small group of us traveled together in one car to the wedding. I don't quite remember how I ended up with this group, since I didn't know them—it was probably a result of one of those you-call-so-and-so and somebody's-putting-a-group-together kind of things.

I don't think I spoke more than ten words on the entire trip; I was completely in my head, lost in one fantasy after another about Mrs. Jones, and how to keep from leaving her. Mrs. Jones and I had agreed that it was time for me to go back to the States, to get on with my life there. We had agreed that our work together was coming to a logical end. And yet the mere contemplation of that "end" had started my mind and my anxieties on a collision course with each other.

In the car, everyone else was chatting merrily—on the drive up to Manchester, it was with anticipation for the wedding and the celebration, on the way back, it was retelling various moments and events of the day—but I was completely silent. That was my way. When the fantasies took over, I could see only them. And while lost in them, I would exert as much of my will as I could summon to keep anyone from knowing what was going on.

The ceremony, in a beautiful old church, was somewhat more religious than I'd expected, and I was surprised to find myself in tears as the bride and groom exchanged their vows. Not tears for myself, but for Patrick, who had always been quite dear to me, a good and kind friend. He deserved happiness, and I truly wished for him to have it. But for the most part, the wedding, and the reception afterward, went by in a blur. It simply felt like an endless passage of time in which I could not engage and could play no part.

I go to my session. I threaten Mrs. Jones with a knife. I am very psychotic and out of control. Mrs. Jones is kind and gentle. She asks me for the knife and I give it to her. I start screaming. I throw myself against the wall. Mrs. Jones and her husband restrain me. The ambulance arrives and takes me to the hospital. I become out of control again and am subdued. I am crying and sobbing that I will be leaving Mrs. Jones.

With psychosis, the wall that separates fantasy from reality dissolves; inside my head, the fantasies were real, and everything was actually happening. The images I saw, the actions I took, were all real, and it made me frantic. Mrs. Jones had been the glue that held me together. With that glue soon to be gone, would I not shatter into a thousand pieces? The anxiety was overwhelming, and our sessions became more intense and hallucinatory:

Me: "You can't leave. I won't let you. Plupenitenary issues must be addressed. That's a dress. Come home with me, please?"

Her: "I think, you see, that you make yourself confused because you want to avoid the pain of separation. It's upsetting to think I have a life of my own, apart from you. You are trying to live inside me."

Me: "I *am* inside you! Your organs are slimy, just like you are. You think you own me, but I own you. My every command is your wish. You don't exist."

Her: "You would rather kill me off than think I am separate from you."

Me: "I see truth. You see lies. In my mind I'm going to Carolina."

Her: "You are so upset about leaving because it disrupts your fantasy that you own me. You have had the fantasy that I was totally under your control. Your possessiveness then spoils me. But I must remain under your control at all costs."

Me: "You *are* under my control! You go where I go. There will be no separation. I've killed people before and I will kill them again. I give life and I take it away. You have no choice. I am God. Nothing comes from nothing. Nothing. God. Taken away."

Her: "Your fantasies help you avoid the pain of separation."

Me, raising my voice: "They are not fantasies! It's real. I am God. I am the One. One. Two. It's a mess."

It was indeed. I left each session completely drained, and wandered around for hours trying to summon enough calm (or enough energy to fake it) to go back to Janet's house, where I would have tea, sit on the floor, and read a fairy tale to Livy.

After a lot of thought and research, I finally decided to apply to law school, rather than to graduate school in psychology. My list of schools was ambitious—Yale, Harvard, Stanford—and in preparation for the upcoming LSAT exam, I was reading more intensely than ever, plus attending the lectures in law, psychology, and one that combined psychiatry and the law. But I was getting only a few hours of sleep each night, and it was making it difficult to concentrate the next day. I needed to calm down, to rest, and to somehow focus my mind. For the first time in my life, I actually *wanted* to take drugs. I went to my doctor and explained what was going on, and he gave me Halcion to help me sleep. This time around, no one needed to convince me to take meds; in fact, each night, when the drug kicked in and I felt myself falling into unconsciousness, I was, for just a moment, deeply grateful.

The exhaustion may well have been a factor in what happened next: another moped accident. Two days before I was to go to London to take the LSAT exam, a cyclist came around from behind me, then turned abruptly in front of me. I hit his bike and fell again to the ground, this time breaking my collarbone. If there was a worse pain than this to be had, I could not imagine what it might be. The doctors said I would be in a sling for six weeks. It meant postponing the LSATs, and doing my best to keep my restless body as still as possible while the bone knit itself back together.

Things with Mrs. Jones were going from bad to worse. During session, I paced restlessly back and forth, or sat curled up in a corner, moaning in pain and grief. At times, I lay on the floor and clutched her legs, muttering that I could not live without her. When would I see these rooms again, how would I cope? I even took to locking myself in the bathroom. That problem was quickly remedied when Mrs. Jones's analyst-husband, a transplanted American named Dr. Brandt, simply removed the lock from the door.

Often, I couldn't leave the office at all when our sessions were over. Mrs. Jones would say a very calm good-bye, then Dr. Brandt would walk me out the office and out of the house. More than once, I stood out front, rocking back and forth, keening and moaning quietly. Inevitably, Dr. Brandt came out and asked me, gently and firmly, to please go home.

Finally, the time came to go to London for the LSATs. The night before, I stayed in a bed-and-breakfast, where a couple on the floor below me managed to argue with each other, loudly, throughout the entire night, the ebb and flow of their fight rising through my floorboards like some kind of toxic air. At the most, I got two hours of shredded sleep, and felt stupid and clumsy all during the exam the next day. I was convinced I'd done poorly. Yet when the news came, I learned I'd done as well as I needed to. All my schools accepted me. I chose Yale.

I felt enormous, if momentary, relief. My plans were set for the following year. I needed the structure and the challenge, I knew that much about myself, and now, once again, I had set the bar high for myself. *This is the right thing to do,* I thought. *I'll be fine. I have to be fine.*

My final session with Mrs. Jones arrived. In stunned disbelief, I remained silent for most of that last hour, and when the end of the session came, I ran out into the waiting room and sat down, sobbing. Mrs. Jones came through the door right behind me.

"Elyn, you must go now," she said. "Another patient is coming soon, and our time together has come to an end." She and her husband must have been prepared for this, as he was suddenly there as well—he was a chain-smoker, and the scent that came from his body and clothes filled the room. I felt as though I were fighting for air.

"It's time to leave us now," said Dr. Brandt. "Come now, Elyn, this won't do. We'll just say good-bye here, shall we then?"

"No," I said, hunching my shoulders as though I expected them to hit me. How could they be so cruel to me? "I'm not leaving here. I can't."

"Yes. Yes, you can." The two of them, in chorus now.

I shook my head. I looked up at them, pleading with my body and my eyes. "I can't, don't you understand? I cannot leave her. I will not leave her."

"Other patients are coming, Elyn," said Mrs. Jones, gently but firmly. "You'll upset them. Just imagine if you arrived for your appointment, and came upon a scene such as this between me and another patient. That would not be fair, would it? You can do better than this. Come now, it's time."

Dr. Brandt stepped toward me, gently but deliberately, and just as he was about to take hold of my arm to walk me out of the room, as he had done many times before, I lunged for the pipes lining the wall and grabbed onto them as tightly as I could. Luckily it was summer, since they were heating pipes, and I would have been badly burned. Cool to the touch now, they provided a kind of ballast that made me equal to the strength of both Mrs. Jones and Dr. Brandt. How could Mrs. Jones do this, after all we had been to each other? Surely there was something I could do or say that would sway her, and draw her back to me?

"I'm not going!" I cried, and tightened my grip.

In a gesture that made me feel like I'd been struck by lightning, the two of them suddenly grabbed hold of me and tried to pull me away. But I was taller than both of them, and had the added advantage of the pipes. Dr. Brandt was trying to loosen my grip, and Mrs. Jones was pulling me by the hair. We were all completely out of control, and I was sobbing and screaming wildly. How could this be my Mrs. Jones, yanking at my hair and ignoring my cries for her to stop being so unkind?

"We need to call the police," she said to her husband. Police? For *me*?

"No, no," said Dr. Brandt. "No, they'll only take her to a mental hospital."

"I'm not leaving!" I screamed at the top of my lungs.

Finally, defeated, Mrs. Jones left the waiting room for her next appointment. "This is a shame, for you to do this to her, Elyn," said Dr. Brandt. But I wasn't having it. Stunned at her betrayal, I nevertheless could not leave Mrs. Jones behind.

Ultimately, they decided to leave me be. They each saw several rounds of patients, with me all the while sobbing quietly in the waiting room. Several hours passed, and near the end of the day, Dr. Brandt came back to me.

"Elyn, Mrs. Jones is downstairs, waiting to say good-bye to you," he said. "If you are not able to leave on your own, we will have to call the police. This must end now. Are you ready to go?"

In all my confusion and pain, I knew that he meant it. I knew I'd pushed things as far as they would go, without something or someone getting badly hurt. "Yes, I'm ready," I said quietly, and went downstairs with him, my shoulders hunched over and my legs weighing a thousand pounds apiece. When I put my arms around Mrs. Jones, though, I began to cry uncontrollably, soaking her shoulder. She had been the tether that held me to the outside world, the repository for my darkest thoughts, the person who tolerated all the bad and evil that lay within me, and never judged. She was my translator, in a world where I felt most often like an alien. How could I survive in this world without her?

Mrs. Jones pat-patted me on the back and stepped out of my embrace. "Take courage, Elyn, take courage."

I don't know how I got home, but once I got there, the lights were all out, and Janet and Livy were long since in bed and asleep. I sobbed throughout the night.

My flight back to the States left the next day. In the long hours of the trip, with the stale air and the bad food and the transient sounds of fussy babies and coughing passengers, I was cold, and alone, and awash in fantasy and grief. Over and over, I replayed the previous five years, trying frantically every single moment to keep the demons in my head from invading the plane and savaging the other passengers. From time to time, I considered asking the flight attendant whether she would mind if I jumped out the emergency door. Other than that, it was an uneventful flight.

chapter nine

As always, my family greeted me at the airport in Miami. I noted, barely, that my parents had aged somewhat since our last visit together, although I suspected that to an outside observer, they looked far more hale and hearty than I did. The number of tan and healthy faces that swirled around us as we waited to retrieve baggage and deal with customs felt like a personal rebuke—I knew I had the pallor of someone long indoors, nose in a book, spirit in a turmoil.

Although I would tell my mother and father about my second hospitalization soon after I had arrived back home, I would be intentionally scarce with details. So they didn't know any, didn't ask for any, and in any case I wasn't going to give them any now. What purpose would it serve, except to heighten their anxiety and add to my self-consciousness and shame? So the talk on the ride home floated carefully on the surface: Congratulations on the fine academic work. Glad to have you back in the U.S. finally. Yale for law school, this is so exciting. You're terribly pale and thin, Elyn, it will be good for you to spend some time in the sunshine.

My parents had apparently decided that I could chart my own course and didn't need any help. On one hand, I was always relieved when our conversations turned into nothing; on the other hand, I sometimes wondered what it would have been like, just once, if they'd turned into *something*. But there was a wall of appropriateness between us at all times; in fact, we'd spent years carefully constructing it, I on one side with my particular set of tools, they on theirs, with the tools they'd chosen. As long as nothing gratuitously unpleasant happened (as long as I managed to keep myself sufficiently pulled together to interact with them without making some kind of mess), all was calm, on that first day together, and on all the rest of the days throughout that endless summer.

"How was your day?"

"Oh, it was good, I got a lot done, how about you?"

"Oh, the usual. Here, have some of these wonderful tomatoes."

Nothing, nothing, nothing.

I didn't have any classes that summer; in fact, I didn't have any commitments at all—and the absence of a calendar and an organized structure quickly knocked me sideways. In addition, I was taking no medication, except for sleep, and sometimes I wouldn't even take that. So most of my days were spent burrowed in my room, frantically clacking away on my typewriter as I wrote Mrs. Jones one grieving letter after another. Ten, fifteen pages at a time, and sobbing all the while, with the classical music turned up so no one in the house could hear me. There were moments when I thought the grief of the distance between us would leave me doubled over on the floor. The blinding Miami summer sunshine, the weight of the humidity, the bright chatter and busyness of the people I passed by whenever I ventured out—what could anyone know of the fantasies I had? Or the demons that I wrestled with in the night, and the way I needed to grit my teeth together during the day in order to summon the simplest pleasantries of excuse me and thank you and I beg your pardon? *Please, Mrs. Jones. Please, please.*

Occasionally, I received a letter back from her, measured and kind and cautionary in tone—recognizing most probably that we needed to keep a certain boundary, because we were no longer in an analytic relationship. I was profoundly relieved each time she wrote; it meant that she wasn't dead, and that I wasn't, either, at least in her mind. Her words attempted to soothe me, acknowledging that I was having a hard time in this transition, and that she wished it would all be better soon. She knew I missed her. Steady on, and all would be well.

And then, suddenly, there was a cluster of news stories about a workplace shooting, a disgruntled postal worker, and dead coworkers left in the wake of his rage. The postman left a tape recording of his thoughts; disjointed, psychotic ramblings that didn't sound so very different from my own. The man sounded crazy. *Could I do that? Have I done that? Am I a mass murderer? Am I him? Did I shoot those people? Was the wrong person killed?* It haunted me for weeks, worrying that somehow I'd had a hand in the carnage. *Was the wrong person accused? Should I go to the police and confess? I'm evil. There are voices and commands. One must do what they say. Tell them to get away!*

Kenny and Margie Collins, my old friends from Vanderbilt, were living in Carbondale, Illinois, where Kenny had been teaching English at Southern Illinois University for six years. We'd stayed in close touch, and they invited me to come and visit them. Desperate for a change of scene, and nostalgic for the kind of simple certainty their friendship had always given me, I packed up and left Miami for what I hoped would be a good trip.

The initial stage of the flight was direct to St. Louis; from there, I had to take a prop jet to the airport nearest Carbondale. The plane was smaller than I was used to, and far noisier. It also flew much lower to the ground than the transatlantic jets did, and I was hyper-conscious of the land passing below us, with the farms, rivers, roads,

and vehicles clearly visible. As the minutes went by, I became convinced that something terrible was going to happen, that the plane
would crash and burn, and only my sheer force of concentration and
will could prevent it. Perhaps if I held my breath. Perhaps if I closed
my eyes and counted. No, closing my eyes in the middle of death-
and-destruction fantasies was never a good idea; I needed to be alert.

Nothing happened, of course. The flight was uneventful, we
landed in good order, and the smiling faces of my dear friends when
they greeted me managed to subdue the fantasies. As I began to reclaim myself a little, I did my best to participate in the kind of ram-
bling, catching-up conversations old friends take for granted when
they're together after a long time apart. I chattered like a magpie
about Oxford, my years in England, the difficulties of the relocation,
the upcoming challenges of Yale. It was as though I were scared of
what might happen once I shut my mouth.

Kenny and Margie lived in a big, comfortable old house, and did
everything they could to help me be relaxed and at home there.
Their life together seemed to be so peaceful, so normal. Kenny
seemed to enjoy his job and his students and colleagues; Margie
seemed equally happy teaching at a local nursery school. They'd
known about my hospitalization, but I never did tell them about being psychotic. I wanted them to think well of me. I didn't want them
to look at me and see a crazy person. Most of all, I wanted to stay
with them longer, hoping to absorb their normalcy, to take courage
from their intrinsic trust that I was a good friend and a decent person.
But I couldn't stop writing Mrs. Jones, and at night, I couldn't stop
crying.

Soon after my return to Miami, it was time to prepare to head
north to Yale. As much as I'd anticipated this, when it actually came
to making the necessary plans and decisions, I was completely flummoxed, and panicky as well. I made lists of what I thought I needed
to do, then just as quickly scratched things off and replaced them

with others. Should I fly into New York's LaGuardia Airport, even though New Haven was two hours away? If so, then how would I get to school? Or should I fly into Hartford, which was closer, but had fewer flights? What time of day should I fly? Should I carry everything with me, or should I send luggage and winter clothing on ahead? And what about clothes? Law school, an Ivy League college . . . The thought of a shopping expedition with my mother horrified me (I suspect it horrified her as well), so once again I went to the L.L.Bean catalog for mostly dark and sturdy pants, shirts, and sweaters. My mother raised her eyebrows almost imperceptibly, but I brushed away her concern. I'd never cared much how I looked, why should I start now? Besides, I had no energy to waste on my exterior, when so much of my focus was on the barely managed chaos inside my head.

The Yale Law School—the Sterling Law Building—sits on an entire city block in downtown New Haven, across the street from the main University Library. Built during the Depression, it's a group of imposing gothic structures, with the requisite carvings, sculpture, and stained glass windows, many adorned with brightly colored glass medallions. As grand as that sounds, though, at the time I was there, the complex was drafty, run-down, and very poorly maintained—not until 1995 would there be a badly needed, multimillion-dollar renovation that took five years to complete.

I would be staying in a two-bedroom suite, with a common living room which I'd share with Emily, a vivacious redhead from a wealthy family who was so excited to be there that for anyone else, her cheerful enthusiasm might have been contagious. But not for me. I was in no shape to start all over anyplace, let alone someplace so daunting as Yale Law School.

Once classes began, the amount of work I had to do required that I stop writing letters to Mrs. Jones. We were in class nearly twelve hours a week, with additional hours in the library before, after, and well into the night. The law school and the living quarters formed a sort of quad, so for most of us, it was almost a case of rolling out of bed and right into a classroom. Although Oxford had been challenging, there hadn't been such constraints on my time and efforts there. Within days of beginning my classwork at Yale, I was on a treadmill that seemed to have no "stop" button.

My social life was as it had always been when I arrived somewhere new. I was meeting people, but not really making friends. I could not risk anyone knowing the truth. There was no one to trust, no one who would not be repelled by the workings of my mind. And, as much as I'd always felt like an alien, it was particularly pronounced those first months in New Haven. It was 1982, and I'd been out of the country for five years. I knew almost nothing about American culture, or the latest trends and celebrities, and cared even less. Political conversations went right over my head; someone had tried to assassinate President Reagan while I was away, and it had barely entered my consciousness. People on campus were listening to music on small tape cassette players with headphones, and talking about rock videos. I'd never seen or heard of rock videos (or the fledgling rock television station, MTV, let alone cable television), and I'd missed five years of movies—I don't know why my friends and I didn't go to any at Oxford, but we didn't. I was still wearing navy blue docker-type sneakers, while everyone else had moved on to running shoes, the fashion at that time. I spoke with a slight British accent (which many Americans recognized as British, but which a Brit would immediately know as American), and no doubt it made me sound like I was putting on airs. In fact, I'd unconsciously adopted a lot of British behavior—I was arm's-length with people I didn't know, and was somewhat taken aback when students addressed some faculty members by their first names, or asked personal questions or made casual comments that seemed rude or invasive to me. For the last five years I'd been referred to as "Miss Saks" in any professional setting; the shift to "Elyn" felt odd and a bit disorienting.

My correspondence with Mrs. Jones had provided me with a kind of safety valve or repository for all my ravings. I knew that the person who was reading my letters knew me, understood me, and understood the context in which I was writing. But once I had no time to write her, there was no place for the craziness to go, and the pressure slowly began to build. In addition, I wasn't in any sort of treatment or therapy, or taking any kind of medication. There were plenty of indications that I should do something—talk to somebody, take some kind of pill. I knew that much; I was not, after all, stupid. But pills were bad, drugs were bad. Crutches were bad. If you needed a crutch, that meant you were a cripple. It meant you were not strong enough to manage on your own. It meant you were weak, and worthless. For me, my worth was defined in and by *work*.

I need to work. I tried to ignore the fact that I was convinced the person teaching legal research was making derogatory comments about me during lectures. I tried not to pay attention to the other students, who of course believed me evil and defective, and talked about me when I was out of earshot. There was no peace or respite to be found in my living quarters—that's where my endlessly cheerful roommate studied. I wanted to call Mrs. Jones, but Emily was always there, and the thought of her overhearing that conversation appalled me. If I just tried hard enough, concentrated hard enough, I could defeat this thing by myself.

And then I started to have intensely psychotic thoughts about my contracts professor, a young, smart, and funny woman, full of verve, whom I quickly grew to idealize. *She's looking after me. She's God. She has the power to make everything all right for me. She knows about the killings and wants to help. I won't let her kill me, though. She wants to help me. She'll take care of me. She has the power because she's God. I will bask in her God-like glow.* I spent hours each night awash in these thoughts, wondering if I should thank her for everything she was doing on my behalf. Should I bring her a gift of some kind? Or should I write a note instead?

And always, my head hurt from thinking these things—a pounding, searing, real pain, not like the physical pain of a headache, but an intense throbbing inside my skull someplace; sound waves. There were days that I feared that my brain was actually heating up and might explode. I visualized brain matter flying all over the room, spattering the walls. Whenever I sat at a desk and tried to read, I caught myself putting my hands up to either side of my head, trying to hold it all in.

One day, as Emily and I were talking, I turned away from her to see a bearded, scrawny, wild-eyed man behind me, holding a large knife and poised to pounce. Terrified, I gasped. The hallucination immediately disappeared.

"Elyn, what's wrong?" Emily asked.

"Nothing," I said. "Nothing's wrong."

Only two weeks into the semester, I couldn't bear it anymore, and decided I needed to take myself off to Student Health Services. At my first appointment, I met the American version of Dr. Barnes, the rather hapless young psychiatrist who'd treated me in Oxford. A beginning intern, Dr. Baird was visibly taken aback at my near-incomprehensible blabbering. The technical term for what I was doing (where one says words that sound similar but have no real connection with one another) is "word salad"—although in my case, "fruit salad" might have been more apropos.

"My name is Elyn. They used to call me 'Elyn, Elyn, watermelon.' At school. Where I used to go. Where I am now and having trouble."

"What kind of trouble?" she asked.

"There's trouble. Right here in River City. Home of the New Haveners. Where there is no haven, new or old. I'm just looking for a haven. Can you give me haven? Aren't you too young? Why are you crying? I cry because the voices are at the end of time. Time is too old. I've killed lots of people."

"Well, er, now then, Elyn," she began, looking first at her notebook, then back at me. "I think you're having some psychological difficulties. There's a word called 'delusion,' which refers to a fixed and false belief that's not based on evidence. This appears to be what is going on with you."

I thanked her for the lesson. She closed her notebook and said she would see me the following week.

When I left that appointment, I left scared. Things were out of my control and I didn't know where to turn for help. The one person who I knew could make me feel better was an ocean away. I became especially concerned with who might get hurt if my head literally were to explode. *The innocent bystander problem.*

A couple of days later, on a Friday afternoon, I became convinced that I couldn't last the weekend, and went to see the on-call person at Student Health Services. The psychiatrist on call there was nice, and a bit more with-it than the first young woman I'd seen; this young mental health professional spoke with a Latino accent and seemed extremely empathic. Within minutes of meeting her, however, I quickly decided that I needed to conduct my end of our conversation from inside her small coat closet. I stood up and walked over to it, then squeezed myself in. She wasn't having any of it.

"If you don't come out now and talk with me, Elyn, I'm going to have to hospitalize you."

Dutifully, I came out of the closet and sat down. "There's a war in China," I said. "One needs to be heavily armed. Are you God? Have you ever killed anyone?"

"No, no, I haven't," she said quietly. "Elyn, after we speak for a while, if you go back to your room, how do you think you will manage for the rest of the weekend?"

I shook my head. More gibberish came out of my mouth.

She called another therapist into the office, a young male social worker, small and wiry, with a no-nonsense manner. *He's nice*, I thought. *Not scary. Not scary yet.*

After asking me a few more questions, and basically getting nothing for their trouble, they announced that they thought it best to give me a little medication.

"It's called Trilafon," the woman said. "It's a neuroleptic. It'll help with your confused thinking."

I knew exactly what a neuroleptic was—antipsychotic medication, with terrible side effects, like heavy sedation, arms or legs that won't stop trembling (sometimes irreversibly), and a worst-case scenario that included death. There was no way I was going to take their stupid drug. *Why should I take a drug, when all I'm doing is saying what other people think but for some reason don't say? We all think like this, our brains are all like this; it's not as though I'm psychotic or something.* Did I say this out loud? I wasn't sure.

The two of them called in a third person—the chief of psychiatric services, a short, older man with white hair. Somber. Distinguished. All three urged me to take the medication.

"No, no," I said. "I can't do that. Call my friend Jean's husband. Richard. He's a neurologist. They used to know me in England, but they're in Washington, D.C., now; they'll tell you. Richard knows all about my brain, he will know what's best to do."

They shook their heads. They began to look like dolls to me. Puppet dolls. "Elyn, if you don't agree to take the medication, we might have to put you into the hospital."

That sent a shock through my body that forced me to focus my mind, forced me to tighten my speech and manage the words that came like marbles out of my mouth. "None of this is necessary," I said as firmly as I could manage. "Simply being here, talking to you—I'm feeling better now. If you take me to a hospital, they'll let me go. You can't hold someone who's doing as well as I am. I'll get out right away."

It was an act, but it worked. They agreed to let me spend the weekend in the Student Health infirmary instead. And while they kept arguing for the Trilafon, they promised not to force it on me.

I'd won the battle. But I was about to lose the war.

The social worker accompanied me back to my dorm room to get my things; then we walked back and I checked into the infirmary, on the highest floor of the Student Health building. I wasn't happy, but I tried to comfort myself as best I could. *At least you're not in the hospital. That was a close call.*

I sat on the edge of the bed for what seemed like long minutes, then decided I ought to take a look around. To my surprise, I discovered that I could easily walk to the elevators with no interference from anyone, and take them all the way down to the ground floor, which is exactly what I did. I stood outside on the front steps of the building for at least a half hour, smoking a cigarette and thinking about what I should do next.

It was a beautiful New England autumn evening, with a clear sky full of stars. The air was fresh and bracing, and there was a sense of peace and order on the campus. *I don't belong here,* I thought. *I should be in the library working; this is all a big mistake, a regrettable misunderstanding. But it's at least ten o'clock, too dangerous to be walking around this neighborhood alone. They might get upset or angry if they notice me missing. Oh, what the hell, best to go back upstairs and spend the night here.* Sighing, I went back inside and headed for the elevators, leaving the lovely night behind.

As I walked back onto the unit, one of the nurses saw me. "There she is!" she shouted.

Startled, I bolted like a fox who'd heard the bay of the hounds. Hurtling through the nearest door, I ran down the fire stairs, and heard them running after me. Their voices echoing down, their shoes thumping on the metal steps. Barely one flight ahead of them, I made it down to one of the lower floors, where I found an open door. It seemed to be a child's playroom. Panting, I crouched down and crawled under a tiny table, folding myself into the smallest ball I could. I heard the commotion outside, people calling out my name, running back and forth down the halls looking for me. Eventually, someone came into the room where I was hiding and switched on the lights.

"I found her!"

I pleaded with her, incoherent. "Masses of mastiffs are coming! These masses, diseases! Why are they doing this to me? Why?"

The staff quickly gathered to confer with one another, and stayed close to make sure I didn't get away. By the time the on-call clinicians arrived, I was back in my room, sitting calmly on the bed, and able to form an intelligible sentence.

"What's going on, Elyn?" asked the social worker.

I shrugged. "I was bored, I decided to take a walk."

"I see," he said. "And were you thinking of leaving while you were taking this walk?"

"I was thinking of it," I admitted, "but I decided to stay."

"A good decision," he said, and then he smiled. "And how are you feeling now?"

"Fine. I'm fine. It's all OK."

"Yes, you do seem OK to us now," he said. "But the infirmary staff think you're too difficult to manage, so you can't stay here."

As nice as he was, his message was clear: I was being kicked out of Student Health. Shameful. I couldn't decide whether to burst into laughter or burst into tears.

The psychologist and social worker instructed me to spend the night at my dorm and come back the next morning, so they could see how I was doing. I agreed. They gave me a small packet of Trilafon, with the encouragement that it would make me feel better.

I would never take any of that Trilafon; the only time I really even thought about it was days later, when the packet fell out of my pocket after constitutional law class, and my professor, rather embarrassed, returned it to me the following day.

However, I was dutiful about returning to Student Health the next morning. I hadn't slept, my fantasies filled the room, and I couldn't seem to get my mouth to work when it came time to meet with my psychologist and the social worker.

"One. Tempo at the time. Time is a number," I told them.

"You seem upset today, Elyn. Can you tell us how you're feeling?"

"There's the killing fields," I said. "Heads exploding. I didn't do anything wrong. They just said 'quake, fake, lake.' I used to ski. Are you trying to kill me?"

"No, of course not, we're only here to help you. Have you thought any more about taking some of the medicine?"

At that point, I crawled under the desk and started to moan and rock. The faceless creatures hovering near, invisible to everyone but me, were about to tear me to pieces. "They're *killing* me. They're *killing* me! I've got to try. Die. Lie. Cry."

"We want to get you some help, Elyn." The psychologist said she was going to her office to make some calls and that the social worker would stay there with me. I huddled right where I was, rocking and moaning under the desk. The creatures wanted to kill me, and the doctors wanted to send me to a hospital. I knew this for an absolute fact. I had to get out of there.

Crawling out from beneath the desk, I quietly told the nice social worker that I needed a drink of water. He followed me out of the room and toward the water fountain. Suddenly, I darted for the side door, hoping to make my way down the stairs, but he moved fast, caught me in a few steps, and put me in a restraining hold. Although small, he was very strong, and I couldn't move in his grip as he brought me back into the room.

"I'm sorry I did that," he said apologetically. "It had to be done, you know, but I do feel bad about it." As fragmented as I was, I believed him. He wanted to be kind to me, but for some reason I was making it hard for him.

The psychologist came back into the room and reported that it was difficult to find a hospital bed on the weekend. The social worker then replied that maybe he could make a couple of calls and see if there was anything out there. He left to make the calls. The psychologist stayed with me.

I was going to the hospital for the third time, I knew it. I was going to be an inpatient again, and they would make me take drugs. Every nerve in my body was screaming. I didn't want a hospital. I didn't want drugs. I just wanted help.

Struggling to control the terror in my voice, I politely asked the psychologist if we could go into the hall so I could get a drink. She followed me out of the room and toward the water fountain, and once again I darted for the side door and the stairs. The psychologist called out to me, "Stop, Elyn. I won't be able to catch up with you. Please stop now." *No no no no no.* Unseeing—of obstacles, of other students, of anyone who might have been staring at me—I ran all the way across campus back to my room. Thankfully, my roommate was not there.

It was an inauspicious beginning to my legal career.

chapter ten

FULLY EXPECTED THAT someone from Student Health would send the campus police after me, and I braced myself for their arrival. *They'll take me away. They'll lock me up.* I cowered in my room for a long time, waiting for the inevitable knock on the door. But no one came. Scared, but restless, I decided that I could remain hiding in my room or take my chances out in the world. And knowing exactly what would calm me down, I did what I always did whenever my back was against the wall—I gathered up my books and headed for the library.

I began to breathe easier the minute I walked through the doors. I spent the entire day there, reading and going over my notes, trying to focus my thinking about the coming week's classes. Every so often, I'd glance over my shoulder, but nobody was paying any attention to me. By the day's end, I'd managed to calm myself down.

When I returned to my room that evening, I discovered a telephone message that Emily had left for me. The psychologist from Student Health Services had called, and I felt it both professional and kind that she had not identified herself. She asked that I call her back. I thought about it for a few minutes—what's the worst that could happen if I didn't do as she'd asked? But then I decided that given the state I'd been in the previous few days, it was probably a good idea to make the call.

It turned out that I'd been reassigned to another doctor: Hans Pritzer, a senior psychologist and psychoanalyst who, I discovered later, had a formidable reputation for tackling "the most difficult cases" at Student Health.

Dr. Pritzer was Austrian, with a compact frame, reddish hair, and fair complexion; he spoke with a thick accent, where ssss's often came out as zzzzz's. "You caused quite a commotion this weekend," he told me at our first meeting, shaking his head slightly, a concerned father to a truant daughter. *Zis veekend.* For some reason, I relaxed a little. "We need to try to work together now, Elyn, so that we can avoid that kind of thing. How are you feeling today?"

As I almost always did when someone I didn't know asked me that question, I quickly responded, "Better. Much better, thank you."

"No, I don't think that is quite the truth," he said. "I think that there are things going on inside your head, and that you must tell me what you are thinking, so that we can work through this and ad-dress the problem." *Ve can vork zzzrooooo zis.* I wondered if this is what Freud sounded like, with his vvvvv's and his zzzzz's eliding as he led his patients through the thickets of their own minds. My own mind was again speeding up to such a degree that I could barely sit still.

"People are controlling me, they're putting thoughts into my head," I told him. "I can't resist them. They're doing it to me. I'll have to kill them. Are you controlling me? They're making me walk around your office. I give life and I take it away."

Pacing as I muttered, I suddenly stopped in midsentence, trans-fixed by something or someone unseen, and then I began to rock and moan. I wanted to lie down on Dr. Pritzer's couch, but I was astonished to discover that he wouldn't allow that. "Lying down causes people to regress," he said. "You're too regressed already."

Surprisingly, he told me that he didn't think I was schizophrenic. "You seem to be working very hard to connect with me," he observed. "And you've been operating successfully in the world, whereas one of the chief markers of schizophrenia is *not* connecting, and not being able to function. At least, this is what I think so far."

"What about medication?" I asked. "Are you going to make me take pills? Because I don't want to do that. I cannot do that. Drugs are bad, you know."

"We'll see how it goes," he answered. "We will discuss it, and as I learn more, we will come to that decision together."

I wanted so much to trust him, this straight-talking old-world gentleman whose only crime, so far, was that he was not my beloved Mrs. Jones. We agreed that we would meet twice a week.

And then Dr. Pritzer said it was time for me to go.

"I . . . I can't," I said. My legs, so restless before, had turned to stone.

Again, the slight head shake. "Ah, Elyn, you must. It is time now. I have another patient, we will meet again quite soon."

Very reluctantly, I trudged slowly out to the waiting room and sat down. Forces were keeping me from leaving, I could not get to the door that led back outside. A few moments later, Dr. Pritzer came into the waiting room to greet his next patient and usher her into his office. Then, suddenly, he reappeared. "Do you think you can go now, Elyn?" he asked. I was relieved to discover that if I put my mind to it again, I could. And so I did.

Every appointment after that, I spent extra time in the waiting room by myself when our session was finished. It was as though I needed to marshal my forces to leave a safe place. But Pritzer allowed me to judge for myself when I was ready to go, and each time, I managed to make that decision on my own.

In the meantime, I continued going to my classes, straining to focus my mind sufficiently to get my work done. But I was still convinced my contracts teacher was taking special care of me. *Perhaps she and Pritzer are working together on my case. Are they married? Perhaps there's something sinister. That's it, it's an experiment! Contracts teacher works with psychologist. They have a contract on my life. Experimental therapy with messages sent via contracts cases.*

In one session with Dr. Pritzer, I was frantically pacing from one side of his office to the other, growing more agitated as my thoughts became more violent. "I've killed people and I will kill again," I announced. I was almost growling at him. "Who else is in the office with us? Are you human?" I walked over to a big, leafy plant in the corner and snapped off one of its leaves. "See? This is what I can do to people!"

"You should *not* have done that, Elyn," Dr. Pritzer said sternly. "I like that plant. You are not to do that again."

Chastened, I sat down, and tried to be still for the rest of the session. He was setting limits; I was trying to observe them. But the limits never held, at least in my mind. As the days passed, I felt more and more in peril, as though I were hanging from a ledge as my grip weakened.

In class, I was assigned to prepare my first legal memo. Its purpose was to explain a very specific area of law, in a succinct, cogent manner. In a memo, you address a question from both sides; in a brief, you argue only for one side. The assignment was announced two weeks before it was due, with a prescribed format, and the length was to be no more than fifteen pages. As with all my other limits, I went right past this one, too—in addition to the course work for the three other classes, I worked on the memo day and night, for hours, without sleeping. And when I was finished, my paper was nearly fifty pages in length. I later learned that the person in charge of grading papers thought that it was one of the two best pieces of work turned in by anyone that year. But it was not what I was assigned to do. "It's very good," said the teaching assistant. "But it's not a memo—it's more of an article than anything else."

The law is precise; I was expected to be precise as well. And I wanted to be. But each time, something inside me pushed me farther than I was supposed to go. The work was unacceptable. I was unacceptable.

And then I was assigned a second law memo. At this point, it was like being instructed to climb Everest in sneakers. Too anxious to read, I saw only words jumbled on the page, with no coherence. What's worse, I couldn't remember anything I'd read up until this moment, and when I tried to write, only gibberish came out—threads of nonsensical words and phrases that meant nothing, in or out of context, exactly the same way it had happened at Oxford when I was at my worst. *Mrs. Jones, where are you? I need you. We've been in this place before, and you led me out. Where are you?*

All my life, books had been the life raft, the safe haven, the place I ran to when nothing else worked. But now books revealed only page after page of nothing that made sense. Panicked, I picked up my worn copy of Aristotle, but even it betrayed me. *Nothing, nothing,*

I greeted my two classmates in the Yale Law School Library. It was ten o'clock on a Friday night.

One of them was an Alabaman named Rebel ("because I was a breech birth," he'd explained), and the other was a woman named Val. They were both in my "small group"—the only small class a first-term law student has at Yale. And neither of them was particularly happy about being in the library; it was the weekend, after all, and there were plenty of other things they could have been doing at ten on a Friday night. But at my insistence, we'd made the date to work on the second memo assignment. Although each of us was responsible for his or her own memo, we were allowed to strategize together. We had to do it, to *finish* it, to *produce* it, to . . .

"Memos are visitations," I informed them. "They make certain points. The point is on your head. Pat used to say that. Have you ever killed anyone?"

Rebel and Val looked at me as if they, or I, had just been splashed with ice water. "A joke, right?" quipped one. "What are you talking about, Elyn?"

"Oh, the usual. You know. Heaven and hell. Who's what, what's who. Hey!" I said, leaping out of my chair. "Let's all go out on the roof. It's OK. It's safe."

I hurried to the nearest large window, opened it, then climbed through and stepped out onto the roof, a flat surface and not at all scary. A few moments later, Rebel and Val followed me. "Course, the police may see us and bring in a SWAT team," I said, laughing. "Can't you just imagine? 'One-niner-niner, one-niner-niner, there's an APB out for people trying to break into Yale Law Library.' Yeah, like there are lots of valuable things *there*."

They couldn't help but laugh back. They asked what had gotten into me.

"This is the real me," I announced, waving my arms above my head. And then, late on a Friday night, on the roof of the Yale Law School Library, I began to sing, and not quietly, either. "Come to the Florida sunshine bush. Do you want to dance?"

The smiles quickly faded from their faces. "Are you on drugs?" one asked. "Are you high?"

"High? Me? No way. No drugs! Come on, let's dance! Come to the Florida sunshine bush. Where they make lemons. Where there are demons. Is anyone else out here with us? Hey, wait a minute, what's the matter with you guys? Where are you going?"

Rebel and Val had both turned away and were heading back inside. "You're frightening me," said one.

I shrugged. "OK, I'll come in, too. But there's nothing in there. Nothing."

As we clambered back through the window, one of my classmates said something about the Student Health Center. "Maybe you should, um, go see someone there."

"I'm already seeing someone there," I said. "Twice a week."

"Oh. Well. What about maybe going over there right now, though?"

I shook my head. "No. Not now. I need to work. We've got this memo thing."

Once we were all seated around the table again, I began to carefully stack my textbooks into a small tower. Then I rearranged my note pages. Unsatisfied, I rearranged them again. "I don't know if you're having the same experience of words jumping around the pages as I am," I said. "I think someone's infiltrated my copies of the cases. We've got to case the joint. I don't believe in joints. But they hold your body together."

This was more than either of them had bargained for. "It's nearly midnight, we're not getting anything done here. Let's get out of here; we can try it again sometime tomorrow."

"No, no, I can't go home yet. I need to work. Quirk. Of nature."

"Elyn, we have to leave," they said, gathering up their books and looking nervously around the room. Something was obviously scaring them. "Please. And you need to come with us."

"No, I can't. I have to work. I'll stay here, and hide in the stacks."

I stayed long after they'd gone, sitting alone on the floor between two towering stacks of books, muttering to myself. The library grew even more quiet; section by section, the lights were being turned off. Finally, frightened of being locked in overnight, I got up and left, keeping my head down so that I wouldn't have to make eye contact with any of my classmates, which wasn't likely at that hour, since the last remaining person seemed to be the clueless security guard at the front door.

Of course, it was completely dark outside. I'd never been comfortable in that kind of dark—at least not on the ground; the roof had been much more pleasant. My whole body shook as I made my way back to my room. And once there, I couldn't settle down. I couldn't sleep. My head was too full of noise. Too full of lemons, and law memos I could not write, and mass murders that I knew I would be responsible for. Sitting on my bed, I rocked back and forth, moaning in fear and isolation.

I had finally done it: cracked in public, in front of colleagues, my law school classmates. Who I was, what I was, had been revealed. Now everyone would know the truth—of my worthlessness, my evil. When things were this bad at Oxford, knowing I would see Mrs. Jones each day helped me contain my psychotic thoughts when I was with other people, or when I needed to get work done. But with no Mrs. Jones to take my craziness to, and no comfort to be found in my studies, there was no balm in Gilead. Something was prying my grip loose, finger by finger, and very soon now, I was simply going to fall through space.

After a sleepless night, I doggedly went back to the library and tried again to tackle the memo, but I could not make my head work. Panicked, I practically ran to my professor's office. There was no one there. I waited. When Professor M. arrived, he looked at me askance.

"I've come to talk to you about my memo," I said. "I'm sorry, but I need an extension."

"Why don't you come into my office and we'll discuss this," he said. When I sat down in the chair in front of his desk, I hunched over, drawing my shoulders up to my ears as though I expected to be hit.

"The memo materials have been infiltrated," I said, looking at my shoes. "Jumping around. I used to be good at the broad jump. Because I'm tall. I fall. Is anyone else in this room? It's a matter of point. There's a plan. People put things in and then say it's my fault. I used to be God but I got demoted. Are you God?"

Professor M. stayed perfectly calm. "You seem quite upset, Elyn."

My head was buzzing. Lemons and memos and mass murders. "Well, with all the killings, it makes sense that I'd be upset," I said. Then I launched into my little Florida juice jingle, twirling around his office, my arms thrust out like bird wings. Then I went to a corner in his office and sat down, continuing to sing.

Professor M. looked at me. It was hard to decipher the expression on his face. Was he frightened of me? Was he confused? I couldn't decide. Maybe he couldn't decide, either.

"I'm very concerned about you, Elyn," he finally said. "I have a little work to do here at the office, and afterwards, perhaps you might want to come and have dinner with me and my family. Do you think you could do that?"

How reasonable that sounded. "Yes," I said. "That would be quite pleasant. But if you don't mind, I think I'll just go through this window and wait on the roof for you, until it's time for us to go." If that didn't seem a good idea to Professor M., he didn't let on. I proceeded out his window onto the roof.

I spent the next hour or so laughing and singing and gibbering away on the roof of the Yale Law School. I found several feet of loose telephone wire up there, and made myself a kind of belt. I picked up all sorts of metal objects lying around on the roof and attached them to the belt. The best find was a rather long nail, six inches or so. I put it in my pants pocket, just in case I needed protection. *You never know when you might need protection.*

"Elyn? Can you come back in the office now, please?" It was Professor M. at the window again. "I've spoken with my wife," he said, "and we'd like not only to have you join us for dinner, but perhaps to spend the night with us as well."

I thought the offer was exceedingly generous, and told him how very much I appreciated their kindness. Having a home-cooked meal, having nice people to talk to, to spend time with . . . perhaps that might prevent my head from exploding and splattering the walls.

And so Professor M. and I took a leisurely walk across the Yale campus that lovely fall Saturday afternoon, me wearing my telephone-wire belt. Dinner at his house didn't go so well, so Professor M. decided to phone the Student Health Center to speak with the psychiatrist on call—whom we'll call The Doctor.

When Professor M. handed me the phone, The Doctor briskly informed me that he'd received a call from someone at the law school last night who reported that I seemed extraordinarily disturbed. He then asked me a number of questions, to which I gave irrelevant answers, and then he suggested that I might want to come in and see him. He sounded like the kind of person who was looking at his watch and tapping his foot while waiting for my answer. "I don't know," I said. "No, actually, I don't think I do."

I think The Doctor was surprised, and suggested I might want to reconsider. (And by the way, in my experience, the words "now just calm down" almost inevitably have the opposite effect on the person you are speaking to.) "You know, you really are a jerk," I said, and hung up the phone.

"I don't think he handled that particularly well, either, Elyn," said Professor M, referring to his own interactions with The Doctor.

"I think I need to talk to my friend Richard," I said. "He's a neurologist, you know." Something was about to happen to me; I wasn't sure what it was, but I knew it wasn't going to be pleasant. It seemed imperative that I start marshaling my forces.

When Professor M. put the call through, and my old friend Jean answered the phone, I said, "It's me, I've called to talk to you and Richard."

"Your voice sounds funny," said Jean. "What's going on? How are you?"

"Oh, well, I'm up. And down. And all around," I said. "It's a matter of the commands put in my head." I then whispered to Jean as quietly as I could, but with great urgency, that I was trying my best, I really was. "But nefarious things are going on. I've been cornered and the points are pointed. There's an effort under way to kill me." I put my hand in my pocket; the nail from the law school roof was still there.

Richard's voice came through the phone. "Elyn?" he said. "Is something wrong?"

"Come to the Florida sunshine tree," I greeted him.

A moment's silence, then, "What do you mean?" he asked.

"Fresh tasting lemon juice naturally. There's a natural volcano. They put it in my head. It's erupting. I've killed lots of people. I've killed children. There's a flower on the bookshelf. I can see it blooming. Have you killed anyone, Richard? My teacher is God. I used to be God but got demoted. Do you think it's a question of Kilimanjaro?"

"How long have you been feeling like this?" Richard asked.

"It's not a matter of feeling," I told him. "It's a matter of things happening to me. I give life and I take it away. Don't try to fuck with me, Richard, I've killed better men than you. Children. Lemon juice. Point."

"Elyn, you should know by now, there's nothing to fear from me," he said. "Jean and I want the best for you, we'd never hurt you, or allow anyone else to do so, either."

"But people are trying to *kill* me," I moaned. "What am I going to do? They're in the sky. They're killing me. I didn't do it."

In a kind and tender voice, Richard said that he understood how upset I was. "Let me speak to your friend Professor M. now, please." Dutifully, I handed the professor the phone.

I could tell from the look on his face that what Professor M. heard from Richard was unnerving. I was having a psychotic break, Richard said, and needed to go to the hospital as quickly as possible. There was a chance I could be dangerous, possibly even to Professor M.'s child. (I have never harmed anyone. Still, it was not unreasonable at that point, given what I had been saying on the phone, for Richard to fear that I might.)

Not surprisingly, Professor M. immediately called The Doctor and told him he was going to bring me to the emergency room right away.

"Please, no, no," I begged. "Don't take me to the hospital. It'll make me worse, please don't make me go there. I'm fine. I felt a little upset before but I feel fine now. *Please* don't take me to the emergency room."

Professor M. was reassuring, but adamant. "No, I think we have to go to the emergency room, Elyn. You're a smart young woman, and you're not yourself. And Richard, who knows you and cares for you, believes you should go, too. At any rate, you can't be alone, and I'm sorry, but I can't allow you to stay here. At the hospital, you'll be able to talk to someone who can help you."

I tried to calm myself, to focus on convincing him to see it my way. "Thank you, but no, I don't think so. I'd like to call a cab now, so I can go back to my room."

But he was determined—he walked me out to the car, opened the door on the passenger side, and gently but firmly put me inside.

I chattered nervously all the way to Yale-New Haven Hospital. "My goodness, it's so late, you needn't stay with me," I said. "But maybe could I borrow some money from you? I'll need to take a taxi home as soon as this appointment is over. It will only be five, ten minutes at most, they'll tell you I'm perfectly fine, I'm certain of it."

"Yes, of course," he said. "I'll loan you the money."

When we pulled up to the ER entrance, before Professor M. had a chance to shut the car off, I jumped out and took off running in the other direction. I hadn't planned to run, but I was scared. Everything was closing in. Students knew, teachers knew, Richard knew. *This is the end. The end.*

It was not the kind of neighborhood where a woman—or anyone for that matter—should have been running around alone, in the dark, without money or any sense of where she was going. Thankfully, Professor M. caught up with me by the end of the block, placed his hand firmly under my arm, and steered me back to the ER. "This is best," he said.

We both sat down with the admitting nurse to do the necessary paperwork, and I quickly explained that my friend, Professor M., was having terrible stomach pains and needed to be admitted immediately. I laughed hysterically.

A few minutes later, I found myself in a small private room, waiting for The Doctor. Professor M.'s role as guardian angel was over, and he'd gone home. In his place was a hospital attendant, a massive man with a gentle face and a softly moderated voice. "It will just be a few minutes, miss. Don't worry now."

"Would you like to dance?" I asked him. Smiling, he declined.

"Well, then, I'm going to, if you don't mind," I said, and while I pranced around the room, I attempted to explain my situation. "People are trying to kill me. They've killed me many times today already. It might spread to you." I unwound my telephone-wire belt and started to snap it through the air. "This is a very powerful weapon," I said.

"I see that," the attendant said. "You know, miss, I think I have to take it from you. Probably not a good idea for you to have it in here."

I stepped back. "No," I said.

"Yes," he said. "I'm sorry. May I have it, please?"

Reluctantly, I gave up the belt. "But you can't have my nail," I said, patting my pocket.

The attendant asked what I did in New Haven.

"I'm a law student," I said.

"Oh, that's interesting," he said. "Must be very hard work. You know, we had another law student in here the other night with mental problems, his name was————."

Would this nice man soon be telling someone about *me*? If my head exploded, its contents blown all over the room, would that be someone's idea of idle chatter? I thought health stuff was supposed to be confidential. (And indeed, even Professor M.—though no doubt out of good motives—would reveal to my seminar classmates that I had been hospitalized with a breakdown.)

"What happened to him?" I asked. "The law student, I mean?"

"Oh, they just gave him some medication and sent him home." The answer almost erased my confidentiality concerns: The student wasn't admitted to the hospital? He just took some meds and was then allowed to go? It had never occurred to me to think about it like that. I hadn't been in a hospital for three years and didn't intend to end my streak now; if taking medication were my only bargaining chip, I'd consider it.

Then The Doctor arrived.

He was everything I'd imagined in our telephone conversation: short, bureaucratic (right down to the ballpoint pen he kept clicking), authoritarian, and short on patience. *The man who makes the trains run on time.* I slipped my hand into my pocket and wrapped my fingers around my weapon nail. His eyes followed my hand.

"Give that to me," he said.

"No," I said.

He immediately called for security. Another attendant came in, this one not so nice, with no interest in letting me keep my nail. And once he'd pried it from my fingers, it was all over. Within seconds, The Doctor and his whole team of goons swooped down, grabbed me, lifted me out of the chair, and slammed me down on a nearby bed with such force that I saw stars. Then they bound both my legs and arms to the metal bed, with thick leather straps.

A sound came out of my mouth that I'd never heard before. Half-groan, half-scream, barely human, and pure terror. Then the sound came again, forced from somewhere deep inside my belly and scraping my throat raw. "*Noooooo*," I shouted. "Stop this, don't do this to me!" I glanced up to see a face watching the entire scene through the window in the steel door. Why was she watching me? Who was she? I was an exhibit, a specimen, a bug impaled on a pin and helpless to escape. "Please," I begged. "Please, this is like something from the Middle Ages. Please, no!" Somewhere in the midst of the chaos, a single thought occurred to me: If Mrs. Jones were here, this would not be happening. She would never have allowed such a thing. With Mrs. Jones, the tools we worked with were words, not straps. She never would have stood by while someone hurt me, terrified me, or made me feel helpless and alone.

"I want you to count backwards by sevens, starting from one hundred," intoned The Doctor. I looked at him as though he were nuts. Count? For *him*? Do *anything* for him? I had come to the hospital frightened, confused, and paranoid. Nothing he'd done so far had improved the situation. And look, there it was again, the face on the other side of the window. Had someone paid admission to see the crazy woman?

A nurse came into the room with a tray, and a tiny little paper cup on the tray. "Please drink this," she said.

"No," I answered. "You drink it."

"If you don't drink it, I'll have to inject it instead," she said, her face impassive. Bound hand and foot, I had no choice. Choking and gagging, I tried to lock my teeth against the liquid, but could not. It was my first dose of an antipsychotic drug.

Terrified that I was disappearing, I struggled against my restraints, needing to convince myself that I was still there. *I'm shrinking, I'm shrinking.* Being restrained hurt, a lot. But at least the pain meant I hadn't vaporized yet.

The Doctor was as understanding and insightful as ever; he made one of those school-teachery tsk-tsk clucking sounds and rolled his eyes in disapproval. I wondered why he'd gone into psychiatry. "You are acting like you want to be in the hospital," he said, "so we are going to find you a hospital bed."

So, then—it was all a matter of simply behaving myself? He spoke as though the most I had to fear was being sent to bed without milk and cookies. "No, thanks," I replied. "And can you please remove these restraints? They hurt. And they're degrading."

"No," he said. "I want you to admit yourself into the psychiatric hospital."

"Are you *nuts*?" I shot back. "You're the one who belongs in the hospital. I'm fine. And I'd like to go home now. I have work to do. Let me out of these things."

The Doctor said that he was about to write out a "Physician's Emergency Certificate," which allowed the hospital to hold me fifteen days. I would later learn that on that certificate he called me "dangerous to herself and others"; he also described me as "gravely disabled." His reason? I was not able to do my law school homework. After the fifteen days had passed, I would be entitled to a commitment hearing, if I wanted one.

Of course, I didn't learn about the ins and outs of all this until later. All I knew at that moment was that I was going into a hospital. No matter what.

However, it turned out that there was no room for me at the psychiatric unit in Yale-New Haven Hospital, so they were shipping me across town—to Yale Psychiatric Institute. YPI. "You'll be safe there," said The Doctor.

"I'd be just as safe at home. Safe from you, anyway," I said.

When the EMTs came in to take me to the ambulance, I was struck by how handsome one of them was. "Are you a movie star?" I asked. "I'm quite sure you're a movie star. Your name's on the tip of my tongue, I just can't think of it right now."

My relief when they undid the bed restraints lasted about ten seconds; they immediately strapped me down on the ambulance gurney.

"Why?" I asked the young and handsome EMT. "Why do you have to do it like this?"

He looked a little embarrassed, and turned away from my gaze. "It's the rules. I'm sorry."

The rules. New rules. I would have to learn so many new rules. "Can you put a blanket over my face before we go out there?" I pleaded. "I don't want anyone to see me like this."

Very gently, he covered my head with a white sheet, and the gurney left the ER and rolled toward the ambulance. *Maybe this is what it feels like to be dead.*

chapter eleven

ONCE WE'D ARRIVED at YPI, the EMTs took me by stretcher upstairs, where nurses and attendants were waiting. The hallways were narrow and dingy, classic institutional interior decorating. *The people here are all crazy, so who cares if it's ugly?*

I was taken to the "seclusion room"—empty except for a lone bed. Observing the surroundings, I only barely reacted to them, since it was long past midnight, and I was woozy with the effects of the drug. All I wanted to do was go to sleep; this bed looked as good as any.

The psychiatrist on call that night, Dr. Griffith, was a young woman with light brown hair, and an attitude light-years removed from The Doctor's. A gentle smile, a reassuring manner. That is, until I actually heard what she was saying. "We'd like you to put yourself in restraints, Elyn." Dr. Griffith motioned toward the bed.

No. I can't. "Please, it's not necessary," I begged them—a group of strangers, in a strange place, in the middle of this strange night.

A rather large man, who I would later find out was a divinity student,

sort of loomed over me and grumbled, "Either put yourself in restraints or we'll put you in them. It's up to you."

I may have been psychotic, but my antennae for where danger lay
were still pretty good. "Are you the heavy here?" I muttered.

"OK, OK," Dr. Griffith said, motioning for the enforcer to step
back. "Just lie down then, and we can talk. No restraints."

A wave of relief came over me, and I sagged back on the bed,
thinking only of getting my head on that pillow—at which point
everyone in this room did exactly as the others had done in the hospital emergency room. In seconds, my arms and legs were grabbed,
pinned, and bound to the bed by leather straps.

I screamed at the top of my lungs and struggled against the group
of hands pinning me down, but I was no match for them, and soon
the bands were fastened tight. Then it got worse, since apparently
binding my arms and legs wasn't enough. They arranged a net over
me—an actual *net*—from the top at my neck to the bottom at my ankles, covering my legs, my torso, my chest. And then they pulled it
snug at the four corners. I couldn't move at all, and felt like all the
breath was leaving my body.

"I can't breathe, I can't breathe!" I cried.

"Yes, you can," said the voices in unison. They were standing over
me, watching. I continued to gasp and beg, and eventually they loos-
ened the net somewhat, and I could actually inhale. (I later learned
that a hundred or so people die each year in the U.S. while being put
or kept in restraints.)

After I was secure—"made safe," as The Doctor might have
phrased it—people left, even Dr. Griffith. The divinity student stayed,
sitting sentry outside the open door to my room.

Nothing at the Warneford had horrified me as much as this did.
No single hallucination, no threat of demonic forces or impulses I
couldn't control had ever held me hostage like this. No one I knew, no
one who loved me, knew that I was here, tied to a bed with a net over

my body. I was alone in the night, with evil coming at me both from within myself and from without. It was unimaginable to me at that point that the ancient meaning of the word "hospital" is "shelter." Refuge. Comfort. Care. *No.*

As frightened as I was, I was equally angry, and frantic to find a way to show defiance—not an easy task, when you're in four-point restraints and pinned under a tuna net. I was bound . . . but not gagged! So I inhaled as deeply as I could, and started belting out some beloved Beethoven. Not, for obvious reasons, "Ode to Joy," but rather Beethoven's Fifth Symphony. BABABA *BA!* BABABA *BA!* Look, there, see how he created such power out of those four simple notes! It echoed nicely down the halls, so I did it again.

For hours, I sang it and shouted it and hollered it with all the power remaining inside me. I fought off the beings who were attacking me, I yanked against the restraints, and I sang my heart out. Every once in a while, a nurse came by with another little demitasse of antipsychotic liquid. I swallowed it passively, then fought to swim above the fog it created. BABABA *BA!*

Finally, exhausted, I slept, sweaty and fitful and sore. I may have slept an hour or so when Dr. Griffith returned with her supervisor, Dr. Green. He looked surprisingly young to me, for someone who clearly had power over what happened next. "How are you feeling now?" he asked.

I wanted to snap, "Hey, it's tough to feel perky when a room full of people tie you to a bed and pour drugs down your throat." But I didn't do that.

"I feel much better," I said, struggling for the appropriate tone of subservience and penitence. "I'm so sorry for causing such a ruckus. Do you think I might be able to be untied now? Because these hurt."

No. "We'd like you to stay in them a little longer," came his cryptic reply.

At that point, I'd been restrained for six hours. My muscles ached and my skin was chafed from struggling. I longed to stretch an arm, a leg, anything. I couldn't even wiggle my feet. The light inside the building seemed gray, almost as though it were leaking in from someplace else. "What's wrong with me?" I asked.

"You were very psychotic last night," Dr. Green replied.

"But what *kind* of psychosis? Why is this happening?"

He shook his head. The institutional head shake was becoming very familiar to me. "It's really too early to tell," he replied.

"But couldn't I please get back to my work, while we figure it out?" I asked. "Like an outpatient thing? I've done that before. I need to get back to school, I'm losing valuable time here."

"It's too soon," Green said. "You're still quite sick. And we need more time to monitor how the meds are doing."

"I think they're working," I said, ever the good student. "Because my thinking really is clearer." And, in fact, it was.

He agreed—it seemed to be the case that I was improving. The bad news was, he thought it was time to contact my parents.

"What? Why? No, under no circumstances! It's not OK with me to call them, do you understand? It's not OK to tell them about this! They don't need to know this!"

I thought Green understood, I thought he agreed to respect my wishes. But the hospital *did* call them; as it turned out, Connecticut had a law that required it.

The two doctors asked me some more questions—about my feelings and my history—but repeated that they weren't willing to take me out of restraints yet; I had to demonstrate an ability to stay calm. Then they left me alone.

For the next three hours, I stared at the ceiling, felt my pulse beating in my wrists and ankles where the straps held me down, and managed to keep myself from shrieking like a banshee. I somehow managed to control my demons as well. Any sign of weakness, there was no telling how long the hostage situation would last.

When Dr. Griffith finally returned, it was with good news. "We're going to release your legs from the restraints, Elyn, and see how it goes," she said. It went, by their lights, just fine. I managed to stay acceptably calm, and by seven that night I was finally untied altogether. I was moved to the Intensive Care Program, a room with staff and a small number of patients who the hospital felt needed constant monitoring. Ever conscious of the eyes on me, I stretched and moved my arms and legs. Freedom of movement, once it's taken away from you and then restored, is a remarkable gift. Why didn't I ever realize this before?

Not knowing the hospital had already called my parents, I asked if I could call them myself. I needed to try to tell them what was going on—or, at least, a version of events that I thought they might be able to accept. I was allowed to go to the nearest phone on the floor and call Florida collect. Monitoring my own language and tone of voice, I cautiously told my mother and father that I'd had a bit of the old trouble, much as I'd had in England, and that I was in a hospital for a few days, being treated by competent physicians, very nice people, really, it was all going well, and I was very confident that the situation would right itself soon.

"No, really, it was just a small setback. Probably because of all the pressure; it's very rigorous at the law school, you know. Maybe I just needed a rest, a chance to get my bearings."

In response, my father was calm and logical. He asked me a few practical questions, and seemed satisfied with my answers. But my mother's voice wavered a bit, and I could hear the uncertainty there.

Her younger brother, my uncle Norm, had been struggling for some time with serious psychological problems. He'd gotten his medical degree in his thirties, but was unable to pass the boards and never practiced. He had been diagnosed with depression. He was a handsome, sweet man, very shy and quiet. Although I had never discussed his illness with my mother to any great degree (it wasn't then in either of our natures), I knew she worried a great deal about him. Now, hearing that I'd once again been ill myself, she sounded fragile, and frightened—at which point I became even more upbeat, determined to comfort her and keep the anxiety from climbing any higher. "Really, I'm feeling so much better now," I said, "I'll probably be released in another day or two."

Nevertheless, my parents said they were going to come and see me, at which point my own anxiety shot ceiling-ward. "No, no, there's no need for that, it's not necessary, everything here is fine." But they were insistent. So was I.

Oddly, however, I was becoming aware of a kind of yearning inside me. I did need them, I did want them to come, I did want to see them. I needed somebody to be here, someone on my side. But if they came, then it meant there was an officially declared medical and mental-health crisis—and so far, I'd avoided looking that reality in the face.

Since the earliest days of my illness, I had kept most of the details (of my behavior, of the various diagnoses, of all the doctors' opinions, of my therapy sessions) away from my parents. The reasons were, and remain, complicated. First, I was ashamed; surely someone of my intelligence and discipline should be able to exert more power over herself. Second, I didn't want to worry them; they had two other children, a business to run, and their own lives to lead. After all, I was an adult, and so far I'd managed not only to handle things on my own, but also to accomplish two fairly rigorous academic degrees.

Third (and this is the most sensitive of my reasons), I did not want them interfering in my life. I already had many more people than I could handle weighing in on the state of my brain and all the possible treatments and outcomes, and there hadn't even been a clear diagnosis yet. Why increase that burdensome cast of characters if I could possibly help it? Why do that to myself? And besides, what could they do to help?

So—up until now, by my own choice, my parents had been on a need-to-know basis about my illness, which both shielded them and protected my privacy and autonomy. Now that was over.

Later that day, as I was getting ready to leave the Intensive Care Program room, I asked one of the attendants if I could get a pack of cigarettes from my purse; it had been more than twenty-four hours since I'd had one, and I was craving both the nicotine and the physical feeling and ritual of lighting up. The nurse said that was fine.

Maybe it was the nicotine craving; maybe it was the aftereffects of the phone call with my parents. Whatever the reason, I was suddenly overcome with fear again, and when I opened my purse to get my cigarettes, I spotted a small piece of metal, in the shape of a ring, about the size of a Life Savers candy, something I'd retrieved in my rooftop ramblings with my telephone-wire belt. Not sharp at all, not weaponlike in the least. More a talisman, if anything. Quickly, I slipped the metal ring from my purse into my pants pocket, and, after smoking one cigarette, I slipped another—together with my lighter—into my pants pocket as well. All of these, of course, were contraband given my status at the hospital.

A short while later, I was told it was time to prepare for bed, and instructed to change my street clothes for a hospital gown. As I was getting undressed, the piece of metal and my lighter dropped out of my pocket to the floor, catching a nurse's attention. Panicked, I stooped down and grabbed them, then ran to the back of the small room where I'd slept the night before.

"Give me the metal and the lighter, Elyn," the nurse asked.

Oh, God. "No," I said. "I need to keep them, for protection."

"You won't need them," she said. "We'll protect you. Hand them over."

"No!" I insisted. "You're not going to get them unless I want to give them to you, and I don't want to. Actions will be taken if you try to take them away."

I don't know where this came from. I don't know why I felt about the metal ring and lighter as I did, or why I threatened the nurse. I had no intention of hurting her, or anyone else; in fact, I felt small and helpless, unlikely (and unable) to hurt anyone. Nevertheless, out of my mouth came the words, unbidden and scary, and I'd pulled myself up to my full height while I spit them out.

The nurse turned and left the room. When she returned several minutes later, she had a number of staff with her. A posse of four or five in fact.

"Elyn, we want you to put yourself into restraints," the nurse said firmly. "And if you don't do it willingly, we'll put you in them."

I couldn't believe it. "I'm sorry, I'm sorry," I begged. "Please don't tie me down again. I'll be good. Anyway, I was just kidding. *Please!*"

But I'd already lost the battle, and I knew it. So I passively lay back on the bed while the staff did their handiwork. This second round was almost worse than the first, because now I knew what the next hours would bring.

Despite being given dose after dose of Trilafon, I was attacked by my delusions, which swarmed thick and fast. The creatures in the sky wanted to kill me; the creatures here on the ground were on the attack. No one protected me. No one helped me. And as the night wore on, my psychosis deepened. I sang, I shouted, I cried out in terror. I was being *attacked*. And I struggled against the restraints until my back ached and my skin was raw. All the while, the door to my room was left open; anyone who walked by could look in, and a lot of people did.

Eventually, exhaustion and the drug dropped me into sleep—a black pit of dreams and nightmares and a lonely, aching body.

By the time daylight staggered in, I'd been in restraints for the better part of thirty hours. "Please let me out," I wailed, but the answer was a flat no. If they had a timetable as to when I might be set free, they weren't sharing it with me. The day passed, and at eight o'clock that night, I was still bound hand and foot.

Finally, the nurse I'd threatened the night before came in, again with a stern-looking posse. Or maybe, in this instance, a jury. Summoning whatever will I had left, I picked my way through an apology—because I was learning that an apology for bad behavior, made specifically to the person one had threatened (or insulted or offended), was the down payment on a ticket out. And indeed, they released the restraints. I struggled to sit up, and the room swam around me.

"But you cannot leave the room," I was told. "We're waiting for a bed to open up on the evaluation unit at Yale-New Haven Hospital. When it does, we're sending you back there."

Was this all a dream? Was I doing this to myself, for some reason that up until now had been so deeply buried that no one could pinpoint it? Or was I, finally, just another crazy person? Would my life be spent going in and out of mental hospitals, tied to a series of beds, trying to fend off attacks from both without and within, and inevitably losing on both fronts?

Fifteen hours later, I arrived once again at Yale-New Haven Hospital, this time at the Psychiatric Evaluation Unit. Memorial Unit 10, aka MU10. One more stop on a journey that had become, on every level, completely beyond my ability to comprehend.

chapter twelve

FOR A PLACE that existed ostensibly to promote the mental health of the vulnerable people in its care, YPI had been a brutal experience for me. I'd spent the better part of two days locked up, tied down, and forced to swallow a medication that (while not without its benefits) quickly made its side effects apparent: my face felt wooden and looked like a mask; my gait had slowed until it resembled a stroke victim's shuffle more than my own long-legged stride. And I couldn't track even the simplest conversation. "How are you feeling today?" might as well have been coming from ancient Sanskrit.

I desperately hoped that MU10 would be an improvement. The hospital itself, New Haven's largest teaching hospital, was new and modern, and the unit (on the tenth floor) was small, usually holding fewer than a dozen patients. I was placed in a room directly opposite the nurse's station (where anyone in it could be easily observed), and there I waited to meet my doctor. For hours.

Finally, I was directed down the hall to the office of Dr. Kerrigan. "Our plan is to work up a full evaluation and come to an actual diagnosis," he said. "I know this has been a very difficult and confusing time for you, Elyn, and we want to answer some of these questions. And then get you referred as quickly as possible to a facility that can help you." He gave every sign of someone warm and encouraging, but appropriately authoritative. I wanted to trust him—I wanted to trust someone—but I was learning to bide my time until people showed their cards. So I listened as best I could (not easy to do inside the fog of medication). But he seemed to be saying my future meant only more hospitalization.

"No, you don't understand," I said. Inside my head, my voice sounded like an old LP record on a very slow speed. "I need to get back to law school. I'm losing valuable time. I agree about evaluation and figuring out a treatment plan, but I can't stay in a hospital." I could have both treatment *and* school, right? After all, that's the way it had worked with Mrs. Jones. And we weren't talking junior college or adult extension courses, either—I'd managed *Oxford. Graduate* school. And I'd done well.

Dr. Kerrigan responded with what I quickly learned was his favorite verbal tic, the highly annoying "I hear you"—in spite of the fact that either he did in fact not hear me, or he did and didn't much give a damn. "I hear you," he said, nodding solemnly. "And I understand your concerns. But going back to school, I don't think that's going to happen, Elyn, at least in the foreseeable future. You're very sick."

"I'm feeling much better now."

"We can talk about it." The tone of his voice and the expression on his face made clear that the subject was closed.

It felt like Kerrigan had taken his thumb and forefinger and extinguished my single remaining flicker of hope. I was a student, not a mental patient—why couldn't he see that? As the interview continued, his words only made me more frantic and disorganized, and I began to talk over him. "I can go back to school anytime I want," I insisted. "Did you know I was God? But I'm not anymore. What I am now, I can't tell you. Have you killed anyone? I've killed hundreds of thousands of people with my thoughts. It's not my doing. Someone acts through my brain. I give life and I take it away." I stood up and started to pace. "I'm almost as big as you. You can't hurt me. See that hanger with your jacket on it? I can make that into a weapon to protect myself. Do you mind if I take your hanger, please?"

"Sit down," he said.

"I don't want to sit down," I said. "I would like that hanger, though."

"I don't think so," he said. "Please sit down now."

"No, I'd like to go back to my room now."

"I think that's a good idea," he said. "Another good idea is for you to spend some time in restraints. We believe they help patients feel safe, more in control."

I couldn't believe what I was hearing. "Restraints don't make me feel better." I was pleading, but I was angry, too. At the very least, somebody could have *asked* me what made me feel better.

"There's no need for alarm," he said. "MU10's policy on restraints is a little different from Yale Psychiatric's. You can get out of them in as little as half an hour, if all goes well."

Who defines what "goes well" is? I wondered. Kerrigan's tone and expression belied any hope of negotiation once again, I had no choice but to run, which I did, right into the arms of the unit's staff. I struggled, but again was tied to the bed, with a sheet pulled tight over my chest.

MU10 considered tying people up a form of therapy. In fact, in my chart, Kerrigan had written, "Use restraints liberally." And for three weeks, they did.

Since I was considered too disruptive to be in any therapy groups, I had very little to do with other patients, and was mostly kept apart from them. I'd often sit under the little desk in my room and rock and moan, gibbering away under the grip of fearsome delusions.

Much later, when I had the opportunity to read my own chart, I discovered that the staff had actually been frightened of me; in fact, I was so scary that I was "staff specialed," which meant that a staff member was with me all the time, watching my every move. Staff stood outside when I was using the bathroom, and the door was left unlocked. I could shower with a curtain, but my "minder" could come in at any time and pull the curtain back to see that I was OK. Which she did. Which horrified me.

When I was allowed to wander around a little, I met a young college student named James. He'd evidently had a very bad drug experience, which spun him into a manic episode; he said they'd kept him in restraints for three days. When I told him this wasn't my first hospitalization, he reacted almost as though, in our brief friendship, I'd somehow betrayed him.

"Wasn't once enough?" he asked angrily.

"It was, at least for me. I'm not here by choice, you know. I hate hospitals. I hope you have better luck than I did and never come back. At least there's something concrete you can *do:* never take drugs again."

"I just can't believe you let this happen to yourself," he said.

I shrugged. "The killings were just getting me down. The ones with my thoughts. The brain explosions which the crimes caused. Have you killed anyone lately?"

James visibly recoiled. "Please don't talk that way. It really upsets me."

"OK," I said, and thereafter, I tried to stick to it.

I was allowed only plastic utensils to eat with, and at one meal, I jokingly held up my plastic fork and told a staff member I could stab her if I wanted. I was immediately restrained.

When I became agitated and paced the corridors, I was restrained.

I kept careful watch whenever someone came onto or left the unit; an open door was always an opportunity to make a run for it. Each time I did it, staff caught me. And each time I was restrained.

When I voiced my violent delusions (which in spite of my best efforts included thoughts about hurting staff, among others), I was restrained.

In fact, any expression of anything that I was feeling—fear, anguish, restlessness, disorganized and delusional thoughts—led to immediate restraints. Even humor wasn't a good idea. My tendency to bluff or make a wisecrack in difficult circumstances was misinterpreted time and time again, and landed me in restraints.

My friend James couldn't understand why I kept setting myself up. "Just do what they say," he said. "What's so hard to understand about that? Do you *want* to be put in restraints?"

"No," I said. "What I want is to get out of here. That's why I keep running for the door. Last time I made it down a whole flight of stairs. I won't stop until I succeed. Massive unemployment and introjections."

He sighed. "*Please* don't talk like that."

Part of the problem was that I was behaving like a patient in psychoanalysis. When Mrs. Jones and I were working together, I was encouraged to say exactly what was on my mind, always, no matter how crazy it sounded—that was how analysis worked. That was the *point*. Otherwise, how would she know what was going on inside me? But the people at MU10 didn't want to know. If they couldn't tolerate what was in my head, why were any of them in this business? When my scrambled thinking revealed itself, they put me in the hospital version of "time out." Where was the "treatment" in this? Were they wanting to help me get better, or did they just want me to be socially appropriate? Overall, the sole message they seemed to want me to get was "behave yourself!"

This is a classic bind for psychiatric patients. They're struggling with thoughts of wanting to hurt themselves or others, and at the same time, they desperately need the help of those they're threatening to harm. The conundrum: Say what's on your mind and there'll be consequences; struggle to keep the delusions to your-self, and it's likely you won't get the help you need.

Staff decided that my drug regimen wasn't sufficient, so Kerrigan, not wanting to exceed the maximum recommended dose of Trilafon, put me on Valium as well. I hated Valium—it made me feel dopey, and dulled whatever thought processes I had left. I could almost see my cogent mind waving at me from the shore.

One day, I simply refused to take the Valium. Staff held me down and gave me a shot. I later read in my chart that Valium is not effec-tive when given by injection. It just doesn't work that way. Even with-out knowing that, I wondered whose needs were really being met on this unit.

Contacted by Dr. Kerrigan and the MU10 staff, my parents came to see me. (I had been embarrassed one afternoon when I overheard a couple of nurses talking about their absence: "Where are Saks's par-ents?" Despite having told me of their plans to visit, it had taken them a week to appear.) To my surprise, they brought my two broth-ers with them. As comforted as I was by their arrival, I was also com-pletely horrified that they were there. None of them had ever seen me like this. I felt worthless, a failure. But I couldn't tell them what I was feeling and they of course couldn't ask. And as hard as they tried to put a good face on our time together, they, too, seemed stunned that my law school life had come to this, a scant two months after I'd first arrived at Yale.

We were allowed to have our Thanksgiving dinner together, in a small dining area that had been "reserved" just for our family. As we'd done during our summers and vacations together, my parents and I coped as best we could, keeping conversation light and limited to easy, even humorous subjects, while the gravity of my situation ran beneath us like a furnace that held the potential for blowing me apart. We joked that the fixtures on the wall were bugged and we were probably being listened to, and our laughter echoed down the hall. My brothers were somewhat quieter, and I could see by the look in their eyes that they were confused and frightened.

The family therapist would later write that my parents had made light of my illness and didn't seem willing to accept its seriousness. The fact is, until this time, they'd only known as much as I'd told them, and whenever we were together, including this time, I always did everything I could to *hide* its seriousness: I cracked jokes, and laughed, and was gratified when they did the same. It was our way of handling it; it was our habit—and every family has its habits. The levity and irreverence made it possible for us to be together without everyone falling completely apart.

I had other visitors as well. Two of my law school classmates, who'd heard what had happened, came by one afternoon, and although it was obvious to me that they were struggling for the right things to say, I was both comforted and moved that they'd come at all. And my dear friend Sam from Oxford, who was now living in New York, came to see me, too. When I showed him the leather straps on my bed that were used to tie me down, he winced and shook his head. He got it. And that gave me courage. It was so easy to feel isolated and alone here; each one of these people who cared enough about me to come and visit gave me reason to hope that I was worth saving.

Of course, visitors were turned away when I was in restraints (although for obvious reasons they were not informed that was the case). So some people went away believing I didn't want to see them, when nothing could have been further from the truth. That said, having company was sometimes exhausting and even confusing. I'd summon focus and energy to keep the demons away during a visit, and then go to pieces after friends and family were gone.

Young James left after my first week on MU10, and I then met two

new patients, Susan and Mark, and we spent a little time together almost every day (that is, when I wasn't in restraints or trying to run
away). Susan, about my age, was bulimic. This was a condition only
recently recognized by the medical community, but it was far from
being understood—mostly, treatment seemed to consist of variations
of "mind over matter."

"My doctor says I should just stop binging and purging," Susan
said. "There's a simple solution to my problem, she told me—just
stop doing it."

I remembered when my parents, and Dr. Hamilton, essentially said
the same thing about my anorexia. "You know, it's my opinion that
'just don't do it' is usually said by somebody who just doesn't get it."

She nodded. "Now they're going to put me on the ward with older
people, the one-month-maximum unit. Do you think that might
help me?"

"The people here suck!" I said. "So it's got to be better on the
other ward. I hope you'll get what you need over there, I really do."

Mark was barely eighteen, and clearly had some kind of organic
impairment, although I didn't know the cause. He had no short-
term memory (I had to reintroduce myself each time we ran into
each other), was in a state of perpetual confusion, and had difficulty
both in speaking and comprehending what was said to him. He was
so endearingly (and vulnerably) young, it was hard not to feel mater-
nal toward him. *This is a child,* I thought, feeling angrier and more
protective each time I spent time with him. *Isn't there anywhere else he
could be—someplace gentler, with professionals who might take better care of
him?*

One day, Mark told me he was scheduled for an overnight EEG,
which would give the doctors a more detailed picture of his brain-
wave patterns. He barely understood this, and for days he'd fought
having the procedure. (Where were *his* parents? I wondered.) There
was no way he understood the doctors' rationale. All he knew was,

they were going to stick electrodes all over his head, do something scary to his brain inside, and not stop until the next morning.

"Don't worry," I said, comforting him as best I could. "The things on your head aren't needles—they won't hurt at all, you won't feel anything. It's like they're little cameras, and they're taking pictures that the doctors will look at, to help you feel better."

"But why are they doing this to me?" he asked in a tremulous voice. "What if they make a mistake and do it wrong?"

"That won't happen," I said. "They know what they're doing; this will help them fix whatever's wrong." I felt a little hypocritical—I was pretty sure that they *didn't* know what they were doing. "Hey, let's go play cards, OK? We can play any game you like."

Meanwhile, the Physician's Emergency Certificate that had been signed when I was admitted to YPI was about to expire. The certificate allowed the hospital to keep me against my will for fifteen days; once that time was up, one of three things had to happen. The hospital could let me go, which is what I wanted, but that wasn't going to happen. I could agree to stay in the hospital, by signing a piece of paper called a "voluntary," which would be the equivalent of me saying, "Yes, I agree to stay here and get treatment." But that wasn't going to happen either.

The third option was for the hospital to request a formal proceeding called a "civil commitment hearing." When a patient insists upon leaving the hospital, and the hospital insists that the patient needs to stay, a civil commitment hearing is held before a judge, and it's the judge who makes the ultimate decision. The choice seemed very clear to me: I would demand a civil commitment hearing, ask to be released, and the judge, seeing the absurdity of the whole situation, would of course send me on my way back to school.

My parents talked me out of that one, because they understood more clearly than I did that the hospital would prevail. "No, go with the 'voluntary,' Elyn," advised my dad. "You can't be on your own quite yet, but you certainly don't want anything in the record where a judge *orders* you to stay."

Unbeknownst to me then, the consequences of being civilly committed to a psychiatric hospital are severe and can be long-lasting. For instance, many application forms (such as an application to sit for the bar exam) ask whether one has ever been civilly committed. I didn't know it then, but there would a come a day when I would be very happy that I wasn't compelled to check the "yes" box. So, following my dad's advice, I signed the voluntary.

Then I discovered some stunning news—MU10, *without* my permission or knowledge, had called the dean of students at the law school, to confirm that I couldn't return that year, or possibly ever. In effect, MU10 withdrew me from law school.

When the staff told me this, I was overcome with such a sweeping feeling of betrayal that I could barely catch my breath. What had happened to the assurance of confidentiality? What had happened to their sense of my own autonomy? All right, I was certainly somewhat compromised, but I wasn't *comatose*—surely someone could have spoken to me first. Who had done this? Who had taken it upon themselves to release information that was mine alone, and that now, no doubt, had settled into my academic file, probably in big bold black type.

Completely overwrought, I begged my parents to call the dean, to plead my case that I be allowed to return to and resume my classes. And they did. They may not have believed that I was completely ready to return—they weren't unrealistic people, after all—but in this gesture they demonstrated that they absolutely believed in *me*, which was a powerful message for me to get at that point. Their support notwithstanding, of course the dean had no choice but to reject their pleas. Nothing was permanent; I could always try again the following year.

And for the first time, as Kerrigan had promised when I was first admitted, I received an actual diagnosis: "Chronic paranoid schizophrenia with acute exacerbation." My prognosis, I was told, was listed as "Grave."

So then—there it was. A part of me had been waiting for those words, or some version of them, for a very long time, but that didn't lessen the overwhelming impact of them, or what they signified for my life.

In spite of my ongoing difficulties ever since undergraduate school (and, in all likelihood, even before that), I hadn't ever really thought of myself as "ill"—not at Vanderbilt, or even at Oxford, when I was obviously delusional. I truly believed that everyone had the scrambled thoughts I did, as well as the occasional breaks from reality and the sense that some unseen force was compelling them to destructive behavior. The difference was, others were simply more adept than I at masking the craziness, and presenting a healthy, competent front to the world. What was "broken" about me, I thought, was my inability to control my thoughts and fantasies, or to keep from expressing them. In reading everything about mental illness that I could get my hands on, I wasn't looking for a diagnosis per se as much as I was looking for an explanation for my *behavior,* which obviously wasn't acceptable. I thought that if I could figure it out, I could conquer it. My problem was not that I was crazy; it was that I was weak.

The summer before I first came to Yale (when I'd returned from Oxford and had too much time on my hands), I had discovered the *Diagnostic and Statistical Manual of Mental Disorders,* aka the *DSM,* in the Miami library. I read it cover to cover. Knowledge had always been my salvation, but with my immersion into the *DSM,* I began to understand that there were some truths that were too difficult and frightening to know. I was smart enough to read the text—the definitions, the ramifications—and I understood what the words meant. And to a certain extent, I even understood some of the science. But understanding and believing are not the same; I simply refused to accept on any conscious level that this had anything to do with me. And now, here it was, in writing: The Diagnosis. What did it mean?

Schizophrenia is a brain disease which entails a profound loss of connection to reality. It is often accompanied with delusions, which are fixed yet false beliefs—such as you have killed thousands of people—and hallucinations, which are false sensory perceptions—such as you have just seen a man with a knife. Often speech and reason can become disorganized to the point of incoherence. The prognosis: I would largely lose the capacity to care for myself. I wasn't expected to have a career, or even a job that might bring in a paycheck. I wouldn't be able to form attachments, or keep friendships, or find someone to love me, or have a family of my own—in short, I'd never have a *life*.

At that time, there was little encouraging medical news about treatment for schizophrenia; certainly there were no cures, and effective treatment was rare. Save for a few antipsychotic medications that carried terrible side effects in the short term and horrible physical risk in the long term, there was little in the way of medication to offer a person suffering from schizophrenia. The medications worked for some people; they didn't work for others. They had to be constantly monitored by medical professionals and readjusted. What had been an essential part of treatment for me—intensive talk therapy—was falling out of favor.

I'd always been optimistic that when and if the mystery of me was solved, it could be fixed; now I was being told that whatever had gone wrong inside my head was permanent and, from all indications, unfixable. Repeatedly, I ran up against words like "debilitating," "baffling," "chronic," "catastrophic," "devastating," and "loss." For the rest of my life. *The rest of my life*. It felt more like a death sentence than a medical diagnosis.

And then there was the whole mythology of schizophrenia, aided and abetted by years of books and movies that presented people like me as hopelessly evil or helplessly doomed. I would become violent, as the delusions in my head grew more real to me than reality itself. My psychotic episodes would increase, and last longer; my intelligence would be severely compromised. Maybe I'd end my life in an institution; maybe I'd *live* my life in an institution. Or become homeless, a bag lady whose family could no longer care for her. I'd be that wild-eyed character on the city sidewalk that all the nice baby carriage–pushing mommies shrink away from. *Get away from the crazy lady.* I'd love no one; no one would love me. For the first time in my life, I truly, deeply understood what people meant when they said, "It broke my heart."

At much earlier times, people suffering from schizophrenia were viewed as either cursed by the gods or blessed by them. In some cultures, "seers" were revered and given the privileges of high station; in others, they were shunned and driven away from the community like lepers. More recently, one nursing textbook from the 1930s gave an impressive (if unlikely) laundry list for what caused schizophrenia: war, marriage, masturbation, and religious revivals.

The history of schizophrenia is rich in blame for families. According to the crushing weight of a century's teaching, my illness was an indictment of my parents. Years ago, one respected psychoanalyst coined the phrase "schizophrenogenic mother"—literally, the mother who creates a schizophrenic. Such a mother (no surprise) was described as cold, aloof, hostile, and rejecting, which in no way describes my mother or my lifelong experience of her. Yet another theory held that parents caused schizophrenia when they subjected a child to the so-called "double bind," a condition where a child receives intensely contradictory messages such as "Come here, go away," or "You're a good little girl, but you're really bad."

More current theories about the origins of schizophrenia discount or even refute entirely the family-transmission view, focusing instead on the patient's brain chemistry. The rapid expansion of research into the workings of the human genome has helped shift the focus to a genetic predisposition for the disease. As with many families, there is serious mental illness in my extended family as well.

Schizophrenia tends to emerge at different times for men than for women. For men, the first "breaks" tend to happen in the late teens or early twenties. For most women, things begin to fall apart later, usually in the mid-twenties. But before the illness truly manifests, there is a stage—called the prodrome—when it slowly becomes apparent to anyone paying attention that all is not well. It's possible that my own prodromal stage happened during my time with Operation Re-Entry. Certainly, my experience of the houses giving me frightening messages on that long walk home from school was a very loud preview of coming attractions. But the length of time between the beginning of the disease and its diagnosis (and treatment) can range from mere weeks to several years, as it had for me. And recent studies indicate that earlier diagnosis (which could result in treatment at lower symptom levels) may contribute to a more positive outcome. Researchers are beginning to explore the benefits of intervening with young people before the behaviors become destructive and isolating— perhaps even intervening before a first psychotic break.

The problem is that prodomal symptoms, viewed separately or together, mirror what many healthy teenagers experience in their routine passage through adolescence: sleep irregularities, difficulty in concentrating, vague feelings of tension or anxiety, a change in personality, and perhaps a withdrawal from the social life of their peers. Often, parents will realize (after their child has been diagnosed) that there had been an identifiable period of foreshadowing, during which time they'd wondered if their child was struggling with depression. Indeed, these days, teenagers and adults alike are sometimes prescribed antidepressants to combat this part of their illness. As I reflect back, Operation Re-Entry may have served a similar function for me, by giving me enormous amounts of stimulation and attention at a time when I otherwise could easily have retreated into my own world, under the guise of being a sullen or shy teenager.

To make the picture even more complicated, schizophrenia is often clinically confused with bipolar disease (what used to be referred to as manic-depressive disorder) or popularly confused with dissociative identity disorder (also known as multiple-personality disorder). But treatments for these illnesses range widely. And the potential for no diagnosis at all, or the wrong one, is vast.

I wasn't diagnosed early; I wasn't treated early. I stumbled around in the dark for years, clutching my Aristotle and negotiating my life as best I could, until I was blessed by the wisdom and guidance of Mrs. Jones, and given reason to hope in the future. But with Dr. Kerrigan's announcement, those days had officially come to an end.

Everyone at MU10 believed that my next hospitalization would be measured in years, not weeks or months. I didn't believe them, but I kept quiet about that—there seemed to be no benefit for me in being candid about my thoughts. My parents and I considered medical facilities in Boston and New York, but in the end, I argued for going back to YPI. It would keep me in New Haven, close to school; in fact, from YPI to the law school it was only a short, pretty walk down a hill. Maybe I'd even be able to audit a class or two in preparation for returning the next year; maybe I could even nurture the few slight friendships I'd begun to make before I had to leave.

It had been a rough three weeks at MU10. I was exhausted and druggy, and deeply terrified about what would come next. But when I climbed into the ambulance that would take me away from there, I was relieved to leave the place behind. Nothing had happened to me at MU10 that was encouraging or helpful; in fact much of what had happened was inhumane and ineffective. But Yale Psychiatric offered a tether to the life I still, somehow, hoped to lead. Thin as it was, that tether was all I had.

chapter thirteen

THE FIRST PATIENT I met once back at YPI was Eric. An Ivy League graduate slightly older than I, Eric, too, had spent time on MU10. "I was there a little over a year ago, but they let me go," he told me. "I wish they'd made me stay, and then maybe moved me here, like they did with you. I fooled them into thinking I was OK. And I went home. And then I killed my father."

Surely I'd misheard him. "I'm sorry, you did what?"

He nodded. "I strangled him."

I was dumbstruck. And horrified. To actually strangle your father? A laying on of hands that actually kills someone? That was very different from having thoughts that could kill. Besides, entities worked *through* me; Eric, it seemed, was his own agent.

My parents came back from Miami for the first meeting of my YPI care team—doctors, psychologists, social workers, and nurses. When asked about my relationship with my brother Warren, I stopped rocking and humming long enough to correct the inquiring doctor's grammar. "No, it's 'between you and me,' not 'between you and I.'"

I can only imagine now (but was completely oblivious at the time) that it must have been sheer torture for my mother and father to witness the worsening disintegration of their daughter.

I was placed in YPI's Intensive Care Program—ICP. My days would be spent in a small room with a staff member and one or two other ICP patients. I would take my meals apart from everyone else (no socializing for me in the cafeteria) and sleep in a locked seclusion room at night. And I was not allowed to wear shoes. That way, if I escaped the building, staff could be certain I wouldn't get too far. The New England autumn was deepening outside, and it was getting colder every day.

For the first three weeks at YPI, I remained as floridly psychotic as I had been at MU10. My medication was increased, putting me over the maximum recommended dose for Trilafon. No Valium, though—it seemed that staff wanted me on meds that actually helped my psychosis.

Nevertheless, the hallucinations never stopped. Walls were collapsing, ashtrays were dancing; at one point I went into a linen closet and invited the other ICP patients to join me in there for a "housewarming" party, as I laughed and gibbered the afternoon away. Totally lost in my delusions, I warned of the great horrors and devastation that I could inflict upon everyone (most notably the ICP staff) with the power of my mind.

Incredibly, no matter what I said or threatened, I was never restrained. If I expressed a violent impulse, staff encouraged me to rip out the pages of a magazine; if I kept it up, staff steered me to the seclusion room, away from other people. My behavior was no different from what it had been in the ER, or on my initial visit to YPI weeks earlier, or during my three weeks at MU10. But the hospital's response to the behavior most certainly was. Evidently, the question of whether I was to be restrained or not had more to do with where I happened to be than how I behaved.

What I'd gained in freedom, however, I lost in privacy. I was kept apart from almost all the other patients, yet never left alone. Maybe it was ICP policy—I had my own special staff person, my shadow, watching and listening, right beside me, all the time. When I ate. When I slept. When I spoke on the phone with a friend. When I met with my family. A slight reprieve came when I went to the bathroom; the staff member lodged a sanitary napkin in the door to hold it slightly open, then sat down just outside. A staff member even watched as I took a shower.

Not only did they take my shoes away, they wouldn't allow me to wear socks at night, no matter how cold it was on the ward. I couldn't imagine how I could hurt myself with socks, but evidently staff had seen otherwise with other patients. So no socks, even when it meant I shivered through the night.

I was on a high dose of antipsychotic medication, attending a few therapy groups, and in individual session three times a week—total saturation. But there were no miracle cures; instead, there was only the dreary sameness of day-to-day life on a psychiatric ward, and this one was particularly grim. Old, run-down, with shabby, narrow halls, yellowed paint, and grate-covered windows which never drew in any sun (and a pathetically weak sun it was, too). I was followed day and night by my minder, and never allowed to go outside to fill my lungs with some fresh, cool air, or for a change of scenery. I'd made no friends on the ward; other patients never tried to socialize with me at all, no one broke through my isolation, and even Eric, the father-killing Ivy grad, shunned me—who was he, I wondered, to shun anybody? I hadn't been this bone lonely since my early days at Oxford. Every day was the same, and would be for a long time. The years yawned out ahead of me; my hair would turn gray here, I knew it, while every dream I'd ever had would be absorbed into the ugly yellowed walls.

And then something threw a switch in my head, and I got it. I *got* it.

The only barrier between me and the door out was me. I simply had to *stop* it. Stop voicing the hallucinations and delusions, even when they were there. Stop babbling incoherently, even if those were the only words that came to my lips; no, no, it was better to be quiet. Stop resisting; just behave. *Being in a psychiatric hospital is nonsense,* I thought. *I'm a law student, not a mental patient. I want my life back, damn it! And if I have to bite my tongue until it bleeds, I am going to get it back.*

What was happening, of course, was that after weeks of steady medication, the psychosis was beginning to lift. Maybe I couldn't keep the thoughts from coming into my head, but I could organize them, and keep them from getting out. *OK, here I go.*

It took staff a week or so to notice—much too long, it seemed to me—and when they finally did, it took another week before I was off the Intensive Care Program and allowed more privileges. I could sleep with socks. I could use the bathroom in peace. I could shower without company.

Yes, yes, I absolutely agreed with them that I needed treatment. "But not here and not this kind. I want to go back to England," I said. "Mrs. Jones knows what I need to get well again. I can go back into treatment there with her."

The request was met with stony faces and heads shaking "no." YPI didn't like that idea; YPI wasn't going to relinquish control of my treatment to some woman in England who in their estimation likely didn't know what she was doing.

As sudden (and effective) as I thought my change in attitude had been, what happened to me next was just as sudden, only in the reverse direction. In fact, it's a case study—partly—in the ups and downs of heavy drug loads and the complicated biochemistry that results: Soaked in antipsychotic medication, with the psychosis actually clearing, I became profoundly depressed, and felt the brief flash of energy and focus leak right out of me. Suddenly, I couldn't follow the simplest sitcom on the unit TV, or decipher the lines in a book I'd been reading just days before. I was given an IQ test and scored "dull normal" in the verbal portion and "borderline mentally retarded" in the quantitative section. It's not that I wasn't trying—I just couldn't function. I had no way of knowing that depression following a psychotic period is not unusual; I only knew I was sliding backward. I called my parents and pleaded with them to get me out. "It's all going wrong again!" I cried.

They promised to help, and once again we began the search for another hospital, where a stay might be shorter. My parents even contacted Karen, the therapist whom I'd seen the summer after my first year in college, and she suggested a hospital in Philadelphia, where she was now living. I remembered what she'd said to me so many years before: "You do need help. And I just want you to know that when you decide you're ready to get it, you can and should come back to see me."

The staff at YPI did everything they could to dissuade me from leaving, from either going to Philadelphia or back to England. They'd move me to an open ward, they said, with more privileges. I could even have my shoes back. I politely declined.

Five weeks after I had arrived at YPI, my parents came to bail me out. They pulled up the driveway, loaded all my stuff in the trunk of the car, and together we headed out of New Haven. I felt safe, relieved, even a little optimistic; if I closed my eyes, I could almost imagine I was a girl again, safe in the car, on a trip with my mom and dad. But the trip wasn't to Disneyland; it was from one hospital to another hospital, and I was leaving law school behind. Nevertheless, it was still a good day.

The Institute of Pennsylvania Hospital—IPH—was a much more physically attractive place than YPI, in spite of being the oldest mental hospital in the country. Located smack in the middle of a neighborhood in serious decline, the building literally shone, with high, vaulted ceilings and marble floors that were polished daily. I was taken to my private room, with its own private bath. If there was a food chain of treatment centers, it appeared as though I'd moved up. Although I was still trying to get out from under the depression, I was nowhere near as psychotic as I had been (thanks to the hefty dose of Trilafon). I was convinced that I'd only be at IPH a couple of weeks. In the end, it would be three months.

The doctor I'd be working with, Dr. Miller, was a short, round psychoanalyst who had a welcoming Midwestern openness and used words like "swell." It was easy to like him—a good thing, since we met six times a week. In addition, I'd meet with Karen, the former Miami therapist, once a week for several hours. And that meeting would take place off-site, which thrilled me; in fact, I was granted the highest level of privileges, which meant I could even walk the grounds alone.

As is usual in psychiatric hospitals, IPH offered many group activities for patients. On my second day, I went to my art therapy assessment. Not being an artist, I drew what I knew how to draw—a stick figure and a tree. "This is wonderful, primitive work!" exclaimed the therapist. I went to very few groups after that.

Instead, I read my law books in preparation for getting back to school the next year. I'd gotten the course requirements and assigned readings before I left New Haven, and every day I pored through the material so I could be ready when the time came. Because I was going back. Diagnosis or not, I was going back.

Having two therapists would likely confuse many people, because even with the best intentions and the most open communication, they'll probably trip over each other's feet. But I liked the arrangement, and I liked the two of them both as well. And I quickly figured out that it was an arrangement that would work to my advantage.

Miller was the one to decide when I could leave the hospital, so I tried to be as circumspect as possible in terms of what I revealed of the inner workings of my mind: I wanted out, and he was the judge and jury. Karen, however, had no such role or authority. As a consequence, I felt freer to tell her what was going on—my bizarre and frightening dreams, and my ongoing violent thoughts.

The first time I tried to get to Karen's office, however, was a comedy of errors that was far from funny. The cabdriver couldn't find the house, and I certainly couldn't help. We went round and round Philadelphia, stopping for directions at several gas stations, and when we finally arrived, I was more than an hour late and completely discombobulated. Shaking, I knocked on Karen's door.

"Thank goodness you're here!" she said. "I just got off the phone with your parents saying you must have eloped"—hospitalese for escaped. "Now I have to call them right back before we start our session, they're frantic!"

In the beginning, Dr. Miller and I spoke mostly about how I was experiencing and managing daily life, but soon our sessions became more psychoanalytic. I even started lying on the couch and working with dreams again. And I talked a lot about Mrs. Jones, and how much I missed her.

"Why don't you write her?" he suggested one afternoon. "Or perhaps even talk to her on the phone? Would you like that?"

I couldn't believe it. For some reason, I'd thought that he would put up a barrier to that, as they'd done at YPI. "Not at all," he said. "I think it's a good idea."

With his support, I wrote a carefully crafted letter asking Mrs. Jones if she'd consent to our scheduling a transatlantic telephone call. To my great relief, the letter she sent back to me in reply said yes.

When I actually heard her voice on the phone, my heart leapt—and then I immediately felt overwhelmingly sad. So much had happened since I last saw her, most of it bad. I felt as though I'd failed her. I told her how terribly much I'd missed her; she said she'd missed me, too. "Mrs. Jones, do you think I might come over and see you? Maybe this summer?"

There was no hesitation in her answer. "Why, yes, Elyn," she said. "I think that would be perfectly acceptable and fine."

The elation returned—now I had something to look forward to, and someone I knew and trusted who would help me formulate my plan. I began to understand the deep ache I felt in my heart each time I thought of her; I'd been so sad when I left her, so unhinged that day, that we hadn't really shared a proper good-bye. I had not been ready to let go, and wasn't able to find the right words. Perhaps this time, I would be able to do it in a way that I could live with, something that would help me stop looking back and start me moving forward again.

In spite of the side effects, I had to admit that the Trilafon was helping. Nevertheless, I was, as always, anxious to get off meds. Karen was rabidly anti-medication as well, and my parents were, too, so Miller agreed that we could give it a try, but very slowly.

As cautious as he was in reducing my intake, I felt the effects almost immediately. My blank, masklike face relaxed into its familiar appearance, and I stopped doing the invalid shuffle down the hall. I felt less fuzzy, more aware of what was going on around me. "You seem angrier to me, though," said Miller. I'd walked out of a couple of sessions before we'd officially ended, which concerned him.

"I can handle it," I said, impatient. "Let's keep going."

In two months, I was med-free, except for something to help me sleep. At three months, I was one of the old-timers on the ward. In fact, the staff sometimes consulted me in ward meetings about newer patients—which one was doing OK, which one needed watching, and who might deserve more privileges. I wasn't comfortable with this role: Was I a colleague to them? Was I still a patient and, if so, why did they trust me? And which of them could *I* trust? I'd have preferred being left out of it entirely. But I knew that every move I made was still being closely watched; if I was nonresponsive when asked my opinion, I knew I'd pay some kind of price. Once, walking down the hall, I jumped up to touch the ceiling, just to see if I could—and then caught myself, panicky about what would happen if I'd been seen. I'd be written up. My fear of being scrutinized wasn't paranoia. Others really were watching me, and the risk was real.

By early April, I was more than ready to leave IPH, and once again I asked my parents for help in getting out of a hospital. "Don't you think you should stay until Dr. Miller thinks it's time?" my dad asked.

"No," I said. "Besides, he just told me he's going away on vacation for two whole weeks. I want out of here now."

Miller suggested that I might think about going home during the time he was gone—kind of like an R & R, I suppose—and then return to IPH for another month or two in the open ward. There was a nurse on the ward I trusted, and I asked her about this. "Why should I come back if I'm well enough to leave?"

She pondered this for a moment. "In my experience, doctors know much more than patients about what's best for them," she said finally. "So I think I'd come back, if I were you."

My parents, on the other hand, agreed with me—if Miller truly thought I was well enough to be on my own at home for two weeks, then I was well enough to leave the hospital for good. No one else on staff was very enthusiastic about this. Nevertheless, it became the plan: I'd leave the day Miller did. My discharge papers read "AMA"— Against Medical Advice.

As I walked down the hall on my last day, suitcase in hand, one of the custodians who came to the ward daily, a good-looking, wiry man, saw me. Although we'd never had a single exchange during my entire stay, this time he smiled warmly and nodded at the suitcase. "Good for you, getting out."

My own smile stretched as wide as his did. "Thank you," I said, and walked out into the late spring sunshine.

In the taxi on the way to the Philadelphia airport, however, the sense of having made my escape and leaving the hospital behind was more than I could handle. I was alone, and unguarded, and as the emotions piled on top of one another, I was quickly overwhelmed by them. As though they'd slipped by a guard at the gate, the delusions marched in—paranoid thoughts and a strong message from someone, something, insistent upon being heard. I was the center of a massive and intricate plot involving the creatures in the sky. It would somehow involve the plane I was about to take. But the idea of returning to the hospital never crossed my mind. Gritting my teeth, and trying with all my might to focus on what I knew to be real, I grimly boarded the plane for Miami. *Hold it together. Hold it together.* It was, as usual, an uneventful flight.

It was May and I was home, just as a lot of other young people were at the end of a year away at school. September to May—one full academic year since I'd walked across the Yale campus sporting a telephone-wire belt and babbling about my complicity in the impending end of the world. And now here I was back home again, completely off antipsychotic meds and somewhat functional, although just barely on some days. Good days, bad days. More bad days. I went to the beach with my brother and sister-in-law, and the light and heat almost made me cower. In minutes, I was convinced that everyone there had come to the beach to ambush me—they thought I was evil, that I had killed many people. I was certain that if I moved suddenly, they'd leap up and kill me. I sat stiff as a board on my towel down near the water, silently begging not to be noticed. I wished I had brought a gun with me to protect myself in case I was attacked.

Years of this illness had taken a toll. The constant effort to keep reality on one side and delusions on the other was exhausting, and I often felt beaten down, knowing that the schizophrenia diagnosis had ended any hope I'd had of a miracle cure or a miracle fix. I'd disappointed my family; I'd shamed them. I wondered aloud if I would ever amount to anything. "Maybe it's too late," I said. "Maybe I need to be realistic about my life."

"You have to stop thinking like this," said my father firmly. I knew before he'd gotten to the next sentence that I was in for the familiar "buck up—get tough" speech, variations of which I'd heard much of my life. "This isn't terminal cancer, Elyn—and people have come back strong even from that diagnosis, you know. What you've got, that's a piece of cake by comparison. You can beat it with the right attitude. Stop feeling so sorry for yourself!"

I wondered what I would have done in my father's place—if I would have, or could have, given a child of mine that same speech under the same circumstances. I had an illness, it was real, and it was ruining my life—how could he make it all about (or *only* about) pulling up my socks and getting tough? Didn't he get it?

But then I had to concede that yes, I probably would have given my child a near-identical speech—because it reflected what I'd been taught all my life: Intelligence, combined with discipline, could overcome any challenge. And mostly, that belief had served me well. The problem was, it assumed that the intelligence at hand was fully functional, fully capable—but I'd been told by experts that my brain had serious problems. Was my brain the same thing as my mind? Could I hang onto the one while conceding that there was a big flaw in the other? I resented my dad for setting up a standard that I might not be able to meet, yet his opinion meant everything to me—and he believed I could beat this.

I sought comfort in reality as I knew it: I was out of the hospital, off medication. I was reading Aristotle again, and it was even making sense. And I was going back to law school. My determination to go back to school was not part of my delusional thinking; it was part of my self. I believed myself to be the person who would go back to law school and finish it. That's who I believed myself to be, and that wasn't delusional.

In order for me to be readmitted, university policy required that I meet with the head of the University Health Psychiatry Department. And just as I'd done all my life, I studied hard before "the test": I researched the director, and every single article he'd written. In a wonderful coincidence, one of his published articles concerned the questions university officials should ask people who've had psychotic breaks and are applying to be readmitted to school. I couldn't believe my luck—or was it fate? I didn't care what it was; I simply rehearsed my answers to the questions in the article, and sure enough, they were the ones he asked.

I was relieved to hear that my medical records weren't forwarded from the hospital; no one from Yale, to my knowledge, had asked for them, and I certainly didn't volunteer them. Did I have any symptoms? he asked. Did I think I could take the stress of school? And what might I do if I started feeling poorly? As nervous as I was (I didn't sleep well the night before, and I had to fold my hands tight in my lap to keep him from seeing me shake), I didn't actually have to tell a single lie. Instead, I simply strategized, by staying as close to the truth as I could without hurting myself. And in any case, I told him, "With an analyst four days a week, I'm sure I'll be able to handle everything very well." I was readmitted.

The next hurdle would be my upcoming trip to England to see Mrs. Jones. As difficult as travel was for me, and as many challenges as getting well and staying well would present me with, there was no way I could see the trip as anything but promising. Maybe our time together would prove to be exactly the booster shot I needed.

It was a little odd, being back in Oxford again. Summer there was green and leafy and still; it looked and felt as different from Miami as anyplace could have. Janet was renting my old quarters to a lodger, so I stayed in a little bed-and-breakfast near her house. It was a joy to spend time with her, and visit with bright and beautiful young Livy.

For the next couple of months, I met with Mrs. Jones three times a week. It was such a relief to be in that familiar office in her shabby little house, to stretch out on the couch and have no care for what came into my head or out of my mouth. I told her about the restraints, and the drugs, and about my fear that with each episode, I was losing more of myself. I reported my delusions, and the forces beyond my control that were unbearably evil. I was malicious, I was bad, I was a destroyer of worlds.

She was not afraid; she did not look at me with alarm in her eyes. She did not judge, she only listened, and reflected back to me what she heard, telling me what she thought it meant. And she did not embrace the schizophrenia diagnosis, either (although she acknowledged the existence of the symptoms and behaviors; after all, it was impossible to deny them). "Don't focus on it," she said. "Don't define yourself in terms of something which even many highly trained and gifted professionals do not fully understand." To her, the best road to understanding was psychoanalytic. There was little room for biology and therefore little room for medication.

When at last it came time to leave Oxford again and return to New Haven, my faith in myself was shored up. This time, I didn't feel the overwhelming grief at leaving Mrs. Jones behind; she was there for me, we would stay in touch, and I could come back to see her. For now, it was time to get back to my intended life.

I had no way of knowing then that it would be the last time I'd see Mrs. Jones in good health. The following year, she was in a terrible automobile accident that required a tracheotomy and left her in a coma for months. When she regained consciousness, her mind and body were badly damaged; in fact, she was diagnosed with traumatic Parkinson's. When her husband, Dr. Brandt, wrote me about what had happened, I returned to Oxford as soon as I could, and what I saw there frightened me. White as a sheet, frail and trembling, she reached out her hand and said my name. "I love you," she said.

A year after that, I visited again, devastated at how fragile and small she'd become. She wasn't ever going to be well again; she would never be who she once was. Nervously, I began talking about my successful second year at law school and my plans for the future. To my great sorrow, she began to weep. "Oh, Mrs. Jones, what's wrong?" I asked. "Did I say something to hurt you?"

"I'm sorry," she softly cried. "But I just don't remember you."

As I turned away, to leave our brief meeting, it occurred to me how truly beautiful she was.

A few months later, she died. The grief at her loss burrowed deep into my soul; this was, in every way that mattered, a death in the family. For so long, through everything that had happened to me, I'd taken courage in knowing that Mrs. Jones was there, in her house, in that office. She knew me like no other.

chapter fourteen

I RETURNED TO New Haven a few weeks before classes were to start, in order to begin treatment with a doctor who would be new to me—Dr. Joseph White, a senior member of the Yale faculty who'd been recommended to me by one of the doctors at YPI. White had a widespread reputation for his work in psychiatry, but his scholarship also extended to the humanities. He had a great deal of experience working with very sick patients, and he was also a well-known believer in "talk therapy." In short, there was every reason to think I'd be in good hands.

Psychoanalysis was by no means the obvious treatment for my illness; indeed, most of the professionals at YPI cautioned against it. Psychoanalysis, they explained, causes regression, and I was already too regressed; supportive psychotherapy, combined with medication, was the way to go. I needed, in their view, to shore up my psychological defenses, not to delve behind or take them apart.

But to me, psychoanalysis was the *only* treatment that made sense. I had been cripplingly ill in England. Psychoanalytic treatment kept me out of the hospital while I actually completed my Oxford degree. In the States, in exactly the same situation, I was hospitalized, tied up, and forced to drink foul antipsychotic meds—a year of my life wasted, at a cost to my parents of thousands of out-of-pocket dollars, since the thirty days' worth of inpatient care that my insurance covered hadn't even scratched the surface. I may have been crazy, but I wasn't stupid—I was going with what had worked before.

I met with White at his office at a community mental health center (for those who couldn't afford private care, although I'd be seeing him as a private patient) affiliated with Yale Medical School. White was head of one of the divisions, supervising residents in their placements at the center.

A two-story, nondescript gray building, the center was not particularly inviting, and neither was the doctor's office, which was equally gray and nondescript. Nevertheless, I took to the occupant immediately. White was distinguished-looking, with an almost patrician reserve. Then, as now, he struck me as the quintessential Yale professor. For the time being, we would meet four times a week.

White was more classically Freudian than Mrs. Jones. Kleinians go deep and fast, wasting no time to get to the heart of the matter, whereas White's style was to be more attentive to my defenses, those psychological tools we all use to protect ourselves from painful thoughts and feelings. Mrs. Jones quickly focused on my thoughts and feelings; White examined instead the ways I kept certain parts of my mind at bay. Where Mrs. Jones might discuss my envy, White discussed how my being overly admiring of someone allowed me to *avoid* my envy of them. He'd wait, listen, say a word or two, then wait and listen some more. Despite his relative silence, nothing escaped his attention. And he set limits.

"Elyn, I need you to stop pacing," he said one afternoon.

"Why?" I asked. Part of me was genuinely curious; another part felt my hackles rise in defiance. "We can talk just as well if I'm pacing."

He shook his head. "No," he said. "I need you to talk about what you are feeling, I need you to not act." His voice wasn't harsh; his manner wasn't angry. He was calm and knowing, and spoke as a teacher might to a student who was restless in class and therefore likely to miss the lesson. White recognized early on that my own powers of will, which had often served me well, were just as likely to serve me badly when they pushed me to behavior that was destructive.

Once I was set up with White, my next order of business was school, and how to deal with the awkward "story" of my abrupt departure the year before. I'd learned an unpleasant lesson that long-ago day when I'd tried to volunteer at the Warneford. Any attempt at telling the truth would condemn me, both socially and professionally. So I made up a story about how I'd taken a leave of absence to decide if law school was really for me. The story worked well enough, but whenever a classmate said how impressed she was that I'd actually taken time away to consider this decision, I felt like a fraud. Piling a lie on top of a secret didn't feel particularly good, but mental illness comes with a price tag—and I was willing to pay it.

And then classes began. I walked into my first class of the new year and sat down with a quiet, almost fragile joy and a near-audible sigh of relief: I was back.

I especially liked the professor of my "small group," the seminarlike class of about fifteen required of all first-years. His name was Bob Cover. At the age of forty, he'd won the Ames Prize (given by Harvard Law School for a book deemed of profound legal scholarship) for *Justice Accused: Antislavery and the Judicial Process*. In addition to being a wise and compelling teacher, he was also a scholar of philosophy, literature, and Jewish history, as well as a civil rights activist—a leading supporter of the unionization efforts of Yale's clerical and technical workers, and active in the movement to get Yale to divest itself of South African investments before the end of apartheid. Engaged, passionate, and genuinely humane—everything I hoped someday to be. Later that year, I'd be fortunate enough to be Cover's research assistant on an article for the *Harvard Law Review* entitled "Nomos and Narrative" (*nomos* is the Greek word for "law"); I was thrilled to see that he'd thanked me for my efforts in the article's first footnote. (Sadly, at the end of my third year of law school, in 1986, Cover died of a massive heart attack at forty-two. His loss profoundly touched the legal community at Yale and far beyond.)

With years of practice, I'd learned to keep my symptoms mostly hidden from view; I was becoming adept at *acting* normal even when I wasn't feeling it. Perfecting this acting, this *seeming*, was vitally important if I were going to make my way in the real world. Yet in spite of my vigilance, periodically my psychosis surfaced. One day, a classmate received high praise from one of my professors; fortunately, I had a session with White shortly after. "Someone's trying to kill me," I said. "He's a friend, he's an enemy, and he sent soldiers to the front where I was to explode my brain. I'm scared."

"I think you're talking about your competitive feelings toward your classmate," White said. "You sort of started there, but then you felt scared to have such strong negative feelings about a classmate—so in your mind, you made your classmate attack you. It's sometimes easier to feel attacked than to feel angry or sad."

He also helped me understand that I retreated into thoughts of my own violence when I felt cornered or upset; even to me, that made some sense. "I think you're talking about threatening and scary ideas, because you feel threatened and scared yourself," he said. "The violence is your defense against fear. You are safe here."

So I went back out into the world, shoved the violence and the delusions into a closet, and leaned against that closet door just as hard as I could. I was determined not to lose any more time, not to lose any more of my self . . . and then Professor Cover assigned our small group its first memo. I was startled at how quickly my body reacted: hot, cold, clenched fists, some trouble with concentration.

Memos are what threw me the last time. For two weeks, I worked on my arguments, burrowing down into the research while managing my other classes. *It's OK. Calm down. Focus.*

My memo came back with only three words on it: "Generally very good." I had no way of knowing that this was high praise indeed coming from Bob Cover. Some students were required to completely rewrite their memos; all I had to do was fix a few footnotes. But those three words weren't enough; to me, they meant *I* wasn't enough. By nightfall, I was more disorganized in my thinking and behavior than I'd been since early in the summer. *The library's the only safe place,* I thought. *I'll go work.*

Once settled in, I looked up to see a classmate approaching. "What year is it?" was my greeting. "Do you know where your schoolchildren are? Who's in the library with us? Have you ever killed anyone?" It had simply never occurred to me that others didn't also kill people with their thoughts. My classmate (with impressive practicality, not to mention quick thinking) asked if there was a doctor or therapist she could call for me. I gave her White's name and number, then revealed that the law book I was carrying had no "no's" in it. Then I started reciting Aristotle in Greek.

"Elyn, stay here. Stay right here, I'll be back as soon as I can." When she returned, she told me that White was on the phone; then she led me to the phone itself.

"What's going on?" White asked.

"There's cheese and there's whizzes," I told him. "I'm a cheese whiz. It has to do with effort and subliminal choice. Vertigo and killing." Suddenly, I was terrified.

White's voice was calm. "You sound as if you're not feeling too well," he said. "Your friends are concerned about you."

"Oh, they're nice. Do you like spice? I ate it thrice. They're all hurting me! They're hurting me and I'm scared!"

"I know," White said. "But it's not you, Elyn. It's your illness acting up. Everything is going to be OK. I want you to go to the ER now, the doctors there will be able to help you."

Like a laser beam, his suggestion focused my mind: the ER? No. I'd been given a second chance, I wasn't about to repeat the events of the previous year. "No way," I told him. "No way in hell am I going to the emergency room."

"But I think you need to," he said. "They won't hurt you, and they may be able to give you some medicine that will help."

"Or they may tie me down and lock me up," I argued. "No emergency room."

"I know you're frightened because of last year," White said. "But that's not going to happen this time. And I think you need their help."

"I'll think about it," I muttered. I was fragmented, leaking out at the edges, but I was determined: It'd take police and significant force to get me back into an ER again.

I left the library in a panic, headed back to my room, and attempted to sleep, but it was futile; the very air in the room seemed to swirl around me with threat. *Danger. Evil.* Exhausted, I headed for the Student Health Center the next morning, and once again found myself sitting with a doctor whom I didn't know and who didn't know me. "I've been talking funny," I told him, along with only the barest-bones medical history. He gave me some Trilafon, which I slipped into my pocket. YPI had loaded me up on Trilafon to the point where I couldn't walk and couldn't read—why should I take it now? I had a standing appointment with White the next day; we'd talk about it then.

By the time my appointment rolled around, I was deep in psychosis and almost speechless. I rocked in his chair, rolled my eyes, and stared at the floor.

"How's everything going today, Elyn?" White asked.

"Two and the division of time." Silence.

"Can you tell me what you mean?"

No. More silence, more rocking and gesticulating.

"Everything's going to be OK," he said. "It's good that you went to Student Health; I was concerned that you were going to resist treatment when you didn't go to the ER."

There was a drug, he said—Navane, an antipsychotic whose side effects were milder than Trilafon's. We'd start at a low dose, ten or twelve milligrams. "No," I said. "Not a good idea."

"It will help you concentrate," he said. "It's milder than the other, it works quickly, and please, it will help."

Finally, desperate, I agreed. Only one memo and I'd already crashed. How on earth would I make it through all the memos to come?

The Navane worked as quickly as anything I'd taken. Within a few hours, my mind had calmed. I could read. I could think.

Different bodies respond differently to different medication; finding the magic potion is pretty much hit-and-miss. This seems obvious, even simplistic, but it's the only consistently true fact in treating mental illness. This time, Navane worked. I stayed on it for about ten days, got a lot of work done, then decided that while it was helpful, it was making me a little druggy, and besides, it probably wasn't necessary. *I'll take it when I get sick, but not for long; I don't want to be drugged.* Within two days, I'd stopped altogether. I'd fooled them. Which of course raises the question: Fooled *whom*?

It would take me another fifteen years to learn the lesson of what happened each time I withdrew from drugs. It had been much easier to learn ancient Greek, and not nearly as self-destructive.

One of the worst aspects of schizophrenia is the profound isolation—the constant awareness that you're different, some sort of alien, not really human. Other people have flesh and bones, and insides made of organs and healthy living tissue. You are only a machine, with insides made of metal. Medication and talk therapy allay this terrible feeling, but friendship can be as powerful as either.

Steve Behnke was a first-year student, with a boyish face, a head full of thick sandy hair, and a runner's body. We first talked in the law school cafeteria sometime in early November, on one of those New England evenings when leaves are turning colors and you can taste fall in the crisp air. A group of seven or eight of us sat down to dinner on a Friday.

Steve and I were in contracts class together, and a couple of times he had asked me about an assignment. Other than that, we'd never really spoken. The dinner conversation that night was casual and pleasant, drifting from one subject to another—classes, and law journal, and summer jobs. I noticed that Steve seemed engaged enough—he nodded, he smiled—but after a while, it began to look more like simple politeness. As the others got up to leave, I realized I wasn't ready to go just yet.

And there began one of those conversations that last for a lifetime, one in which there is immediate comfort and acceptance, the equivalent of someone's strong hand offered to you when you most need to grasp it. That first talk flew far and wide: how we got to Yale, who our families were, how we felt about them. Then philosophy, then religion, and what mattered to us, and why. Steve had majored in classics at Princeton, where he was named salutatorian of his class and spoke, in Latin, at graduation. The summer after graduation, he'd worked as a janitor at a small-town airport, then gone to Rome, where he lived with a group of Benedictine monks and read Latin at the Vatican, with a monk who served as the Pope's Latinist. He'd considered entering the monastery and studying medieval philosophy, but decided against it—because he couldn't marry as a monk (he very much wanted a family) and because medieval philosophy had ceased to hold his interest, at least as a life-long endeavor. Instead of becoming a monk, Steve came to Yale Law School. And so did I. And neither one of us was quite sure why.

Sometime later, it occurred to me that at the very moment I was being tied to a bed in a psychiatric ward, screaming bloody murder and afraid for my life, Steve was singing Gregorian chant in a monastery overlooking the ancient city of Rome. And here we were now, come to the same place, from two very different directions. It was past midnight when we said good night, and as I walked back to my room, I had the distinct feeling, in the middle of my usual muddle, that I'd been unexpectedly blessed.

I don't know why I decided to tell Steve the truth about myself; I don't know why I thought I could trust him. But I did. I believed from our very first conversation that this man would be a significant friend and a force for good in my life. Once the possibility came to my mind, I realized how very much I wanted it to be so. But I didn't believe that could happen unless I revealed the truth about myself and let him "see" me in full. So much of what I did on a daily basis was about faking it; I knew that I would never fake it with him.

And so, on a rainy Sunday afternoon, at a pizzeria in New Haven, I shared my history. Aside from doctors and therapists, it was the first time I'd ever done this with anyone, anywhere.

Steve's a naturally curious man and a gentleman as well. So he asked a lot of questions, but in a very gentle and noninvasive way. He told me he didn't know much about mental illness; there'd never been much of a reason to study up. But he listened, and he was empathetic, and little by little, every detail came out. Speaking as a Jewish woman, I suspected he probably would have made a fine priest.

When Steve and I first came to know each other, romantic relationships were so far off my radar that it never even crossed my mind to look for one or, more particularly, to look for one with him. As our friendship progressed, I realized it was becoming exactly what I wanted. He was, for lack of a better term, brotherly—that is, if you can find a brother (or a sister, for that matter) who reads the same authors you do, has the same political and philosophical beliefs, is staggering under the same load of books, and is comfortable making tactless jokes about mental illness. Specifically, mine.

It was late one blustery fall night, in the bowels of the law school, when I was struggling badly, not so long after I'd told Steve about myself. "You can't imagine what it's like in an emergency room—it's god-awful, the way they tie you down and make you wait all night till someone has time to see you. They walk into your room at the crack of dawn, because they're ready to talk. What do they possibly expect you to say except '*Let me f'ing go!*'"

Steve looked at me with an impish grin. "Quote *Hamlet*, perhaps?" And in his best Shakespearian accent he intoned, "Lo, noble physician, the 'morn in russet mantle clad walks o'er the dew of yon high easterward hill. So loosen my chains, kind sir, for the tasks of the day await me."

He smiled. I laughed. He got it. I knew this man, whose depth of heart was equal to the speed of his mind, would be a lifelong friend.

chapter fifteen

URING SECOND SEMESTER, we were free to choose whatever classes we liked. I chose the mental health law clinic and another in criminal law. Steve was in both as well.

As part of the mental health law clinic, students represented actual patients in psychiatric hospitals. Professor Stephen Wizner was the head of the clinic. Tall, with curly black hair, he was often moody and mercurial (sometimes, he gave advice one day that he contradicted the next); he nevertheless helped me feel confident in my early forays helping folks who often looked and sounded like me at my most vulnerable.

Joe Goldstein, a law professor who was also a psychoanalyst, taught the criminal law course. Joe looked like the quintessential "mad professor": baggy clothes that looked like he'd slept in them, plus wild, Einstein-like hair and a distinct, eccentric way of speaking. He only assigned a very few pages of reading for each class—and his syllabus made the course look like a breeze—but he wasn't fooling around. He expected us to read every page, every paragraph, and every sentence; to do otherwise could earn Joe's wrath, which was considerable.

Yale's Legal Services Organization—LSO—always had students work in teams, so Steve and I worked on our mental health law cases together, and from the beginning we represented psychiatric patients and children. One of our first cases involved the two young sons of a man then in prison for multiple rapes. The boys' mother didn't want them anywhere near the dad, an obvious psychopath with a certain quality of persuasive charm. While there's a significant body of evidence that argues that keeping ties to an incarcerated parent is good for a child, there's an equally strong argument on behalf of deferring to a custodial parent—and in this case, the custodial parent was a very good one. The boys were healthy, happy, and well taken care of, in a stable home, by someone whose judgment could be trusted. In Connecticut, children are entitled to their own lawyers in custody and visitation issues, and as attorneys for the boys, we explored what would be best for them, drawing as well on the expertise of the Yale Child Study Center.

Increasingly, Steve and I and our small band of friends hung out at Yorkside Pizza in New Haven—red vinyl banquettes, Yale memorabilia and team pictures on the walls, a jukebox upstairs, a Pac-Man machine downstairs. Over meatballs and sauce, or calzones, or endless slices of cheese-and-pepperoni pizza, we strategized our cases and talked about our classes. It was about as normal as I'd been, and felt, since college.

At the end of spring semester, the academic work grew more intense, and exams loomed. Possible grade range at Yale: honors, pass, low pass, and fail. For the in-class exams (which were open book), I always earned honors, except for my first. For the take-home exam in Joe Goldstein's criminal law class, we were given a choice of topics to write on, and I chose to discuss whether there should be a special law for mentally ill mothers who kill their children. I spent hours consulting with Steve (which we were allowed to do) and hours more putting it all together. When our exams came back, Steve's rated honors—mine got a pass. Like most of the students around me, I cared intensely about my work. Unlike them, however, that work was all that I had. I didn't play sports, I didn't play a musical instrument, I didn't have any hobbies, and whatever social life I'd managed to construct was small and fragile. So the grades I earned were the only objective signal I ever received about how I was doing in the world. The task of setting and achieving academic goals operated as a sort of adhesive; I needed it to hold myself together. Failing (or, at least in this case, failing my own expectations) tore that adhesive off and further splintered my fragile sense of self.

After I retrieved my exam in the department secretary's office and noted the grade, I went directly back to my dorm room, closed the door behind me, and crawled into bed. There, I curled up in the fetal position and spent the rest of the day moaning and babbling, totally convinced that faceless, nameless beings were controlling ("interdicting" was the word I had begun to use in my psychotic ravings) my thoughts. I was in danger of daggers; they were aimed at my flesh, and would slice me in pieces if I dared go to sleep. Afraid to leave the room, afraid to stay in it, I dragged myself to my afternoon appointment with White, who took one look and knew immediately that something was very wrong.

"I only got a pass," I said. "They passed me up. From Jo-Jo. Interdictions are flying everywhere and the other children ate the porridge. No news is good news, bad news brings a flap. Like flipper." The evil presences were in the room. "They're killing me! Tell them to get away!"

White tried to get me to explain what had happened, but it was beyond me, and I grew angrier by the second. "Murders are necessary and evil or necessary evils! The orders will come from elsewhere!" I was pacing frantically around the room, clenching my fists.

"We need to take this seriously," said White. "Do you think you need to be in the hospital?"

"No," I shot back. As if any other answer were possible. As bad as my devils were, the specter of the hospital was worse. *Mrs. Jones, oh, Mrs. Jones, I need you need you need you need you.*

Dimly, I was aware that White was wrestling with his decision and my obstinacy. He could have insisted on hospitalization; in all likelihood, he probably could have had me locked up immediately. But he didn't do that. "All right, no hospital," he replied in a measured and thoughtful tone. "But I want you back on Navane, double your usual dose. And I'd like to meet twice a day until this levels off."

For the next two weeks, I shuffled back and forth to his office twice a day, head down, shoulders hunched, eyes on my feet. I spent the intervening hours sitting on the floor in my room or curled up in a ball on the bed, alone and muttering to myself, accompanied only by my demons, and the occasional knock on the door, which I didn't answer. Few showers, very little food. Gradually, the increased dose of Navane kicked in, the demons receded, and the fog lifted. I got up off the floor, cleaned myself up, and one more time I went back out into the world and started all over again.

Many of my classmates spent the summer after first year in New York City, where impressive law firms paid them lots of money to be summer associates, all the while wining and dining and courting them for the future. That kind of summer was the last thing I could imagine— the stress of a big law firm and the dislocation of a frantic summer in the city seemed too much for me to handle. Besides, I needed to stay near White.

Through one of his clients at the mental health law clinic, Steve found out about a halfway house for the homeless mentally ill and decided to volunteer there for the summer as a live-in counselor. So we both stayed in New Haven and continued our work at LSO, representing mental patients and poor children for a few dollars an hour.

One of our clients that summer was a young anorexic woman, not quite twenty, who had been a patient at a private psychiatric hospital in Connecticut for almost two years. She wanted to get out—her parents wanted her to stay. Their concern was understandable; both physicians and the lay public were learning the truth about anorexia, that it was neither a disease of choice nor a case of weak will, but was real, and potentially fatal. But even that didn't automatically mean the young woman had surrendered her right to have a say in her own treatment. One of her old friends from high school, now a Yale undergraduate, called us about the case, and when we met the young woman, I quickly identified with her, not only because of my battle with my parents around my own weight loss, but also because of the great frustration that comes when your fate is completely in someone else's hands and you're helpless to exercise any control.

Psychiatric patients always have someone (or a whole chorus of someones) telling them what they're supposed to do. In my own experience, I had discovered that it was much more effective to be asked what *I'd* like, e.g., "If you could arrange things your way, what would that look like and how do you think we could help you get there?" Indeed, the young woman accepted that she did need treatment—she just wanted, and was entitled to have, a voice in the decision-making about where and how that treatment would happen. It was my job to help her get that. And as empathetic as I felt toward her, I also began to understand, as the case progressed, that as her legal representative, I was not advocating for *myself*—I was using my skills to advocate for someone else. Ultimately, Steve and I were successful in finding a place for her at a different hospital, where we were hopeful that her disease would be well treated and her autonomy better respected.

. . .

I stayed on the increased Navane dose for the rest of the summer, and took an antidepressant as well. I had to concede that the medicine was working—I could do my schoolwork, I was functioning reasonably well in the world—but I was still looking forward to the day when I'd be able to stop taking meds.

With September came the challenges of second year, and new classes, and a lowered Navane dose—back to ten milligrams. The meetings with White were back to four times a week. But in spite of the meds and meetings, I was having some brief hallucinations, mostly at night—once of a large spider crawling up my wall, but mostly of people standing and staring at me. *They're not there. They're not really there. And even if they are, they're not really looking at you.*

Our work at LSO representing children and psychiatric patients afforded Steve and me easy access to Yale's Medical School and the Yale Child Study Center. We both did an "intensive semester" at the Child Study Center, participating in almost all the classes that the psychiatry fellows and psychology post-doc students were taking. For law students interested in the psychoanalytic approach, there was no more ideal setting. There were times, though, when reminders of my own history as a hospitalized psych patient popped up unexpectedly— like walking past Dr. Kerrigan in the halls. He was the one who'd kept me hospitalized at MU10; he was the one who'd ordered the restraints. Every time our eyes met, I wondered whose bad idea it was that this man come to the Child Study Center. I'm sure he wondered the same about me.

"I think I want to get off my medication now," I told Dr. White. Things were going well; I was feeling fine. I could manage without drugs. "I don't need it."

"Well," he said, and then paused for a moment. I was suddenly aware of trying to read his mind. "How about this: you slowly taper down, and we'll see what happens. Let's say we reduce by two milligrams a week."

Too slow—at that rate, it'd be five or six weeks before I was done with them completely. But whatever I did, I knew it had to be with his knowledge and support. "OK," I said. "I'll start with that."

It wasn't just my usual reluctance to be med-dependent; it was the side effects. Until a new class of antipsychotic meds was developed in the 1990s, the drugs to treat psychosis carried the serious risk of tardive dyskenisia—TD—a neurological disorder that causes involuntary movements, first in your face and around your mouth, and sometimes through your entire body. People with TD twitch and jerk—in short, they *look* like mental patients, and once they've got TD, it generally doesn't go away. I'd spent enough time in and around psychiatric hospitals to know I wanted no part of that.

The first week, I didn't feel any different. "This is working well, don't you think?" I asked White.

"We'll see," he said.

By week two, I was a little shaky. Tightrope walking. *It's ordinary stress, everybody has it. Stop thinking about it. Stop.*

By week three, I was visibly fragmented and struggling to hide it, even from White. I was going to melt. I was about to be attacked and ripped apart. *Stop. It's not real. It will pass.* "I'm feeling a little stress," I told White, "but it's probably just my imagination. Pation. Which is related to being both patient and a patient. Don't you think? Pink?"

He raised an eyebrow. "It sounds as if you're having a bit of a hard time," he said. "Should we up the Navane?"

I shook my head. "No. Too early. I'm doing OK. A-OK. I just need to try a little harder."

"I don't think it's a matter of trying, Elyn. I think it's a matter of whether you need the meds. But if you want to give it a little more time . . ." There seemed to be a question mark at the end of his sentence. Was he asking me?

"Yes," I said with whatever firmness I could muster. "A little more time."

I don't know why he was so accommodating. Maybe he thought I could really do without medication eventually; maybe he wanted to respect my wishes. Maybe he, too, didn't want to see me with the TD shakes. Whatever his reasons, this wouldn't be the last time White would agree to be my copilot while I tried to fly without the meds.

By week four, I'd arrived in the land of full-fledged psychosis. *The people in the sky poison me. I in turn will poison the world.*

"I think you're having thoughts that are scaring you because you need to be on more medication now," said White.

"No!" I was practically shouting. "It has nothing to do with drugs. It's a massive attempt at medical and physiological, not to say psychological, derailment which was a result of deregulation of the rail!"

"It's hard to admit you need medications," said White. "But you do."

Defeat, defeat. "There's no need. I'm not sick. I'm wicked. La di da. I'm ever so well, thank you, ever so well."

But we both knew I'd hit the damn wall again. And as soon as he increased the Navane, I started feeling better. *But this has nothing to do with me or being sick. It's just about being able to study. I'm not sick, I just need some help so that I can study.*

More than once while working with Steve on our LSO cases, I was struck with the absurdities of the mental health care system. Almost every time, there'd come a moment where we'd ask each other, "Wait a minute, just who are the crazy people here?" In one case, the patient's chart said he was restrained *because he wouldn't get out of bed—*

which was hardly an instance of "imminent danger to himself or others" as required by the laws of Connecticut.

In another case, we represented a young man who'd been in the hospital for months, refusing to take his medication for religious reasons. There was no question that our client was seriously ill (although he himself did not agree with that assessment); for instance, he'd severely mutilated himself because he thought the Bible required as much of sinners. At the time, Connecticut permitted forcible medication of involuntary patients, but we wrote strong and well-researched letters to the hospital arguing that our client should not be medicated if he chose not to be: Freedom of religion required as much. The hospital agreed.

Eventually, our client was moved to a new ward. There, he spoke to no one, most especially staff, because he didn't trust the doctors or anyone else. On the other hand, he would call us almost daily, or we called him, to discuss his case; in fact, there were some days we could barely get him *off* the phone, he was so engaged with the legal details.

After several weeks of back-and-forth calls, the hospital scheduled a hearing to appoint a guardian for our client. As preparation, Steve and I went to the hospital to meet with him and explain how the procedure would go. We were met by one of his nurses.

"He's psychotic," she said with absolute certainty. "If you don't believe me, take a look at the record."

So we did. A typed evaluation, and entry upon entry, stating the following: "Patient is very bizarre. He is totally mute. However, we know that he's able to speak, because many times he's been overheard talking on the telephone about his legal rights with his imaginary lawyers."

Steve began to sing under his breath the Temptations song "Just My Imagination."

No one had bothered to notice that in addition to making phone calls, sometimes our client *received* them; no one had bothered to inquire whether he actually may have had a lawyer or lawyers. He was crazy—ergo, his lawyers were imaginary. Imagine the staff's consternation when the imaginary lawyers began introducing themselves to their client's doctors and nurses.

One of my favorite cases, involving someone I would end up working with on and off for six years, was Jefferson, a young man barely out of his teens. When we first met him, Jefferson had been on a back ward in a state mental hospital for many years, after spending even more years before that at a state hospital for adolescents. In addition to having been diagnosed as mentally ill, Jefferson was moderately mentally retarded. And therein lay the problem: Retardation is not equivalent to mental illness, and there seemed to be no current evidence that he was still mentally ill. And if he wasn't, a state mental hospital was absolutely the last place he should have been living.

After our first visit, it took Jefferson another three or four to recognize us and remember who we were; soon, he actually seemed to enjoy our visits, and seemed to have decided to trust us. Whatever his limitations, he had, we believed, "dignity interests" that required us to try to find out what *he* wanted.

"Do you like it here?" we asked.

A stony face. "No. Don't like it here. It's a bad place."

"Why?"

"John, he punched me once, but I whupped him."

"Do you want to stay here?"

"No," he said. "There's nothing to do here."

"Do you have any friends here?"

"No, don't like anyone here. The other people, they're not like me."

"Have you met with any teachers? To do some schoolwork?"

"What schoolwork?" he asked. "We don't get no schoolwork."

It was clear as day that Jefferson needed to be with people who knew how to help him; he needed a group home. But his long history of being in mental hospitals, together with his size (well over six feet

tall and weighing more than three hundred pounds), made us cautious and concerned—was there anyplace that would actually take
him on now?

We started looking for someplace for Jefferson, and the search
went on for weeks—this one was too small, that one too large, others
had no openings (with long, long waiting lists) or housed residents
who appeared neglected. The whole time we were looking, we kept
going back to the mental hospital to check in with our client, just so
he'd know we hadn't forgotten him. "Can I please leave yet?" he
asked each time. Inside that large body was a lonely child who knew
he was in the wrong place.

Finally, we heard of a vacancy in a very pleasant group home in
west New Haven, where most of the other residents were both autis-
tic and retarded. The right size, with competent staff and a good
track record. Could this be Jefferson's new home?

After several overnight and weekend visits in which he did very
well (and was obviously very happy), Jefferson was finally released
from the mental hospital, a warehouse where he hadn't belonged in
many years—if, in fact, he had ever belonged there. I wondered:
How was that first diagnosis made, so many years ago? Who made it?
And how many more Jeffersons were locked up inside places just like
that—lost, or misdiagnosed, spending whole lifetimes waiting for
someone to really see them and recognize them for who they were?

chapter sixteen

AS THE END of law school drew near, I knew only one thing for certain: I was never going to be able to stand up in court and orate like Perry Mason. And I probably wasn't ever going to deliver an impassioned closing argument to a jury on behalf of a good guy or in prosecution of a bad guy. Nor was I going to orchestrate the legal machinations of a Fortune 500 corporation as its counsel, or be one of many names on some prestigious law firm's fancy letterhead. But I *was* going to have to find a job. Finish school, navigate the bar exam, and then a job. Some job. Someplace.

This was . . . daunting. Aside from selling Cokes and popcorn at a movie concession stand, my brief stint as staff trainee at the Center, and summers working at LSO, I'd only ever been a student. And I'd had to battle some terrible demons even to be consistent at that.

I was excruciatingly uncomfortable speaking up in class, so I rarely, if ever, did. After one final exam, the professor called me on the telephone and said that he had no idea of who I was—but that

I'd written the best exam in class. Each time it happened, in spite of the grades I'd earned in the past, this kind of comment came as a surprise. I had to replay it repeatedly in my head, before I could effectively shut off the tape that ran almost all the time: *There's been an unfortunate mistake, they've confused me with some other student, in fact my true performance was less than stellar, and it's only a matter of time before everyone finds out the truth.*

Commenting in class was not the only thing almost impossible for me. I was also terrified of research papers, which scared me right up until the time I became an actual academic. One paper that still resonates for me today was for a class on Freud taught by George Mahl. I was so afraid of having to write a paper that I almost didn't take the class, and did so only after Steve managed to persuade me that it would be a wonderful course despite the paper I'd have to write— and it was, one of the best I've ever taken. The subject of the paper was Daniel Paul Schreber, who at one point in his life had been the chief justice of the supreme court of the German state of Saxony. Schreber had a schizophrenic breakdown, which he wrote about in *A Memoir of My Nervous Illness.* Freud wrote a case study of Schreber, and I constructed a somewhat different interpretation of his delusional system, his principal delusion being that he was being transformed into a woman to be fertilized by the Rays of God in order to bring forth a new race of man and woman. (When describing this in a job interview with Notre Dame Law School, I was met with a hilarious comment by one of the nuns: "What's wrong with that?")

When my paper on Schreber came back to me, it contained a note from Dr. Mahl, telling me that the paper was "publishable." (Later the professor wrote that my final exam was the best he'd seen in twenty-five years of teaching.) This meant a lot to me, particularly because I found Dr. Mahl one of the finest lecturers I'd ever heard, or have heard to this day. There were no class discussions in Mahl's course, but his lectures were so amazing nobody missed having discussions—and nobody skipped his classes, either.

Professor Mahl's feedback had an enormous effect on me— positive at first, then almost immediately negative: I stopped taking my medication again. *I'm publishable, I'm not mentally ill at all—which means I don't need to take medication for the mentally ill. I'm done with this.* The last time I'd tried to stop the meds—using White's "weaning" method—I only became more anxious as the weeks went by and the dosage went down. *That was the wrong way. This time, I'll do it all at once. Just pull the bandage right off!*

I felt fine for a day or two; ecstatic, even. By day five, I was completely and floridly psychotic, convinced that evil beings were about to destroy me. I gibbered; I cowered. I couldn't work, and the end of the final term was coming up. Finally, White insisted: back to the Navane, and increase it again. The effect was almost immediate, but instead of being relieved, I was angry. *I'm sick of this.* It all came down to supporting the patient's choice—didn't it? If I was competent when I decided to stop taking the meds, then it was a competently made decision. A decision made by a competent person. Wasn't it?

One tragic example of supporting a patient's choice was the case of my close friend Dan, whose first client in the mental health law clinic was an adolescent named Tony, who'd been institutionalized most of his life. When Dan took his case, Tony was at the state hospital for adolescents with mental illness, although oddly, his only clinical diagnosis at that point was attention deficit disorder—ADD. Tony wanted out of the hospital, and Dan got Tony released to his reluctant parents, who only after much pleading had finally agreed to take Tony in.

Some months later—at a point at which Tony would perhaps have been out of the hospital anyway—Dan got a phone call from Tony: He was being held in prison on a murder charge. He had burned down the family trailer with his mother, father, and seven-year-old brother still inside; they'd all died. Dan was devastated; indeed, the

entire mental health law class was. For a bunch of idealistic law students, some lessons were harder to learn than others, and this one—
that "helping people" isn't always a good thing (or, maybe, that
"helping" translates differently from case to case, and must be cautiously scrutinized)—was tragic for all parties. The caveat, of course,
is that there is no way of knowing whether Dan's intervention made
any significant difference in how Tony's story turned out.

Generally, though, helping psychiatric patients felt pretty good to
me. There were so many factors in their various hospitalizations, and
so much potential for error and neglect in the way they were treated.
Some damage *could* be undone; some lives *could* be changed for the
better. I realized early on that going to the mental wards sometimes
set me off emotionally—it probably aroused my own dependency
needs, as well as my anger at how I had been treated when I was being held in the hospital. But I was convinced I understood more than
most people did (medical professionals as well as man-on-the-street
people) about what it was like to be the helpless patient in that bed, or
the terrified patient in four-point restraints.

And yet, even as I adamantly denied my illness, I understood all
too well my limitations. If I couldn't even speak up in class, it wasn't
likely that I'd be capable of being an impassioned advocacy soldier
slugging away in the courtroom trenches, trying to get either a hospital administrator or an intransigent legal system to pay attention to
me. If I were really going to make a change in lives of mental patients, I had to find a different way to do it.

The *Yale Law Journal,* established in 1891, published (and continues
to publish) "original scholarly work in all fields of law and legal
study." Its articles and essays have always been contributed by the
leading professors and legal minds throughout the world, but the
Journal also includes shorter pieces, called "Notes," written by
student-staff members. In order to be a member of the *Journal,* I had
to submit a topic statement on the subject I wished to write about in my

Note—the use of restraints in psychiatric hospitals. When my statement was accepted, I asked Steve if he'd help me revise and prepare the Note for publication, and of course he said yes. I wanted my argument to be as cogent and powerful as possible; in fact, on some level, I wanted the words on the page to do the *im*possible—go back and change the outcome for that young woman tied to a bed at the Yale Psychiatric Institute and Yale-New Haven Hospital's MU10. I wanted my words to change the minds of all the doctors who had ever treated me and gotten it wrong. It might have been too late for me. But perhaps it wasn't too late for somebody else.

The research I did showed that restraints hadn't been used in England for more than two centuries; certainly I'd never seen any sign of them when I was there (and I'd been neither a docile nor a particularly cooperative patient). Yet they were used liberally in the United States. Was this truly the best we could do? What were the rules, what were the parameters, what was reasonable (and unreasonable) care when treating patients who were already terrified at that moment when someone in authority forcibly tied them down? In my Note, I proposed a Model Statute (a statute that could serve as a model for legislation in individual states); in addition, I argued for a greater degree of negligence before a doctor could be held liable for *not* restraining someone—in short, I wished to change the incentives for doctors. My doctors, everyone's doctors.

While I was preparing my Note, I spoke to one mental health professional then on the Yale faculty. "Wouldn't you agree that being restrained is incredibly degrading?" I asked. "Not to mention painful. And frightening."

The professor looked at me in a knowing way. "You don't really understand," he said kindly. "These people are different from you and me. It doesn't affect them the way it would affect us." *If only he knew,* I thought to myself.

My Note, "The Use of Mechanical Restraints in Psychiatric Hospitals," was published in the *Yale Law Journal* in 1986. The pride I felt was almost too enormous to be borne. A few months later—after graduation—I received a call from a lawyer at the Bazelon Center for Mental Health Law, then and now considered the premier public interest law firm representing people with mental illness. Bazelon, located in Washington, D.C., advocates in both the courts and in Congress on behalf of a constituency that in most cases is unable to advocate for itself. "I read your Note with great interest," she said, and then went on to explain that she'd used the information in it to form and bring a major class action lawsuit challenging the use of restraints in a certain Midwestern hospital. My Note helped someone. My work had made a difference. It helped another attorney and it helped patients who were no different from me. No different at all.

Graduation was (as it is, I suspect, for almost everyone) a time for reflection. For me that meant asking how I had gotten here, what had kept me out of the hospital and in the classroom, and how I could ensure that safety in the uncertain time ahead.

First, I was in consistent talk therapy, with a psychoanalyst who understood me and treated me with respect. With his painstaking interpretations of my behaviors, White helped me open a window onto myself, showing me that my psychosis served to protect me from painful thoughts and feelings. My psychosis actually played a role in my psychological life—the unconscious mind serving as a defender of the conscious mind. For some reason, knowing that made everything less toxic, more malleable. I may not have been in complete control of my psychosis, but I wasn't totally at its mercy, either.

In addition (as with Mrs. Jones, but unlike all the medical doctors to date), White did not recoil from me. He never put me in the hospital (under the guise of protecting me while actually protecting himself), but stood his ground when I was most frightening, and vowed to protect me. He knew better than anyone that most of the time, I was literally scared out of my wits.

When it came to the difficult issue of medication, White encouraged but never forced me. For all my intense ambivalence about taking drugs, I nevertheless did take them most of the time—because in White, I had a medical professional who actually listened to me, trusted me, and rewarded my trust in him.

In Steve, I'd finally found a true friend, almost a soul mate, who saw and accepted my illness, yet viewed it as not at all central to who I actually was. That connection—to a good person, a smart person, an affectionate, funny, and accepting person—made me feel truly human. And it made me feel hopeful that I'd find other people like Steve, and that they, too, would see past my illness and value the real me.

I'd been in an academic program that offered equal parts structure (which I needed) and unstructured time (which I needed to learn to manage). Everybody, on some level, needs a good day-care program: Mine was the Yale Law School.

So I'd made it through, and managed to construct some survival tools. I'd found a school that helped me flourish, a psychiatrist who made me feel life might well be worth living, and a friend who made me feel human. And while it might be a long time before I'd find a man who made me feel like a woman, what I had on graduation day was not half bad, given all I'd been through. Graduation was a victory— and in fact, the administration chose me and another student to be class marshals, the students who go up on stage to receive a diploma on behalf of their graduating class. My entire family was present when I made that walk, and I couldn't help but think how far we'd all come.

It was a very good day.

.   .   .

And yet. There was the not-insignificant matter of the law boards, and the job hunt, and having to move out of the dorm, and finding a new place to live. The day after graduation was all about change, and I'd never been good with change.

I decided to stay on in Connecticut for a while; I wasn't yet ready to leave White, and he concurred. And Steve was staying around, too. He was intending to apply to graduate schools in clinical psychology, but needed to get some more experience with clinical work first. So he took a live-in job at the halfway house for the severely mentally ill where as a law student he had worked with the residents.

My law board exam was scheduled for July; the job hunt had to wait until I passed. I was somewhat sleepless in the days leading up to the exam, and just a little nervous—anyone would have been, not just me. But I'd done well in the practice exams, and besides, for three years everyone at Yale had reassured us, "Don't worry, the bar review course will teach you everything you'll need"—I had no choice but to trust that they were right. I did receive one additional piece of advice: *don't think.* So I didn't, and managed to score in the ninety-ninth percentile of those taking the exam that day.

Steve and I had a few more cases at the Legal Services Organization to finish up. One day soon after the bar exam, when the structure of exam preparation and the anticipation of the day itself had passed, I walked into the LSO office and greeted Sally, one of the secretaries there who'd become a friend.

"How's everything?" I asked. "Do you want to vandalize the law school with me? I don't know who's listening to this, but it's a master plot to do with the questions. Points. Points of view. Should I jump out the window?"

"What are you talking about?" Sally asked, half laughing.

"I'm just kidding around," I said. "Kidding has to do with sheep. I'm sheepish. Have you ever killed anyone? I've killed lots of people with my thoughts."

The smile left Sally's face. "Elyn, you're scaring me a little here."

"Don't be scared," I said. "I'm just a cat. The fish is delicious. I'll just go do my work now."

"Oh, no, wait," she said. "I think you should stay here for a few minutes . . ."

I sat down, then started singing, then stopped. "Do you mind if I make a hat out of that clothes hanger?" I asked Sally. "And after that, I think I might jump out of the window."

Quickly, Sally and another secretary, Maria (who'd become a friend as well, thankfully), called Steve Wizner, the Legal Services director. Wizner came immediately from wherever he'd been, was briefed by the others for a few moments, and then called me into his office. "So what's going on, Elyn?" he asked. "You seem to be a little upset—everything OK?"

"I'm ever so well, thank you, ever so well," I chirped. "I've been making up songs for the films. There's a bootleg traffic in legal briefs going on. We'll be sued, but my name is not Sue, thank you very much. How did you get to be so tall? Don't fall." I was laughing hysterically, and having trouble not falling off my chair onto the office floor.

Nearly two years before, I'd told Wizner about my illness and my history, and he'd known all along about the treatment I'd been getting. "I'd like to call Dr. White," he said.

"I don't think that's necessary," I said, "but you can if you want."

When he'd reached White, Wizner told him what had been going on, and then handed me the phone. "Up the Navane to twenty milligrams, Elyn," said White's calm voice. "Now, please."

Handing the phone back to Wizner, I reached into my bag, pulled out the bottle, and obediently popped the appropriate number of pills. "All better now!" I cheerfully informed Wizner—and we both started laughing, him with relief, me still delusional but cogent enough to be embarrassed at the scene I'd caused. My actual recovery, however, took a little longer.

In the three years since I'd last been hospitalized, this was only the second time I'd become overtly psychotic with anyone other than White or Steve, and it was part of the pattern: I'd set goals for myself, meet them successfully, then fall apart at the seams. Once again, everything familiar and comfortable in my life was going away or being left behind. What was ahead was new and frightening. The scaffolding had been removed, and I wasn't sure that I could sustain the structure all by myself.

When I become psychotic, a kind of curtain (of civilization, of socialization) falls away, and a secret part of me is revealed. And then, after the psychosis passes, I suffer overwhelming shame: I have been seen. *Now they know.* But something about this episode was intrinsically different from the ones that had come before. I'd worked with Sally, Maria, and Wizner for three years; I trusted them, and they trusted me—as a friend and also as a professional who'd been judged competent to handle patients and cases in a responsible manner. So, in retrospect, I think it was somehow almost normal that I'd go to that office to fall apart. When you're scared, on the verge of a meltdown, you instinctively know to head someplace where you'll be safe; when you reveal something so intimate as psychosis, you want the witnesses to be people you trust.

In the days to come, I was oddly reassured to realize that my instinct for survival seemed to have gotten better over the years—instead of having the episode in the street, or the grocery store, or in line at the bank, I'd somehow managed to stave it off until I could get to a safe place. Although my colleagues there were not necessarily prepared for what happened, the relationship we'd all formed gave them the tools to manage it, and manage me as well. They were calm, they did the right thing, and the moment passed.

My first "real" job interview was with New Haven Legal Assistance, probably the best such job in Connecticut. I was nervous, but no more medicated than usual. My record was good; I thought I had a decent shot at it. Afterward, the office's lawyers called Steve Wizner to say that notwithstanding my strong record and my seeming to be a nice person, they couldn't offer me the job. Basically, I'd flunked the interview—I was, they said, "practically comatose."

At my next appointment (with Connecticut Legal Services— CLS—in Bridgeport), I was advised by the staff attorney who first interviewed me to "act perkier" when I met with the executive director. Now, "perky" had never been in my playbook—and I'd never seen it listed anywhere as a job requirement. Maybe I just needed an extra cup of coffee. Whatever the case, I managed to make a credible impression and was offered and accepted the position at CLS.

The office was in an old, run-down house in what had been a nice part of Bridgeport years earlier but was now in the heart of the slums. I began representing clients immediately, half-time on family law cases, half-time on housing cases. At a typical legal services office (and Bridgeport was that), there's little time to reflect, to learn, to think or strategize. Resources and staff are minimal, and the clients themselves are usually in such dire straits by the time they make contact with the office, there's often very little the lawyers can do for them. My first day on the job, I was asked to go—alone—to Father Panik Village, at the time the sixth-largest public housing project in the country, and notoriously one of its worst, with forty-six brick buildings on forty acres, and a population of nearly five thousand people, low-income families who grew more embattled every day: with guns, drugs, domestic abuse, and overall mayhem and chaos.

Panik was the name of the priest who'd originally championed this Bridgeport Housing Authority project during the Depression; nevertheless, the word's connotations were apt. I said I would go there only if someone else accompanied me, which was quickly arranged. I was also assigned a case that first day that was scheduled to go to trial in just a week. No preparation had been done. No one had actually seen the client. The case settled.

I quickly realized I'd been spoiled at LSO. We handpicked our cases there, and chose only the most interesting ones, or those that might elucidate some point of law. We worked with experts in the various fields (who were happy to return our phone calls when we identified ourselves as Yale students), we had ample time for research and strategizing, and we had staff support. We had time to work, and time to think; in fact, thinking was actually prized.

At CLS, I spent most of my time negotiating with slick lawyers who represented sleazy slumlords or wife-batterers. I had no time to make or return phone calls; I had no time to research or think about the law, and it was the thinking part that was so integral to my love for the law. Though I liked and even admired many of the people I represented (when I could find the time to really talk with them), I found the work itself unrelentingly grueling, and was soon overwhelmed. I wasn't Perry Mason, I certainly wasn't Joan of Arc, and at the end of each day, I was barely sentient. I worried that I wasn't helping my clients as I should. Frantically, I began to look for some other place, any other place, that would have me. I felt somewhat guilty about wanting to go, but not guilty enough to stay.

In 1993, the last of the Father Panik Village residents were relocated. A year later, the buildings were demolished, a fitting end to the overly optimistic idea of high-rise, high-density communities as the solution for low-income housing—now recognized by contemporary city planners as an unworkable (and often inhumane) nightmare. On the site now, there's a sprinkling of new, single-family homes and duplexes, with recently planted yards and young sapling trees. The word is, Bridgeport's on its way back. I sometimes wonder if any of my clients made it back as well.

. . .

I did continue pro bono with one mental health law case: that of Jefferson. Once Steve and I got him into a group home, we turned to the task of getting him education. Trouble was, he was already twenty-one, and the relevant laws only provided for special education for kids under twenty-one. So we tried a novel theory: Since Jefferson had received no education at all when he was at the mental hospital for five years, he was owed "compensatory education" for that time. That theory is now well accepted in special education law, but it was new when we brought it. And we prevailed, through a complicated and circuitous route. Jefferson received five more years of education, at the premier special ed facility in the state.

During the time I worked in Bridgeport, scheduling analysis appointments with White became difficult. We tried to work around both my schedule and his, but it was often hard to meet all four days. And then one day, the question of my diagnosis came up.

We'd discovered that the medical insurance from my CLS job would pay for some of my analysis. In order for that to happen, however, White had to fill out a form that specified a diagnosis. I'd hoped he might write something innocuous—neurotic anxiety disorder, maybe—so that I could avoid having an official record of serious mental illness. There would be other jobs in my future, I hoped, and I wanted access to them without being hobbled. But White made it perfectly clear to me that it was his intention to complete the form with integrity, and tell the truth. And I quickly understood there'd be no negotiating with him on this point.

When we first began our work together, White had discussed my diagnosis. He thought then that I suffered primarily from depression, not schizophrenia, which was a huge relief to me. "But let's put aside the labels for now," he'd said. "They're a distraction, and we have more important work to do."

Of course, I'd remained intensely interested in his ultimate diagnosis—depression, even psychotic depression, was still primarily a disorder of feelings, and that much I could accept. Schizophrenia (or some variant) was a "thought disorder"—a disorder that was psychotic at its core—and that was another matter entirely.

Within a day or two, White returned the form to me. I could feel my pulse pounding in my ears when I saw it in his hand, stretched out to me. I took it from him, and read the words: "schizoaffective disorder, depressive type." A psychotic illness. An illness only once removed from schizophrenia. Seeing those words—coming from someone I knew, someone whose clinical judgment I couldn't dispute—felt like death. And so, as if to fully inhabit the diagnosis, I quickly started to unravel.

That night, while Steve and I were taking a walk, I told him that I'd seen White's diagnosis and it had startled me. "Mild mental retardation in the presence of overachievement, as manifested by successfully completing Yale Law School," I said quietly, sneaking a look at him out of the corner of my eye, waiting for the reaction.

Steve flushed and began to stammer, knowing how important White's opinion was to me. "Elyn, I realize White is really smart, but isn't it possible he's wrong about this? I just don't think you're mentally retarded." He looked up to see me smiling.

"Gotcha!" I said, and laughed. I could tell from the look on his face that he couldn't decide whether to laugh with me, or turn and walk in the other direction.

Despite my laughter, there wasn't much funny in this situation; any diagnosis starting off with "schizo" damned me, and I knew it. *Why does White think that about me? Am I really that sick? Is everything I've done, all the progress I've made, a joke? Do I really belong in a mental hospital after all?*

As if to mock me, the universe dropped me into the dark hole again, and the delusions came back for a visit.

At White's urging, I again increased the Navane; within days, I was on an even keel. But still his diagnosis haunted me. I was so certain that I'd made real progress; I believed I'd moved past that first diagnosis in the hospital. But now the weight of White's verdict was palpable, even ominous, my own private Sisyphus's rock—I rolled it up the hill, it rolled back down, I rolled it up, it rolled back down. It had all the potential to crush me entirely.

I continued to spend a great deal of time with Steve, who had come to love his work and shared it with me; I found our time together soothing. Steve found the work he was doing at the halfway house enormously rewarding, and compared living there with living in the monastery. I often went over to the house for dinner, or just to sit around the kitchen table and talk to the people who were in residence. One day, I came in the door to find that the newest tenant was a patient I'd known on the ward at YPI. There were a few minutes of awkwardness between us until we realized that the coffee and the conversation meant exactly the same thing to both of us, and for the same reasons.

Spending time at the halfway house reminded me that being ill had its advantages. Staff in ERs and hospitals pay close attention to very ill patients, and people at the halfway house almost always had someone to talk to. But "getting well" means giving up that kind of attention, or finding other, better ways of getting it. It was the familiar lesson: Leaving home is great, but few people make the journey without looking back, at least a few times in the beginning.

That summer I learned of a two-year position at a local law school (now Quinnipiac University School of Law) teaching legal research and writing. The position held no prospect for tenure, but it made my escape from legal services possible; lawyering had never come easily to me and in Father Panik Village I had found myself completely overwhelmed. Plus, with this job, I could stay in New Haven, and continue my analysis with White. And so I applied for it.

In my interview (a vast improvement over the ones I'd bumbled through at the two legal services offices), the very nice dean, as subtly as possible, warned me that this teaching job might be well beneath my talents. I didn't care. I needed to work and I wanted to work; besides, he didn't have all the information about me. And I wasn't going to give it to him, either.

When I received the offer, I accepted it on that very day.

"I have to tell you something." This was Steve, in his gentlest voice. I braced myself, half-knowing already what was coming. "I'm leaving New Haven, and moving to Washington."

He'd become involved with a woman—a woman I liked a lot, someone gentle and kind, who made him smile. She'd completed her degree at Yale and had been accepted into a doctoral program at the University of Virginia in Charlottesville. Steve wanted to be near her, I understood that, I supported it; in fact, I'd known for a long time that it was only a matter of time before there would be actual miles between us instead of only minutes.

Nevertheless, it hurt, deeply. He was my colleague, my confidant, my best friend, and in a complex way, my best witness—to my illness, my darkness, and my struggle to stay in the world and become a contributing member of a professional community. He critiqued my papers, he helped keep my fragmented mind together, he charted my progress (and reminded me I'd made some)—he even finished some of my sentences. And I often finished his as well. There was nothing he didn't know about me. There was nothing we didn't talk about, nothing I didn't want his counsel on, no matter if it was personal, professional, or academic. And now he was leaving me? No surprise that my first response to his news was "No!"

"Yes," he said. "It's time."

"I don't think I can manage without you near," I said. My voice was shaking.

"Yes, you can," he said. "Elyn, your whole life has been the story of you fighting to get whatever you need, and *getting* it. You're the quintessential survivor—you've found friends, therapists, professors who believe in you. And now you're about to begin your professional life. I didn't do that for you—*you* did it!"

"But I had your help," I said.

"And you always will have it," he said. "This isn't the end of the friendship—nothing could make that happen. Come on, admit it, you'll be going someplace else someday soon as well. You have important work to do, and where I'm living when that happens won't make any difference."

We had brunch together on the day he left. I barely got my omelette down, one slow bite at a time, and the coffee tasted like it'd been made the week before. Afterward, Steve climbed into his car, a Ford Pinto he'd bought for $500, and drove away, headed for I-95 South. I stood there watching for a few minutes, thinking back to that long-ago day when Kenny and Margie Collins had driven away from Vanderbilt, and away from me. My heart broke that day, and it was breaking now, but I'd survive—as sad as I was, I knew that. So I got into my own car and drove (crying all the way) back to the law school for a meeting. I parked the car and pulled myself together. Steve was right—I had things to do. It was time to go to work.

chapter seventeen

TAKING THE TEACHING job, even though it was not at all prestigious (as the dean himself had intimated), was one of the best professional decisions I ever made.

It was one of the smaller schools I had been in, with less pressure and tension than Yale; the students were hardworking and aspirational, eager to listen and learn (there was, however, a significant flunk-out rate, unlike Yale). My major responsibility—grading their memos and briefs—was time-consuming, but straightforward, and on some days mostly easy. In spite of my awkwardness about speaking in public, the give-and-take I had with these students helped shore up my confidence. I began to think of myself as a real teacher.

One of my colleagues there was a professor named Sandy Meiklejohn, a grandson of the famous philosopher and First Amendment scholar, Alexander Meiklejohn. Sandy had been a tennis pro in between graduating from law school and practicing law, and had been surprised that he was able to land a teaching job. Once there, he discovered that the family tradition of teaching (Alexander senior had been dean of Brown University from 1901 until 1912 and president of Amherst College from 1913 until 1923) ran deep in him as well. Sandy loved teaching, and in spite of having a reputation of being hard on his students, he was also the favorite professor of many—he didn't patronize and he didn't pander. And he was a wonderful role model for me.

Sandy and I became good friends and shared many working dinners together; he was a kind and intuitive "coach" during my wobbly early days as an academic, and helped me with a paper I was trying to put together for publication. For obvious reasons, I'd become interested in what attributes or characteristics comprised "competency" for people who wanted to decide for themselves to take (or not to take) medication for psychosis. How did the law define it? How did the medical establishment understand it? And how *should* we understand it? Since Sandy had studied contractual capacity, his feedback on another competency topic was vitally important to me.

That teaching year seemed almost to fly by, and I was doing well—better, certainly, than I could have expected. I'd adjusted to the many changes in my life as trouble-free as I'd ever done. The teaching job made it easier for me to schedule my appointments with White, and although I longed to be drug-free, I'd stayed on the Navane and an antidepressant, Elavil (amitriptyline) (but occasionally tinkered with the dosages, of course). I felt confident about my teaching, I'd made some new friends, and my article on competency was coming along nicely, with Sandy reading the drafts and giving me some ideas about where I might send it. My hope was, if I could get the article published in a law journal, maybe (after another year working with White), I'd feel safe enough to apply for a position someplace else and leave New Haven behind.

And then White told me he was going retire very soon—to be precise, in three months.

As though someone had hit a switch, I was almost immediately in

terrible shape—worse than I'd been since Oxford and those first few
horrible months at Yale. Within days, withdrawn and almost mute, I
began rocking and gibbering again, whether I was alone or in
White's office. I was surrounded by destructive energy and unspeakable fear. "Please don't go," I begged White. "You can't. The world is
coming to an end."

Fortunately, the law school was in moot court competition, so I really needn't do anything other than show up—which was a good
thing, since I was incapable of speech. One day, I brought all my jewelry into White's office, along with a check for a large amount of
money—nearly all I had. "I want your wife to have this jewelry," I
told him. "I won't need it anymore. And I won't need the money, either, so you take it."

"Elyn, you know I can't accept this. Do you think it's time to go to
the hospital?"

No! No hospital. Mostly, I stayed in my apartment, curled up and
muttering on the couch. Friends brought me cigarettes and food, but
I couldn't eat. I started to talk about violent things whenever someone was with me. "I've killed many people," I said. "And now that
White has been taken over by the devil, I might have to kill him as
well. And he's not the only one."

Steve was traveling to universities around the country, interviewing
with various psychology doctorate programs. He'd called many times
to check up on me, but I wasn't picking up the phone, so he called
our friends, who told him what had happened. He immediately returned to New Haven.

I opened the door of my studio apartment. Steve would later tell
me that for all the times he had seen me psychotic, what he saw that
day shocked him. For a week or more I had barely eaten. I was gaunt,
and moved as though my legs were wooden. My face looked (and felt)
like a mask. Since I'd pulled down all the shades, the apartment (in
the middle of the afternoon) was in near total darkness. The air was

fetid, the place was a shambles. Steve has worked with many patients who suffer from severe mental illness. To this day he'll tell me that on that afternoon I looked as bad as any he'd ever seen.

"Hi," I said, then returned to the couch, where I sat in silence for about five minutes. "Thank you for coming, Steve," I finally said. "Crumbling world. Word. Voice. Tell the clocks to stop. Time is time has come."

"White is leaving," Steve said somberly.

"I'm being pushed into a grave, the situation is grave," I moaned. "Gravity is pulling me down. They're all trying to kill me. Tell them to get away. I'm scared."

Steve spent several days with me as I listened to music and alternately muttered unintelligibly and threatened to commit violent acts. I didn't want to leave the apartment, except to see White and put in an appearance to try and hold on to my job, but Steve gently insisted that I needed to get out more. I needed to shower, and brush my teeth, and put on some clean clothes, and eat something. In fact, we actually met with friends for dinner one night; blessedly, there was little reaction from anyone as I babbled quietly at the table while everyone else enjoyed their meal.

And then everything changed again. It turned out that White wasn't leaving, at least not yet. Yale had convinced him to stay on an additional year, since it was taking them some time to find his replacement. The cloud lifted. The devils receded; my head cleared. When I had settled, White went back to interpreting. "You are harboring fantasies that this situation has something to do with you," he said to me in session. Of course I was. He *was* staying for me. Wasn't he?

How do I understand why I fell apart so badly at White's telling me he was leaving? Right now, wherever you are—in your room, in a library, on a park bench, on a bus—literally hundreds of things clamor for your attention. On the outside, there are sights, sounds, and smells; on the inside, you have your thoughts, feelings, memories, wishes, dreams, and fears. Each and every one of these, both inside and out, is knocking at your door, all at once.

But you have the power to choose which thing, or combination of things, to give your attention to. Maybe it's the feeling of the book in your hand, or the temperature of the room you're sitting in. You shift and reposition a pillow at your back. You reread the last paragraph on the page, then turn to the next one. You think about getting up and walking into the kitchen, maybe preparing a snack. Even though these actions address only a tiny fraction of what's actually going on inside and around you, you are able to *choose* them and relegate the others to the background.

Now consider this: The regulator that funnels certain information to you and filters out other information suddenly shuts off. Immediately, every sight, every sound, every smell coming at you carries equal weight; every thought, feeling, memory, and idea presents itself to you with an equally strong and demanding intensity. You're receiving a dozen different messages in a dozen different media—phone, e-mail, TV, CD player, friend knocking at the door, ideas inside your head—and you're unable to choose which ones come to the front and which are relegated to "later." It's the crowd at the Super Bowl, and they're all yelling directly at you.

Or try this: Place yourself in the middle of the room. Turn on the stereo, the television, and a beeping video game, and then invite into the room several small children with ice cream cones. Crank up the volume on each piece of electrical equipment, then take away the children's ice cream. Imagine these circumstances existing every day and night of your life. What would you do?

First, you'd desperately look for clarity, a way out of the din— something to focus on, something to hang onto. Medication could be one solution, if your body chemistry tolerates it. You might also strive to make your life as predictable and orderly as possible—to literally control the various ingredients that make up your life—so that you knew ahead of time what was expected of you, what was going to happen, and how to prepare for it. Your basic goal would be to eliminate surprises. Slowly, painstakingly, you would rebuild your own internal regulator, with structure and predictability. What you lose in the way of spontaneity, you gain by way of sanity.

I'd made it through graduation, a difficult public sector job, the switch to teaching, and the learning of new skills. And Steve's departure. And mostly, I'd stayed on my feet. And then, I formulated a plan for getting on with my life. White was central to that plan, and the plan was working. I knew how to work with him and what to expect from him—that provided me with the "something to hang onto" that gave structure to my life. Of course, I knew change was inevitable; I'd learned that. But I was also still learning how to navigate it. White's retirement announcement came as a catastrophic surprise, in the way that a lightning strike is a surprise. In the time it took for him to say the words, the structure and predictability I'd built my life around simply blew up in my face. The regulator—the one I'd created so carefully in order to replace the *missing* regulator—was destroyed. Every sight, sound, smell, taste, memory, emotion, thought, and idea roared in at once and overwhelmed me.

I had always believed that the breakdown I'd suffered in my first months at Yale came about partly because I hadn't been able to successfully complete my work with Mrs. Jones—now, with White's announcement, something inside told me that history was repeating itself. But that worst-case scenario didn't happen. Steve came as a messenger from the outside world, and White's changed plans restored order to my interior world.

However, had White kept to his original plan of retiring and not been able to treat me for the one additional year I'd counted on, I'm certain I would have ended up in the hospital again. I knew full well that the time would come when White and I would agree that our work together was at an end. But for me to stay sane, our "end" had to come at the right time and place. Now that was back to being possible.

It was a frightening slide, however, and my recovery from it, although a relief, was almost as unnerving. I began to understand that my continuing well-being depended not only on my own focus and resolve, but equally on random luck. For someone whose very survival hinged on structure and predictability, this was *not* good news.

In the summer of 1988, I'd finished my teaching year and was gearing up for my plunge into the law-school teaching market. I'd completed the manuscript of my journal article on competency to refuse medication and was confident that the article was good enough to use for my "job talk" in upcoming interviews. The plan was back on track.

That Fourth of July weekend, I'd planned a quick trip to Miami to visit my family. But the night before my flight, I suddenly had a horrible headache.

As many medical problems as I'd had, headaches had never been on the list. And this one didn't seem to want to go away. It lasted for two whole days. My head hurt, my neck hurt, my back hurt, and I was on the verge of nausea much of the time.

I tried to be philosophical, and patient with my body. I had friends who got migraines; maybe now it was my turn. Maybe, for once, what I was experiencing was normal—garden variety stress. Or maybe it was the heat. Or the humidity. In any case, just as suddenly as it came, the headache was gone.

Two weeks later, it was back. I was stunned at the pain, and my inability to get above it. A friend whom I'd made through Steve—a man named John, who was not only a wise priest but also a gifted psychiatrist—finally convinced me to see my doctor. I learned later that John's mother had died young after experiencing symptoms similar to mine.

The doctor concurred with me—yes, the problem was migraines, possibly brought on by stress. He gave me a prescription for Tylenol with codeine. After my appointment, I drove back to Yale to see my friends at Legal Services; the last thing I remember was violently throwing up. Even now, I remember nothing else that occurred for the five days that followed.

According to what I've since pieced together, after I was sick, Maria and Sally drove me home and told me I needed to go straight to bed. The following morning, they called to check on me, but the line was busy. For hours. By noon, they were concerned enough to come back to the apartment, where they found me in the same clothes I'd been wearing the day before. My bed had not been slept in, and I kept repeating one sentence—"Why are you here, why are you here?" They'd tell me, and a few moments later I was asking them again, literally unable to keep the thought in my head from one moment to the next.

Quickly, they bundled me into their car and took me to the emergency room. Where a completely predictable disaster happened: The ER discovered that I had a psychiatric history. And that was the end of any further diagnostic work.

Stigma against mental illness is a scourge with many faces, and the medical community wears a number of those faces. A psychiatric patient at a program where Steve once worked went for weeks with a broken back; none of the medical people the patient saw took the man's pain seriously—he was a mental patient. So once the ER learned I had a mental illness and was on antipsychotic medication, the diagnosis was written in stone: I was "just" having an episode. Poor Maria was literally jumping up and down, trying to tell anyone who'd listen that she had seen me psychotic before and that this was different. But her testimony didn't help—I was a mental patient. The ER sent me away.

Maria decided that I needed to come home with her; whatever was going on with me, it was obvious to her that I wouldn't be safe alone. By the time we arrived at her place, I had no recollection of going to the ER and didn't know where we were, or why. Trying to get me settled, she called my parents. My mother flew up from Miami immediately—my father was recovering from eye surgery and would follow as soon as he could.

My mother came directly to Maria's, spent half an hour or so there with us, and then drove me back to my little apartment. She stepped out for a few minutes to pick something up for us to eat at a neighborhood store. When she came back and knocked at the door, I opened it and was surprised to see her and her groceries. "What are you doing here?" I asked.

"I just went out to get groceries," she said. "Don't you remember I picked you up at Maria's and drove you home?"

"No. But why are you here? Is someone in the family sick?"

"No, Elyn, no one's sick. Except maybe you. So I'm here to see what's happening with you, and if I can help."

Five minutes later: "What are you doing here, Mom?" And five minutes after that: "What are you doing here?" And then again: "What are you doing here?"

My mother took me back to my internist. At first, he seemed not terribly concerned—until he realized that I had no recollection of coming to see him before, discussing my headaches, or picking up a pain prescription. Immediately, he told my mother to get me back to the hospital.

So we went to the ER. For several hours, I sat on a gurney in the hall. Eventually, I answered the standard questions, and once again, it appeared as if they were going to send me home. But then the attending physician asked if it hurt when my legs were raised and I tried to touch my toes with my fingers at the same time. It did.

The spinal tap he quickly ordered came back yellowish, with dried blood. I was diagnosed with a subarachnoid hemorrhage—my brain was bleeding.

The mortality from this kind of hemorrhage is about 50 percent, although I didn't know this at the time. I was thirty-two years old, and so far, my brain had been both very good and very bad to me.

It was three o'clock in the morning when the brain surgeon walked into the examination room. He wanted to do a procedure, called an angiogram, which would allow him to look at the blood vessels in my brain. Angiograms are risky procedures in any case, but this time it was absolutely necessary. If the angiogram revealed an aneurism, I'd need immediate brain surgery.

I do remember hearing those words—with the overhead lights glaring, the institutional smells and sounds of the hospital, and both my mother and me in tears. "If anything happens to me, please, you and Daddy should go on with your lives, and have good lives. That's what I want." My mother's sobbing became louder. As scared as I was for myself, I was even more frightened for my parents. If I died . . .

The angiogram was inconclusive. Often, an angiogram can't detect the cause of a bleed, at which point the doctors assume that some structural abnormality—such as a very tiny (thus undetectable) aneurism or an arterial venal malformation (AVM)—has bled out and destroyed itself. In any case, I wouldn't need surgery after all. When I heard that news, I was so relieved I cried almost to the point of hysterics.

My dad arrived soon after I was admitted to the hospital. I stayed there another three weeks; within a day or two, my memory had improved, although it took longer for the headaches to go away. There was an endless round of tests—CAT scans, MRIs, one more angiogram, and a spinal tap every day, until at last my spinal sac simply collapsed, and they could do no more taps.

While I was hospitalized, they took me off antidepressants; with all the other sedatives I was taking, the doctors believed that an antidepressant would be too much for my system. So in the midst of being poked and prodded and having medical personnel standing around going "hmmmm" and "well, on the other hand, it could be thus and so," I was incredibly sad and frightened. And, inevitably, psychotic.

One night, I came to believe that I was the so-called "wood chip murderer," a man then on trial in Connecticut for dismembering his wife with a chain saw and putting her body parts through a wood chipper. Hooked up to the IV pole, I wandered down to the nurse's station and told the nurses there that they needed to call the police and tell them my whereabouts. Very gently, they walked me back to my room and put me back to bed.

The next day during rounds, one of the resident doctors asked me about what had happened. "I heard you were upset last night, what was that about?"

"Actually, I thought I was the wood chip murderer," I told him. "I'm still not sure whether I am or not. In any case, I'm a very bad person—evil, in fact."

The doctor's response was a burst of laughter so loud that the nurses down the hall could hear him, and it immediately made me feel ashamed. *He thinks I'm crazy.*

It was summer, and Dr. White was out of town on vacation; luckily, he'd asked a colleague, a consultation-liaison psychiatrist at the hospital, to stop by and see me. Dr. Feinstein came by my room almost every day, and was very gentle and soothing, which was exactly what I needed.

"I'm really scared," I told him. "I see now that life can be snatched away just like *that*," and I snapped my fingers in the air.

He nodded. "That's true. And it's very sad. But you know, Elyn, most people come to that realization when they're in their fifties—you've just learned it early."

Feinstein's visits, along with the frequent presence of my parents, who came to visit each day for the three weeks I was in the hospital, helped immensely. My New York brother and his family came up to spend a little time with me as well; we all went together to the cafeteria for an occasional snack or for meals. Late at night, after everyone had gone, I'd wander down to the lounge while hooked to the portable IV pole. There, I'd have a cigarette and listen to classical music on the music channel on the lounge TV. My parents tacked a sign on my door that read, "AWOL risk," and while it made us laugh, the doctors were obviously annoyed. We were treated as though we weren't taking this hospitalization, and the event that had caused it, with sufficient seriousness, when in fact we'd been terrified, and jokes were our way of protecting ourselves from that terror.

As the days went by, the memory impairment lifted somewhat, but it lingered, as did the headaches, so the hospital ordered some psychological testing—the results were handwritten in my chart and quite easy for me to read. Several people, from different disciplines, weighed in on my condition and status, and the variety of opinions fascinated me. According to one, the testing suggested that I "may be bothered by consistently delusional thought and self-persecutory processes." No news there.

Another tester, who gave me a lengthy memory test, a master's-level psychologist who signed "MA" after his name, came up with an odd formulation: The results suggested I was deliberately intending to *appear* impaired, particularly around memory loss. His supervisor noted that rather than suggesting that I was trying to *look* impaired, the test results might also be read to suggest that I was *indeed* impaired. The MA also suggested that my headaches could be due to poor nutrition, while another person opined that the headaches were due to my "disturbed thought processes." So: I was either faking, or crazy, or not eating properly. Somehow, the existence of an actual brain hemorrhage had disappeared in its importance.

The MA also questioned my ability to care for myself in my own apartment, "nutritionally and hygienically"; a third person kindly referred me to the social services department "for assistance with long-range care needs." I would have *loved* assistance with my long-range care needs, since my long-range plan was to publish many books with major presses, write a dozen or so law review articles, and obtain a tenured faculty position at a major university's law school. Even under the best of conditions, and in the best of health, anybody setting out to do that could probably use all the help they could get.

At the end of three weeks, I was finally discharged from the hospital, without any clear conclusion about what had caused my bleed. Although my memory never filled in the blanks of the days before the hospital, the headaches receded. My parents returned to Miami; I returned to my life, as flawed and confounding and mysterious and promising as it was. I felt fragile for a while; I knew that what had happened had been genuinely frightening, even threatening. But the fact is, I didn't die; I survived, and I told myself that fact every single day. It's a little like having a meteor land in your backyard without hitting the house. You can either focus on the meteor, and what almost happened, or you can focus on the fortunate miss and what didn't happen. I decided to do my best to focus on the miss.

chapter eighteen

IN SEPTEMBER, I went back to my second year of teaching at the small law school and prepared my application for a tenure-track teaching position elsewhere. In spite of my not having gone the traditional law-school route to an academic position—clerking for a judge and working as a summer associate at a large law firm—I was gratified when the reaction to my applications was overwhelmingly positive, with over 35 law schools responding with interest.

I wanted to be optimistic—and on paper, there was every reason to *be* optimistic—but there was a small biochemical obstacle. Since my hospital adventure, I still hadn't resumed my usual drug regimen. Within days, I'd gone from feeling a little blue to being seriously depressed, and then I started sliding toward suicidal. White recommended that I immediately go back on the amitriptyline (Prozac was still a few years away), and Steve gave me a stern lecture on the phone about the stress I'd encounter during the job hunt, and how I needed to be focused and steady. "I know you, I know what you're thinking," he said. "But this is no time to fool around with your meds." As much as I longed to be totally drug-free, I had to accept that he was right.

It was too easy for me to slip up in other ways, though. On the brief trip to the University of Miami for a day-long interview, for example, I was so distracted and stressed out that I didn't eat well, and during the interview and job-talk I did very poorly. "Practically comatose" again. Even worse, I fainted as I tried to leave the plane when it landed in New York, and had to be taken out in a wheelchair. Horribly embarrassed, I filed the experience under "poor self-care—Elyn, pay more attention!"

The rest of the interviews went considerably better, and ultimately I received a number of attractive offers. The one that appealed to me most came from the University of Southern California in Los Angeles. Academically, USC's law school had a wonderful reputation, ranked among the top fifteen to twenty in the country. My interview visit there was comfortable and surprisingly tension-free; the faculty I spoke with were friendly and easygoing, given how brilliant they were (I'd done my research—I knew to the person what each one had published, and in what journals). And (no small factor), the campus was lovely, sunny and warm, and kind to my body. So when the offer came from USC, it was a quick and easy decision—I accepted.

But the actual move remained months away. In the meantime, I still had teaching responsibilities in New Haven, and the ongoing case of Jefferson, whom I'd continued to represent as he made his way through the state system.

I tried to visit him about once a week—we'd meet at his group home and go off to a local soda shop for ice cream and a good talk. As a big man with obvious impairments and limited judgment, he often scared people, but with me, he was always gentle and soft-spoken. He was doing well, and he was happy.

In fact, he'd been making such good progress in his group home and with his schooling that the staff in both places thought he was now able to move to a higher-functioning group home. Since it would take a while for there to be an opening for him, I had ample time for some due diligence on his behalf, with many long and hard conversations with the staff at both houses and at his school. I also spoke with his mother, who'd recently come back into his life. And I had serious conversations as well with Jefferson, who'd not only come to trust me, but saw me as friend and confidante. He'd had a few successful overnight and weekend visits to his potential new home; he liked it. Yes, he told me, he wanted to make the move.

On paper, it looked good. Nevertheless, I had to battle skepticism—my own. Mentally retarded adults with the same behavioral dysfunctions as Jefferson's are well known for trying to please others, especially those who carry some power in their lives; basically, they want desperately to say the right thing and make everyone around them happy. He seemed preoccupied with what would please me, and please the staff as well. So I worried: Was I seeing the situation in its true light? Was this really the right thing for him to do? Was it the right time, and was that the right place? Yes, yes, yes, everyone kept saying. Finally, I agreed—OK, it's the right thing to do. And so we moved him.

Things went well for a few weeks; everyone began to relax. And then, something set him off. It was never quite clear what the trigger was, but in any case, it made him mad. He began shouting and screaming, and making threats to his housemates and staff. The police were called—and when confronted with a large angry black man, inarticulate and out of control, the cops forcibly subdued him and hauled him off to the local mental hospital. There, the worst-case scenario actually happened: restraints, forced medication, and isolated confinement—everything we'd managed to spare him since

Steve and I acted to move him out of the state mental hospital. Everything in my own experience that had terrified me had now happened to Jefferson.

Sadly, it set off a chain reaction and downward momentum that for a while seemed irreversible. His stay in the hospital was brief that first time, but it wasn't his last. He couldn't go back to the old group home; his spot had been taken by someone else. And he couldn't return to the new one—it clearly hadn't worked and they didn't want him back. The word "violent" started showing up in his chart; he bounced from group home to group home, until something would go wrong and he'd have to be hospitalized again. By the time I moved to Los Angeles to begin my new teaching job, Jefferson still wasn't stabilized.

Eventually, things settled down somewhat—a few years later, when I visited him, he was in a group home situation that appeared to be working. But for a while it was as though some kind of switch had been tripped in him, and he would never again do as well as he'd done in that first group home. All of us do-gooders—had we let him down? "Did I do this?" I asked Steve. "Did we do this, is it our fault?"

No, no, he said. We'd used our best judgment and done what seemed right at the time. But I feared we'd fought for what seemed best from our point of view, not necessarily from Jefferson's. Maybe what happened with Jefferson would have happened anyway, there's no way to know. Once again, a hard lesson for fledgling lawyers to learn.

As spring came and my time in Connecticut was coming to an end, I scheduled a trip to Los Angeles for April spring break, to meet with my future colleagues, familiarize myself with the campus and the city, and find someplace to live. In addition, I had some names of psychoanalysts on the West Coast, so that I could continue my treatment with no interruption. I was determined to build a good solid structure for what would be my new life.

Just before I was to leave for the trip, a phone call came from my father. "Your uncle Norm has passed away, he's taken his own life," he said. Uncle Norm, my mother's younger brother, was just forty-seven when he died. It was no secret that he'd had psychiatric problems for much of his life—seriously depressed, he'd spent a year in the Menninger Clinic in Topeka, Kansas. At one point, at my recommendation, he also spent some months at the Institute of Pennsylvania Hospital with my doctor there, Dr. Miller; when he left, it was Against Medical Advice. And now, it had come to this—death by his own hand, from an overdose of pills.

I was stunned and sad, yet somehow not surprised. And as calm as my father had been, my mother was another story. She was overwhelmed with grief—her own father had also died not long before, but this loss of her brother, after so many years of struggle, was worse. My handsome, sweet young uncle, gone. Just like *that*. But I couldn't go to Florida to mourn him; I was scheduled to leave the very next morning for Los Angeles, booked solid with appointments there, and had only this small window of time to get everything done. I wanted to go to his funeral; I regretted (and continue to regret) not being there for my mother, and to honor my uncle's fight.

Suicide almost always leaves shipwrecked survivors in its wake, feeling as though there were something else they could have done, *should* have done, to keep the one they loved alive. "If only I'd said this, if only I'd done that . . . What did we miss, how did we fail?" In those first awful days, there's nothing anyone can say or do to ease that kind of sorrow, and any suggestion that it was "inevitable" gets pushed away.

Even worse, I found myself identifying too closely with Uncle Norm. Was that going to be me someday? Would I ever reach a point where the idea of one more doctor, one more test, one more pill, one more episode, one more hospitalization, would simply flip me over the edge?

After I hung up the phone, I stood alone in my tiny apartment, with suitcases packed and the rest of my life about to begin, and I balled my hands up into defiant fists. *No! No!* That was him, in his life, for his reasons; this was me, in mine.

A vital step in my survival, and a key reason for this trip, was to find myself a good analyst. I'd learned, with the guidance of Mrs. Jones and Dr. White, that without the fail-safe of talk therapy securely in place, the rest of it wouldn't matter. I interviewed four (they'd been recommended by friends, by colleagues, and by White), and in the end, my choice was the one whom White had suggested. His name was Kaplan, and his impressive professional resume included working with many seriously ill patients at a Los Angeles–area hospital.

My initial visit to Kaplan's office was reassuring—it was haphazardly decorated, with a collection of objects that didn't seem to go together (lopsided stacks of books and papers and notebooks everywhere, mismatched lamps, nondescript furniture). To me, it gave ample evidence of his standing as a busy academic doing many things—teaching, writing, and treating patients. Since my own office, then and now, has always been a chaotic mess, I took heart in finding Kaplan's to be almost the same. And it reminded me somewhat of Mrs. Jones's—there was an implicit suggestion here that exterior things didn't much matter, but that the journey to the interior mattered a great deal.

It became clear in our first minutes together that Kaplan not only understood my illness but was also comfortable with blending a psychoanalytic approach with medication (which is not the case with all analysts). But I wondered if he was prepared for the kind of intensity and violence my episodes sometimes contained. Maybe the man was getting more than he bargained for. "Don't worry about that," White had told me. "Don't be too scared of her," he told Kaplan.

The rest of the to-do list—lunches and dinners with the people soon to be my colleagues, and the search for a place to live—went better than I could have hoped; in fact, I managed to get through it completely intact. Heeding Steve's admonitions, I took my medicine, ate the right food, got the necessary rest, and actually had a nice time. The apartment I found—a largish one-bedroom—was in a modern four-story stucco building, typical for the west side of LA, and about a half hour to forty minutes driving time from the campus. Since I'd determined long ago to never live on a ground floor—because who really knew what was on the other side of the window?—I was comfortable up in the air. After my high school experience of the talking houses (a memory which unnerves me to this day), I had no interest in a tidy little bungalow or cottage. And no yard, terrace, or balcony, either, with trees I couldn't see around and odd shadows lurking in the corners. I wanted only to be safely sheltered within four inaccessibly high walls.

As for my future colleagues, everyone seemed eager to make me feel at home, and they did. As we walked around the campus and I began to get my bearings—here's the law school building, there's the library, here's the faculty parking garage—I was acutely aware of the warm sun on my shoulders and a kind of softness in the air. *This will be good,* I thought. *This will be very good. Everything's falling into place.*

Except, of course, for the not-incidental matter of my unpredictable brain. In spite of my history, in spite of the diagnoses and the prescriptions, the frequent delusions and the evil visitations—and Kaplan notwithstanding—I still wasn't convinced that I had a mental illness. Nor was I convinced I really needed medication. To admit to any of it was to admit that my brain was profoundly broken, and I just couldn't do that. And I couldn't let others in on the secret, either.

I had decided not to tell people about my mental health status in a professional situation (as opposed to a personal one), unless not telling people would be an outright lie. For instance, in the law school applications, every school except one asked if I'd ever been forced to take a leave of absence from another school as a result of emotional difficulties. Technically, I did *not* have to withdraw when I was ill at Oxford, because I was doing a thesis degree, not attending classes. So the answer across the board was no, and I was comfortable with that. Stanford, however, asked if I'd ever had to take a leave, or reduce my workload, because of emotional problems. There, I had to answer yes, although in my explanation I focused on the depression, not the psychosis. To do otherwise would reduce my hopes of ever having a career—once it was on the record, all of my thoughts and writings would be seen as merely the musings of a madwoman. *Ignore her, she's crazy.* I could not allow that to happen.

My brain was the instrument of my success and my pride, but it also carried all the tools for my destruction. Yes, the pills helped, but each time I put them in my mouth, it was a reminder that some people—smart people I trusted and respected—believed that I was mentally ill, that I was defective; every dose of Navane was a concession to that. More than anything, I wanted to be healthy and whole; I wanted to exist in the world as my *authentic self*—and I deeply believed that the drugs undermined that. And so I kept backing away from them, tinkering with the dosage, seeing how far I could go before I got burned. And of course, I got burned every time—even in my denial, I knew that. But if the fire that burned me signaled my destruction, it was also the same fire that got me out of bed in the morning and sent me to the library even on the most frightening days.

Steve called me "The Little Engine That Could," and I was proud of that moniker. Every time I'd been knocked down, I'd gotten back up again. There was no reason why I couldn't keep doing it. I just had to control my mind, not vice versa, and if I was careful, I would be able to claim and fully inhabit the life I wanted.

When my years in New Haven finally came to an end, I said a bittersweet good-bye to all my friends there, and to Dr. White in particular. We'd made a good team—I was not only still upright, I was moving forward. And so, on July 4 weekend, 1989—one year to the day from the first symptoms of my brain bleed—I boarded the plane for LA, this time for good. And this time, it was a much smoother ride.

The question, of course, was not so much *if* I would have a psychotic episode as *when*.

Packing up your whole life and starting all over again is high on the list of major life stressors—it ranks right up there with divorce, diagnosis of serious illness, being fired from an old job, jumping to a new one, and grieving a death in the family. And then there was the smaller list, the everyday list: Where's the grocery store? Where's my bank? Where's the best place to buy toothpaste, or lightbulbs, or fresh fruit, or to rent a movie on Friday night? When is the telephone guy coming, and where's all my forwarded mail?

Add to this the schizophrenic's "regulator" and the need to rebuild it once again. How, in a new and unknown landscape, does one construct a completely predictable, familiar, manageable life, one in which there are no surprises? And construct it quickly, because your life literally depends on it.

Well, it helped that Los Angeles reminded me of home—the suburban sprawl, the palm trees, the blue sky, the proximity to the ocean. In fact, I soon decided that Los Angeles was a better Miami than Miami was: better weather, better food, better movies, better theater, no hurricanes (albeit an occasional earthquake), and (often) less humidity. That said, everything else was a mess.

Steve was two thousand miles away; he'd begun his graduate work at the University of Michigan in Ann Arbor. We spoke on the phone almost every day, but that wasn't the same as sitting across from him over pizza, talking away the whole afternoon. I missed him, and the way he'd put his hand on my shoulder or gently pat my back, telling me that everything was going to be fine. When was the last time that anyone had touched me, or been able to reassure me, as he did, as only he could?

And while Dr. Kaplan was good, he wasn't White (any more than White had been Mrs. Jones). Everything about him was different; particularly disconcerting was the fact that the chairs in his office weren't in the same position as in White's—trivial to some, but the effect was as though I were blind, had walked into a familiar room, and discovered, by stumbling over it, that all the furniture had been rearranged.

My colleagues on the faculty were friendly and welcoming, but basically, I didn't know any of them. USC Law's faculty is relatively informal and collegial on any number of levels—I watched with envy as they greeted one another in the halls, read one another's papers, and scheduled workshops together. When would that be me? Would that *ever* be me?

I needed a strategy. I needed to get organized. I needed to make another list: my goals and the steps I needed to take to achieve them. First, there was the issue of tenure: USC required at least three lengthy published articles; I would have four years to write them. That part was simple—I'd spend most of my time in my office, working. I knew that work, more than anything else I could do, would steady me. In fact, four years seemed more than enough—in that time, I could easily write four and probably even five papers. It didn't have to be brilliant, it only had to be good, adequate, challenging work, of a quality sufficient to get tenure. And if I worked hard enough and long enough, I'd be able to get ahead a little and give myself some leeway in case I got sick and needed time off—which was almost sure to happen. It would be like putting work in the bank for a rainy day.

USC requires first-year faculty to teach one course each semester; in an academic year, that worked out to one small seminar-type class and one large class. As luck would have it, my first class was the seminar, in mental health law, with only eight students. I knew the material better than any of my students could have imagined; we would consider such issues as civil commitment, the right to refuse medication, confidentiality, and competency. So that was my plan. When I wasn't preparing for or teaching that class, I'd be writing. No problem.

From the very beginning of our first class meeting, I could tell that the students were bright, lively, and engaged—overall, a good group. Being with them would be an excellent use of my time, and theirs as well, I hoped. Our discussions were wide-ranging, as I strove to find the balance between the headlines, the history, the theory, and the canon of law that applied to the mentally ill. One of the cases we read was that of a medical student with a mental illness who'd been expelled for scratching and cutting herself when she was upset at administrators. Sometime afterward, she sought to be reinstated as a student at medical school.

"Should expulsion even be allowed in this kind of case?" I asked. "Or is this impermissible discrimination?"

Some students pointed out that in the interim since this person's expulsion, she'd managed to get a Master of Public Health degree and hold a responsible job. In addition, it wasn't a given that if she became a medical professional she'd automatically pose a risk to patients—for instance, she could choose to go into research. Indeed, even being a hands-on doc was not out of the question: There's little evidence that impulsively hurting yourself puts you at significant risk of hurting others—that's an entirely different psychodynamic.

One student (a psychiatric nurse) made an observation that hit me hard. "Of course mental patients should not be doctors!" she said. "Particularly if they injure themselves. Plenty of people who hurt themselves do go on to hurt others, even if not everyone does. What would stop this patient, so impulsive, from injuring her patients?"

I gathered my wits for a moment, then asked, "Do you feel the same about lawyers, who don't hold others' *physical* integrity in their hands?"

"Would *you* go see a lawyer who was on psychotropic medication?" she said incredulously. "Because *I* certainly wouldn't."

"Yes," I said. "Yes, in fact, I would." *And what would you think about taking a class taught by someone on psychotropic medication?* I wondered.

And then there was the question of competency. "Should patients have a right to refuse medication when they are in the hospital?" I asked the class.

"It would be sort of silly to hospitalize someone in order to treat him," one student responded, "and then not be able to treat him. It would also cost a lot of money."

"But," another student chimed in, "don't we allow competent people to make all sorts of costly and risky choices—for example to skydive?"

Now we're getting someplace, I thought.

So class started well and I was making progress on my first paper, on the concept of competency. But that didn't guarantee anything, and one weekend early in the fall, after the adrenaline of the first days had worn off, I felt myself slipping. I was in my office, alone, working on an article. I started to sense that the others—the beings who never seemed far off when I got sick—were in the office with me. An evil presence, and growing stronger. *Why are they here? Are they trying to take over my mind? Why do they want to hurt me?*

The thoughts grew more insistent; within minutes, I couldn't push them away anymore. It was afternoon; I knew Steve's schedule, and I knew it'd be hours before I could track him down. So I called Steve Wizner in New Haven instead.

"Elyn!" came his voice on the phone. "How nice to hear from you!"

"How are you doing?" I asked. "I'm a her-o, not a him-o. Heroic efforts. Put in one's time. Like prison. I see through the prism of life. I've killed lots of people."

"You need to call your doctor, now," he said. He knew about Kaplan; he knew that Kaplan had taken over my treatment at White's recommendation.

"All right," I said, and called Kaplan's answering service. While I was leaving the message on one coast, Wizner called from the other, leaving an urgent message with Kaplan's service that my situation was indeed an emergency.

Within the hour, Kaplan called me back. "Steve Wizner tells me you're not doing too well this afternoon," he said. "So what's going on?"

"On is a manner of speaking. Off may be more like it. I don't like it at all, thank you very much. I refuse to be killed. I'll kill back. Are people trying to kill me?"

"I'd like to meet with you at my office in an hour," he said. "Can you come?"

"Yes, but it's Sunday," I said. "The Sundance kid. Bearded and gray. With all the interferences."

"My office in an hour, OK?"

"OK," I said. "OK." *Only terrible patients must be seen on a Sunday. Will Kaplan terminate me and make me get lost? He could do better. Who is interfering with my thoughts? What do they want from me? What will they make me do?*

Kaplan was already in his office when I got there. "Come in, Elyn."

I sat down. I was holding myself, rocking and scared.

"You seem like you're having a hard time," he said.

"I'm doing hard time. For all the crimes. They're doing them through me, though. The ones in the sky. I'm an instrument. An instrument of the devil. Please don't let them kill me. My head is so hot on the inside. I'm afraid it might explode."

"You're having psychotic symptoms now," he said. "The things you're afraid of aren't really happening."

"I know they're real," I said. "They seem crazy to you, but they're real. I'll reel them all in. Tell them to get away!" I was rocking and grimacing, flailing my arms as though I were fighting interference from the beings.

"White used to raise your dose of Navane when you were feeling like this," he said. "So I'd like you to go up to thirty-six milligrams for a few days."

"It's not a medical problem," I moaned. "It's a matter of good and evil. Innocent children are being hurt. There's the store and what's in store. Cries and whispers. Fear and trembling and sickness unto death."

"Yes, I know you are in terrible pain," he said. "Do you have Navane with you?"

"Yes."

"Then count out eighteen pills and take them right now, OK?"

"OK." I reached into my bag, fumbled for the pill container, and carefully counted out eighteen on the desk. Then my paranoia turned to Kaplan. "Which side are you on?" I asked. "Are you trying to hurt me or help me?"

He handed me a glass of water. "I'm trying to help," he said. "You're having a hard time now, but you should be feeling better soon. I'll see you tomorrow for our appointment in the morning, and I'll call you at home tonight to see how you're doing. OK?"

"OK," I said, then dutifully took my pills and went home.

Kaplan called that night as he'd promised; I was still having fears, the beings had not entirely receded, so I was reassured to hear his voice. By the next morning, I felt measurably better.

So—now he'd seen it. He didn't get scared or try to put me in the hospital; he did exactly what White would have done, and he talked me through it. I felt comforted in that continuity. They'd both said we would be able to make that transition, but I'd feared it wouldn't happen, and now I saw that it would.

On the other hand, Kaplan was already taking a firmer line on medication than White. This became the theme of our next few appointments. He wanted me on a higher dose of Navane; I resisted, believing that the less medication I took, the less defective I was. I stayed at thirty-six milligrams, just long enough to feel better, and then I started sneaking my way back down again. I didn't miss a class, and was able to get back to my writing in a couple of days.

So, right off the bat, Kaplan and I laid the groundwork for our years-long battle—how much medication he thought I needed vs. how little medication I thought I needed. Our relationship would become similar to almost any other relationship between two strong-minded, stubborn people who see each other often. Some days it worked well, even happily. Other days, it was an unmitigated disaster.

chapter nineteen

I WAS BEGINNING to feel somewhat comfortable with a few of my new colleagues, and when I met with them one-on-one, or in a small cluster of three or four, for coffee or a meal, I thought I managed myself just fine. In fact, I soon became the person who gathered people up to go out for lunch every day. I pushed myself to start doing this because I was so scared that if I weren't the one doing the gathering, I'd be left out entirely. (In fact, I continue rounding up everybody to this day, and have become known in the law school as "the Lunch Mother." I think I should get committee credit, but the dean will have none of it.)

With more than a handful of people at a time, however, I was in agony—the term "painfully shy" was apt. Speaking in or to a large group of people struck terror in my heart. I was convinced I didn't have anything interesting to say. Maybe USC had made a mistake in hiring me; maybe other people were beginning to wonder about that as well. I'd acquitted myself well enough in my interviews, but sustaining that first impression over the months and years it would take to get tenure—I worried that I wouldn't be able to handle it.

Perhaps sensing my struggles, one senior colleague, Michael Shapiro, took a special interest in me and my work. Though he had a gruff exterior, I quickly discovered that Michael had a great capacity for empathy and old-fashioned friendship. A noted scholar in the fields of bioethics and constitutional law, he wrote the first casebook on bioethics, *Bioethics and the Law: Cases, Materials, and Problems* (with Roy G. Spece, Jr.). Michael began to read the drafts of my papers, and he talked with me about ideas for writing. Once every few weeks, he invited me to his home for dinner with his then-wife and little boy (ultimately, there'd be two little boys joining us). To sit around a table with a family—would it even be possible that I might have something like this in my own life someday? I hadn't realized how starved I'd been for the human connection until Michael extended his friendship, and what a timely gift it was. As a tenured professor, he certainly could have spent his time in other ways, but he chose to spend some of it with me. If someone like this finds value in me, I thought, then perhaps there *is* value in me.

Edward McCaffery was another colleague who went out of his way in those early days to be kind and inclusive. Ed was my "classmate" at the law school—we started at the same time, our offices were next door to each other, and we ultimately received our endowed professorships in the same year. As the "new kids," Ed and I spent hours trying to figure out our senior colleagues, strategizing about how we'd get tenure, and sharing ideas about how to develop good reputations in our respective specialties—his was the federal tax system and its Byzantine code. He's widely published, and widely read and respected by legal scholars across the country.

As that first semester went along and I seemed to be managing OK, I began thinking about my second law journal article. One of my colleagues mentioned seeing an article in the newspaper about a man with multiple personality disorder (MPD) who was then on trial for murdering his parents. I was immediately intrigued by the legal issues raised by such a case: How could a court assess criminal responsibility for someone with multiple personalities? If the person had ten personalities, would all ten have to be guilty to put the person in jail? Or would one guilty personality be enough to convict? If there were ten personalities, and only one was cognizant of having committed a crime, what rights to a defense and subsequent protection did the others have?

The more I thought about the case and its practical complexities, the more fascinated I grew with the philosophical questions as well: What is a person? What's the difference between a person and a personality? Can a person have more than one alternative personality? I quickly discovered that while this situation may have been a staple in daytime television soap operas over the years, very little scholarship had actually been written about it. Even before I started any serious research, I drew up a working outline in my mind. If I really work hard, I thought, I could have a completed draft by the end of the next summer. My article on competency would be ready to submit to law journals by then, too.

Thinking about MPD, of course, led me to ask similar questions of myself: Who was I, at my core? Was I primarily a schizophrenic? Did that illness define me? Or was it an "accident" of being—and only peripheral to me rather than the "essence" of me? It's been my observation that mentally ill people struggle with these questions perhaps even more than those with serious physical illnesses, because mental illness involves your mind and your core self as well. A woman with cancer isn't Cancer Woman; a man with heart disease isn't Diseased Heart Guy; a teenager with a broken leg isn't The Broken Leg Kid. But if, as our society seemed to suggest, good health was partly mind over matter, what hope did someone with a broken mind have?

My class for the second semester was criminal law, and I was greeted on the first day with what seemed to be a large, yawning auditorium filled with seventy students, every single one of them looking straight at me. Although it was a lecture class, I was so weak from anxiety that I couldn't stand, and a few minutes in, I just had to sit down. I sat down for the rest of the semester.

I knew going in that I wasn't as adept with criminal law as I was with mental health law, and from the very beginning I fell behind almost as fast as any clueless student. Most of the questions I was asked in class, I had to research afterward on my own. Often, I found myself so anxious and distracted that I missed most of what the students were asking or answering. I didn't like the performance aspects of lecturing to a large class; I knew I'd never be able to master that. And I really didn't want all those people looking at me.

At the end of that semester, the course evaluations (unlike the positive ones I'd gotten from the mental health seminar) showed that I wasn't the only one who felt the whole experience had been torturous. One student wrote, "Professor Saks is a very nice person, but a very mediocre teacher." Another comment was even more painful: "Didn't anyone ever interview this woman before hiring her?" When I first read that, I wanted to put my head down on my desk. In time, I could read it again and find some humor in it. He was right; I'd been just terrible. He'd applied to a good law school, he (or someone) had paid good money to be there, and for all that, he got me.

For the end-of-the-year humor issue of the *Law Review,* my lecture class got a send-up all its own: "Elyn R. Saks, the sitting Socratic method: lessons in dynamism."

I taught criminal law class four years, and although I became a little better at it each time, I never got comfortable there, and approached the evaluation period each time with the same dread. My reviews got better, but I always disliked teaching first-year students. As I liked to say, the neuroses of first-year students conflicted too much with my own.

I was battling my usual demons outside the class as well. I still wasn't talking much, except to the three or four people I was gradually becoming close to. After one particularly difficult faculty workshop, a colleague took me aside and said I really needed to take more part in faculty discussions, both formal and informal. "I don't mean to be insulting, Elyn," she said, "but you're practically comatose in there." If I hadn't been so mortified, I might have laughed out loud at the familiar terminology.

"Thanks," I said, and I meant it. "I appreciate your coming to me with this." I could hardly tell her how hard it was to relax and enjoy a meal or a meeting with colleagues while your demons bang on the closet door and demand to be let out.

When that first year finally came to an end, I was hugely relieved, and Ed and I went out for a nice dinner to celebrate. We each had a drink (something unusual for me, as I don't like the effects and, besides, drinking doesn't go well with psychotropic meds) and toasted each other's success: We'd made it through year one.

With classes ended, I had nearly four months ahead of me to work away at my game plan. And of course, I couldn't let well enough alone. No longer responsible for students, I decided it was time to get serious about stopping the Navane. Kaplan reluctantly agreed to cooperate, and slowly I started reducing my dose. A month later, my psychosis was in charge.

Except for my appointments with Kaplan, I kept to myself. "I'm having headaches," I told him. "Head Aches, Aching Heads. Maybe another bleed. Blood simple. Ha ha ha. Laughter occurs behind the scenes. I'll take the scenic route."

Kaplan knew immediately what was bothering me. "You're worried about your health," he said. "That's understandable, given your history. So why not face that fear head-on and go see a doctor to reassure yourself? I highly recommend an internist, Edwin Jacobson."

"The blood is all over. It's all over for me," I said. "OK, I'll go to see Dr. Jacobson."

When I got to Jacobson's office, I explained that I'd had a bleed and was having terrible headaches. He asked questions; I answered as best I could. Some of what I said made sense; much of it didn't. "I'm worried about my headaches. My brain may come out of my ears and will drown lots of people. I can't let that happen."

Obviously he'd spoken with Kaplan, and the way in which he responded could not have been more on point. "You don't need to worry about drowning people with your brain, Elyn. That can't happen." His voice was calm and reassuring. "It sounds like Dr. Kaplan is right, that you need to go on more medicine. It's just like if you had something like diabetes; you need to be on enough medicine to keep your balance."

He hadn't argued with me; he didn't try to out-doc me. Rather, he reassured me that there was nothing for me to worry about. That is what I needed most—for my medical doctor to quell my anxiety—and he did. And he'd used a metaphor that I could understand. As with diabetes, my illness *was* treatable; as with diabetes, I simply needed to treat it. I'd heard this metaphor before, but it stuck with me this time.

In our next session, Kaplan made it clear that he wanted me to increase my Navane. That session really disturbed me. It just didn't feel good, on two counts: first, because Kaplan was telling me what to do; second, because the increase made me feel like a failure. I resented both things, but grudgingly agreed to go back up to thirty-six milligrams.

Soon after that, I left for a few days of vacation in New York, where I visited with my parents and spent some too-brief time with my little niece and nephew. I didn't expect children of my own, so to have these two as part of my life always gave me great joy.

And I made a special point of getting up to New Haven and seeing Jefferson, who was now in a somewhat more stable position in a group home.

"Hi, Elyn," he said, and there was the beautiful smile I remembered. "I remember you, you're my friend. It's going good. Can we get some ice cream? Where you been?"

"I moved to California," I told him. "It's on the other side of the country so it's tough to come and see you more often. How have you been?"

"Good," he said. "Got a job now. I put things in a box. It's good."

It sounded good; I hoped it was. "Let's go get that ice cream, OK?" I said. "And I'll come and see you next time I come to Connecticut. And you know, you can call me if you want. Your house has my number."

"OK," he said. "Ice cream, and then you'll come see me soon."

I was pleased that he seemed to be doing better—I wanted him to thrive. Given his vulnerability to the vagaries of the system, it was easy to see myself in him. If he was safe and happy, it meant that maybe I could be safe and happy someday, too.

And the news over time got even better: I recently learned that Jefferson had been featured in a local paper for certain artistic achievements, and that gave me a modicum of comfort that perhaps our involvement had been a positive one in Jefferson's life after all.

When I returned to LA, there was still plenty of summer left. I went back to my office, where I spent nearly every waking hour. As long as I stayed on my meds, I was able to concentrate, and by summer's end, I'd completed a first draft of my multiple personality disorder paper. My article on competency, the first piece in my tenure portfolio, was finished. It was ready for law journals to review for publication.

Bob Cover's memo had been my first test as a law student; the competency article would be my first test as a law professor. I put forty copies of the article and a cover letter in the mail, crossed my fingers, and wished them luck.

Law journals accept articles by phone; rejections come in the mail. Within a couple of weeks, my mailbox was full and my phone wasn't ringing. Not having my first article published would end any realistic chance for tenure and crush any hope of my becoming a real professor. I felt as if I had been tested for some fatal disease; at any moment, the doctor of doom would call with the bad news. I watched the phone as though it were alive. And then one day, it actually rang.

The call was from a law journal whose standing was not very strong, and acceptance into which would be little help to me in the tenure process. By the following day, without having heard from anyone else, I was convinced my project to be a law professor was lurching toward failure. I'd end up on the streets, alone and disgraced. In a matter of hours, my disappointment turned psychotic. *They're trying to kill me with faint praise and my head is so hot on the inside it hurts.*

I called Steve and left a message, then headed for Kaplan's office. With laserlike speed, he went directly to the heart of the matter. "You're afraid you'll end up like your uncle Norm who committed suicide, aren't you?" he asked. "If you don't get tenure, you'll have to kill yourself. Or at best end up a chronic mental patient in a back ward of a hospital for the rest of your life."

Steve was equally direct, in a different way. "What the hell's the matter with you, Elyn?" he said, clearly short on patience that day. "You've still got fifteen or twenty places to hear from. It's a great article, it's going to get published in an excellent law journal. You've convinced yourself you're going to fail, you simply need to *stop* this!" Rather than wilting me, his words picked me up. If he thought so, maybe it was true.

Nevertheless, I was stuck in mild psychosis for the next week or so, during which time I increased my medication. Ed, who'd gotten a good offer right away on his first article, understood exactly what I was going through (although he wasn't aware of the demons swirling around my head). He could have been competitive, even gloating, but instead he was, and has always been, kind and supportive; I saw that he genuinely cared. "It'll happen, Elyn, anytime now. Just wait, the call's coming any day."

About ten days after I fell apart, I received an offer from the *North Carolina Law Review*, a well-respected law journal. Publishing there would count in my favor for tenure. I'd done it. The paper had been accepted. I'd been accepted. I could breathe easy; I wasn't going to be Uncle Norm, at least not now.

By second semester that next year, I'd accomplished one more small seminar and was a little more relaxed in the criminal law lecture course. I could actually hear the students; I could actually respond to them. The MPD article was coming along. In March I presented it at a faculty workshop. The response was encouraging; people liked my work.

And then another colleague—one who hadn't had a particularly easy tenure time—quietly took me aside and suggested that maybe I needed another year to work on the paper.

"But I don't understand," I said. "Everybody else says the paper's ready to go."

"They may be saying that to your face, but you can't always believe them."

I was stunned; had I misread the other responses? Did they have some kind of weird agenda, encouraging me to submit substandard work? And speaking of agendas, why would a senior person drop this nasty little bomb on an obviously struggling junior person? The more I thought about it, the more transparent it became. *Trust your gut, Elyn,* I told myself. *It's good work. Your friends told you so.*

I began working on what would become my third article, another on the conditions under which people were incompetent to refuse antipsychotic medication, especially people whose difficulty came about as a result of noncognitive impairments, that is, impairment from something other than disordered thoughts. It was my argument that many people (more than we might think) should be allowed to refuse medication. As someone who benefits from medication, I know that the question of when one should be allowed to refuse is a complicated one. But I also believe that individual autonomy is vitally important, even precious—after all, it's central to who we are as humans on the planet, with free will and self-ownership.

As the work progressed and the time went by, my faculty friendships came to mean a great deal to me. The lunches, the dinners, the casual greetings in the hallway—I was grateful for all of it. I felt less lonely; I felt more competent. Maybe the time was coming when I could even tell my friends the truth about myself.

And then there was Kaplan. Just as I'd always done, I was tinkering with the med levels, lowering them whenever I could, and feeling the effects, to his increasing and obvious annoyance. One evening, late in the summer, I called Kaplan to tell him that the earth was caving in and he needed to take cover. He sighed. "Elyn, take more medication." That seemed to be his answer whenever I became psychotic.

Later that year, Kaplan was preparing to take a long vacation trip—to China, as I somehow knew. Suddenly, I began slipping. Demons were everywhere, and evil began oozing from the walls. I couldn't focus my thoughts, I couldn't write. Within days, I was huddling on the couch in my office, muttering senselessly into the telephone to Steve, who could tell I was in trouble and tracked Kaplan down—not the kind of thing he'd ever been enthusiastic about doing or felt comfortable with. But he thought, in this instance, it was called for.

Later, Steve recited the call to me verbatim: "Dr. Kaplan, I'm very concerned about Elyn. She seems more psychotic than she's been in a very long time, I thought you needed to know. For instance, she told me that she was going to China in advance of your trip, to clear it out of all the bad persons."

"How very considerate of her!" Kaplan dryly responded. And then he suggested that I increase my medication.

There were, in Kaplan's way of thinking, three different lenses through which I viewed myself—three "me's," as he put it, although without any implication that these were actual selves or personalities or people or anything of that sort—it was purely a heuristic device. One me was Elyn, one me was Professor Saks, and the third me was "the Lady of the Charts"—the person who was a mental patient. I couldn't argue with the metaphor, since it pretty much summed up the way my life worked: I was Elyn with my family and friends, Professor Saks when I was teaching or writing articles, and the Lady of the Charts when I was ill. Kaplan believed that it was Elyn who was the most neglected of the three.

There were many days when I believed I was nothing more than the Lady of the Charts—a crazy woman who'd faked her way into a teaching job and would soon be discovered for what she really was and put where she really belonged—in a mental hospital. Other times, I denied that the Lady of the Charts even existed, because my illness wasn't real. If I could just successfully get off medication, the Lady of the Charts would disappear. Because how could I reconcile the Lady of the Charts coexisting alongside Elyn and Professor Saks? Either I was mentally ill or I could have a full and satisfying personal and professional life, but both things could not be equally true; they were mutually exclusive states of being. To admit one was to deny the other. I simply couldn't have it both ways. Didn't anyone understand this?

During the spring of our second year together, the relationship with Kaplan really got rocky. As I'd always been somehow able to do, I saved most of my psychotic thinking for my sessions. On the couch, I could lie down and relax; there, I felt safe. If the closet door that kept my demons in check burst all the way open, and they all came exploding out—well, that was OK. I was in analysis, where that sort of thing was supposed to happen. Say what's on your mind—or so Mrs. Jones and Dr. White had taught me.

But Kaplan had decided that my way of using analysis had itself become a problem; it was my way of not dealing with more pressing issues. The Lady of the Charts was taking up all his time, and Elyn was getting nowhere. I was filling my hours on the couch with psychotic gibbering. I hadn't had a date in years, and certainly had no foreseeable prospects for a relationship or marriage, something I now insisted that I wanted badly. Kaplan thought the analysis had become too unstructured, and he let me know it.

Then, for some reason, he had to be away; during his absence, I saw another psychiatrist, Kaplan's backup, whom I'd come to know and like. When Kaplan returned a couple of weeks later, he told me the backup doc had reported that he'd noticed what appeared to be trembling movements around my lips, a possible first sign of tardive dyskinesia—TD—the movement disorder caused by antipsychotic medications. Perhaps you've seen it among street people with mental illness: lip smacking, tongue lolling out, limbs shaking uncontrollably. TD's an unmistakable sign that something's wrong; it might as well be a placard stuck to your shirt: "crazy person here." Even worse, there's ample evidence that it's progressive and irreversible.

Quickly, Kaplan referred me to an expert, Dr. Stephen Marder, an internationally known schizophrenia researcher. He did indeed diagnose me with a mild case of TD. On what's called the AIMs test (Abnormal Involuntary Movement), my lips were involuntarily moving; my eyes were blinking too hard and too often. Although the movements were subtle, there was no assurance they would stay so. Friends at the law school had noticed something, too, they told me later. But out of kindness (and not knowing what the cause was), they hadn't said anything.

In spite of Marder's diagnosis, Kaplan insisted he'd never seen the movements. "I'm not convinced you have TD," he said firmly. Marder was the TD expert; nevertheless, Kaplan refused to confirm the diagnosis, which felt dismissive of my very serious concerns that had been raised by the expert Kaplan himself had sent me to. Thanks to my doctors, whom I'd trusted, it seemed that I'd been taking medication the side effects of which would now remove any doubt to the outside world of who I really was: the very shaky, mentally ill Lady of the Charts.

I could not remember the last time, if ever, I had been so angry and frustrated. White and Kaplan had *betrayed* me with their constant insistence that I take the medication. Of course I'd been aware of the risks, but still, the word "betrayal" rang in my ears. I was pretty good at hiding what I was thinking, but once TD set in, how was I supposed to hide how I looked?

And then Kaplan added insult to injury. "You can't lie down in session anymore," he said. "From now on, you have to sit up, in a chair."

What the hell? To my mind, he'd just said that I wasn't well enough to be in psychoanalysis. While Kaplan insisted that effective analysis could occur on or off the couch, to my ear he was telling me I was unanalyzable. I was the Lady of the Charts. Good-bye, Elyn. Good-bye, Professor Saks.

"I'm seriously thinking of quitting with you," I fumed to him, and I said as much to Steve on the phone before and after the sessions.

"There's no point to working with him anymore, Steve; he doesn't want me there anyway, that's clear. I annoy him, I don't do what I'm told. Besides, he's not paying any real attention to me—other people see my lips trembling, he doesn't. Other people see my eyes jumping and blinking, he doesn't. What's the point of him?"

"What's the point of you?" I asked Kaplan. "Not only do you think I'm *only* the Lady of the Charts, you seem determined to expose me to the world that way!"

My anger alternated with complete despair. My analyst, the one who was supposed to know me the best, the one whose job it was to help me navigate and understand my world, obviously thought I was ultimately slated to be nothing more than a street person. Well, then, maybe I should just move to the streets and be done with it. *I'm destined for degradation. I belong on the streets. All else is pretense.*

My fantasies of actually living as a street person grew more intense every day; after all, it wasn't the first time the possibility had been raised. The experts at MU10 had predicted as much when I was hospitalized in New Haven. Maybe they'd been right about me all along; maybe I'd been wrong.

Kaplan was immovable, but Steve was my consolation. We spent hours on the phone every day, as he listened to me rant and rave, and tried his best to talk me down from the ceiling. "I think there's method in his madness," he said.

"*His* madness?" I said.

"Yes. It's as though he's setting up a different construct, a different dynamic between the two of you than you're used to. Stay in analysis, Elyn, and sit up if you have to. Would that truly be so terrible? You've been writing, you've been teaching, it's all been going well. Everything you've ever wanted is in your grasp, if you can just get through this hard phase with him. Are you going to throw everything away just because you're angry?"

Then Kaplan delivered the coup de grâce: his diagnosis. Schizophrenia. "In the past, I've diagnosed you as 'atypical psychosis.' But that's only allowed you to minimize your condition. Now I think I was wrong." His delivery was chilling and abrupt, as though he were serving his diagnosis up with a carving knife. Here's the deal, take it or leave it. "When you're ill, you're totally indistinguishable from the worst kind of schizophrenic. It's not going to change, it's not going to get better, and it's not going to turn into something else. It's time for you to stop fighting, and accept it."

"Stop fighting?" If I was angry before, now I was raging. "Stop fighting? I thought *I* was supposed to be the crazy one in this room."

I'd show him; he'd left me no alternative. I'd show Kaplan and the whole world that I was not mentally ill. I was Elyn and I was Professor Saks, but I was *not* the Lady of the Charts; she was figment of *his* imagination, not mine. I'd show them all—I'd get off the damn meds once and for all. And then they'd all see what was what.

chapter twenty

KAPLAN WAS ASKING me to surrender. That's the way I heard it, and that's the way that it felt, deep inside my core. Asking, hell—he was *telling* me to surrender. I'd never surrendered to anything in my life. If the doctors up to this point were right, wasn't I supposed to be in an institution by now? Virtually every single expert, at one time or another, had suggested that this was my destiny. If I had ever truly believed them, if I had ever surrendered to their version of me (instead of doggedly hanging onto *my* version of me), I'd still be crawling around the tunnels under the Warneford, burning my arms and legs with a lighter and waiting for devils to blow the world up by using my neurotransmitters in some inexplicably evil way.

But I didn't believe them, and look where I'd ended up: a lawyer, a scholar, with multiple academic degrees and honors, the promising beginnings of both a publishing career and a teaching career. I was living on my own, making friends, feeling the warm California sun on my back every day and being grateful for it. So—surrender? Quit?

Stop fighting? I couldn't. My parents had taught me, Operation Re-Entry had taught me: No surrender. Fight back. Fight.

The idea that there's any victory in surrender is totally foreign to almost everyone I've ever known, rich or poor, sick or well, happy or sad. Surrender feels like failure, it feels like defeat. Even worse, it feels like *loss*—of self, of autonomy, and of hope. To surrender is to fold up your tent and slink off the battlefield. It's to say, "I'm not enough. I quit." And it simply was not in me to do that. Yet.

So I made a plan. First, I found a cognitive-behavioral psychologist, Dr. Benson, and asked for some suggestions about how to keep my psychotic thinking in check while I was cutting back on the drugs. That appointment and our discussion reminded me so much of Dr. Hamilton at Oxford—he'd helped me get through those first months of severe illness intact, and Dr. Benson had the same theoretical orientation that Hamilton did. Cautiously but clearly, she did her best to explain what might happen in the ensuing weeks. "It will be hard," she said, "and there are no guarantees it will work."

"But I have to try," I told her.

"Yes," she said. "I suppose you do."

I ran through my plan endlessly with Steve, who tried to be as patient as he could, but who couldn't disguise his skepticism. As always, he was willing to support me in whatever I decided to do, but he made it perfectly clear that he thought what I was proposing was a bad idea. Neither of us saw anything contradictory in his holding both positions; it was simply the kind of conundrum that our friendship had always contained—if, in spite of evidence to the contrary, I wanted to do something the equivalent of jumping off a ledge, he'd caution me first and then pledge to be there to catch me. "Be careful, Elyn," he warned. "This isn't like adjusting aspirin levels for a headache."

Since I knew Kaplan would never go along with what I intended, I told him in a vague, general way that I planned to reduce my medication, primarily because of concern for the side effects. I hoped eventually to be off altogether, but would proceed cautiously, I said, making the smallest adjustments possible; nothing major, nothing abrupt.

Finally, I talked to Marder, the TD and schizophrenia expert. He said that if I were determined to lower the meds, I should do so at about the rate of one milligram every six months. I'd already taken myself down to six milligrams; at the rate Marder suggested, it'd take three years for me to be off entirely. Not fast enough. Not clean enough. I decided to drop one milligram each month—six times faster than Marder advised, but much slower than I'd ever dropped in the past. Ideally, I'd be med-free by mid-summer.

And so I began. I was on a mission. At the end I would either be the Lady of the Charts, or a reasonable combo of Elyn and Professor Saks. But somebody had to go.

At Dr. Benson's suggestion that spring, I'd joined a support group, the Manic-Depressive and Depressive Association of Los Angeles— MDDA. I had looked for a support group for people with schizophrenia, but came up empty. MDDA was the next best thing. It met once a week at a nearby hospital.

As apprehensive as I was about what being in a support group might entail—full disclosure, the presence and opinions of people I didn't know, men and women who were battling their own demons—it was surprisingly easy to be there. Nearly everyone in the room was on medicine, or a combination of medicines, and most of them (even those who accepted their illness) deeply resented that fact. We were flawed, we were less, we were not enough. As many problems as we each had, nobody in that room liked knowing that the solution was in a little plastic prescription bottle. Or two bottles. Or three. "I'm just not me when

I'm taking those," said one person. "They turn me into someone else."

Several of the folks at MDDA didn't believe they had an illness at all, much less one that required constant vigilance and medication. Every once in a while, someone would come to meetings in a manic state—for two or three weeks at a time—and then, for whatever reason, he'd decide to take his medication; by the following week, he'd look and feel much better. Nevertheless, he'd say, "Next time, I just have to try harder. I know I can do it next time." I nodded; I knew exactly what he was talking about.

My dogged insistence on "resistance" wasn't always welcomed by others in the group, however. One of my closest friends in MDDA was a man of great intelligence, about my age, who'd been struggling with his illness for years. Although his intelligence and capability seemed largely intact to me, he'd virtually relinquished any hope of achieving anything further in his life. Instead, he'd gone on disability and worked at various jobs, as he felt the need or desire. Although I enjoyed the time I spent with him, I found myself increasingly intolerant of his attitude toward his illness and his work. "I think you've given up," I said one night at dinner. "I think you've given in. You're way too comfortable in the role of a mentally ill person."

The minute the words were out of my mouth, I wanted to call them back. The look on his face was one of transparent hurt, even sorrow. He had trusted me; now he regretted it.

Kaplan sometimes said that I had a Republican superego when it came to mentally ill friends. I'd pushed myself for years; that pushing had helped me survive. So I wasn't yet ready to allow for someone else what I could not allow for myself. In retrospect, of course, my intolerance said more about me than it did about my friend. It caused him pain. And it cost me a friendship.

· · ·

My first month with a lowered Navane dose went by. I felt . . . uncertain. *Are other people in the room with me and Kaplan? Things seem kind of strange. I don't know which side Kaplan is on.*

The second month came and passed. Now I was down to four milligrams. Classes had ended. I could write, but just barely—it's difficult to concentrate when inch-high men are waging a nuclear war in your head. *Someone is slipping anti-antipsychotics in my blood and making me look psychotic. But I'm not. By God, I'll tell you when I'm psychotic, thank you very much.*

With intense effort, I masked my symptoms with Kaplan. To do otherwise would only prove his point. I sat up in the chair; I controlled my ramblings.

Yet another member of the MDDA group had tried and failed to stay off her medication. Yes, yes, she felt better now that she'd taken her pills. "But I think maybe it just wasn't the right time for my body chemistry," she said. "I'll handle it differently the next time I try."

That night, talking to Steve on the phone, I said, "I know the illnesses are different, and the meds are different. But you know, I'm beginning to think there are some interesting parallels between what I'm trying to do and what the people in group are trying to do."

"Gee, ya think?" Steve said. I could almost hear the smile on his face.

"Oh, shut up."

I was down to three milligrams a day. The days and nights were harder now. The sheer physical effort of containing my body and my thoughts felt like trying to hold back a team of wild horses. Sleep was spotty, and filled with dreams that left me awake and sweating in terror. Nevertheless, I dropped down to two milligrams.

Months before, when I'd been invited to attend a workshop at Oxford, I'd accepted. It was too late now to change my mind without making people angry, significantly inconveniencing them, and making myself look professionally irresponsible. As unhinged as I felt, I had to go. Once there, somehow, I held on by the skin of my teeth, although I'm sure everyone at the workshop thought I was one of the strangest people they'd ever met. By the time I boarded the plane for home, I was a complete wreck.

When I walked into Kaplan's office my first day back, I headed straight for the corner, crouched down on the floor, and began to shake. All around me were thoughts of evil beings, poised with daggers. They'd slice me up in thin slices or make me swallow hot coals. Kaplan would later describe me as "writhing in agony."

"Elyn, you need to increase your meds," he said immediately. "You're acutely and floridly psychotic."

"One. Effort. Number. Explosion."

"Will you take more meds?" Kaplan asked.

I was shaking, but I was also shaking my head. I couldn't take more. *The mission is not yet complete.*

Immediately afterward, I went to see Marder. He'd never seen me ill before; he'd been under the impression (and I hadn't disabused him of it) that I had a mild psychotic illness and that my primary concern was avoiding TD. Once in his office, I sat on his couch, folded over, and began muttering. I was disheveled—I couldn't remember when I'd slept, or what I'd eaten. When had I bathed—in Oxford? Before Oxford? Did it matter, if we were all going to die anyway? Anyone who walked into that room would have thought Marder was treating a schizophrenic street person. Weeks later, he told me that's exactly what I looked like.

"Head explosions and people trying to kill. Is it OK if I totally trash your office?"

"You need to leave if you think you're going to do that," said Marder.

"OK. Small. Fire on ice. Tell them not to kill me. Tell them not to kill me! What have I done wrong? All the explosions. Hundreds of thousands with thoughts. Interdiction."

"Elyn, do you feel you're dangerous to other people? Or to yourself?" he asked.

"That's a trick question," I said.

"No, it's not," he said. "I'm serious, I think you need to be in the hospital. I could get you into UCLA right now, and the whole thing could be very discreet."

"Ha ha ha. You're *offering* to put me in the hospital? Hospitals are bad, they're mad, they're sad. One must stay away. I'm God. Or I used to be. I give life and I take it away. Forgive me for I know not what I do."

"I *really* think a hospital would be a good idea," Marder said.

"No, thank you oh so very much," I said.

"All right, then, but if I were you, I'd stay away from work for a while. You don't want your colleagues to see this."

"Thanks, banks, bang, bye. See you soon." Oblivious to the look on his face, I left.

That night, Kaplan called me at home. "Elyn, Dr. Marder told me about your conversation. He's worried and so am I. This is serious, even dangerous. If you want to prevent hospitalization, you have to take your meds now."

"Oh no, oh no, oh, no," I prattled. "I know that if I just try harder, I can get off the meds. Meds and beds. I'm going to sleep now."

Somewhere inside my head, it registered that Kaplan was as upset as he'd ever been. But my mission was not yet over. The Lady of the Charts was still alive and kicking.

I don't know how I slept that night. It felt as if my arms and legs were going to fly off in four different directions. Maybe I just passed out from exhaustion. The next morning, I dragged myself to my office—my hideout, my refuge.

But I ran into Ed McCaffery in the hall. A few months earlier, I'd told him about my illness, but only in the simplest terms. Nothing could have prepared him for the person standing in front of him, fidgeting wildly and looking as if she'd been caught up in a tornado. I tried to hang onto coherent thought, with some vain idea of fooling him, but that thought disintegrated into complete nonsense.

"There's these little people with the explosions. In my head. Voice mail and interdiction and something must be done. Is someone else in here? I went there, and then they said 'x, y, and z,' and there's the killing fields, but who knew about the conviction?"

At first, Ed had smiled a little, thinking I was making some kind of joke, but as I got more wound up, he figured out what was happening. "Elyn, what the hell's going on? I thought you were kidding at first, but you're not, are you? Does anyone else know about this? Is it OK for anyone else to know?"

"I wouldn't mind telling Michael," I said. "Not the Archangel one. The other one."

"Stay here," he said firmly. "Stay here. I'm going to call Kaplan. And Donna." Ed's then-wife, Donna, was a physician.

In a few moments, Ed came back, and as he did, the phone rang. I picked it up and heard Michael Shapiro, my kind bioethics colleague, on the other end. "Elyn, how are you?" he asked.

"Oh, ever so well, thank you. But there's interdiction here, and I'm responsible for many deaths. Have I killed you yet?"

"Give the phone to Ed now, please," he said simply.

I listened attentively to Ed's side of the conversation. "No, no, we can't call the vice dean," he said urgently. "I've talked to her doctor, he's going to call here in a couple of minutes. We'll do whatever he says. But this is serious, let me tell you." Just as he put the phone down, it rang again. Kaplan.

"I'm not going to take more medicine," I told him. "I can do this, I just have to try harder." And then I hung up on him.

If I could just exert control over my wayward brain, if I could just hang on a little longer, my mission to dissolve the Lady of the Charts would not fail. I was fighting for Elyn and for Professor Saks. I had never failed anything, I wasn't going to start now.

"I'm going to drive you home," Ed told me. "And I'll stay with you for a while there. Elyn, you have to take your medicine."

"No," I said. "And yes. No to the medicine, yes to the drive home."

"You're not going to jump out of the car, are you?" he asked.

"No. I'm not. Off we go, into the wild, blue yonder."

Throughout the ride from school to Westwood, Ed kept talking. "I don't understand," he said. "Your career, your writing—it all works when you take your medicine, doesn't it? So isn't it obvious? I mean, that you have to take it?"

I shook my head. "No," I said. "That is not clear. Clear, fear, near, dear. Deer in the headlights. I can't fail."

Once we got into my apartment, Ed called Donna to let her know where he was, and how I was. "What do you want me to do, tackle her to the ground?" he hissed into the phone. He didn't sound happy. I wasn't, either.

I called Kaplan. "I want off the stuff!" I moaned.

"I know you do," he said. "But what you're doing is going to land you right in the hospital instead. You need to accept that you have an illness and need to take medicine to control it. It's not fair, it's not fun, but that's the way it is."

No, no. I can't take the meds and I can't be in the hospital! The room was full of swirling, taunting demons, forces coming through the walls and ceiling. Ed couldn't see them, but I knew they were there. Any minute now, something terrifying would happen to us both.

"I'm being interfered with," I cried to Kaplan. "I'm so scared. Help me, please!"

"Do you have your medications there?" he asked.

"Yes," I said.

"Then it's time to take them. Thirty-six milligrams—eighteen of your pills. Do that now."

I looked up. Ed was staring at me. Steve would be calling soon, as he'd done every day, to tell me it was time to take my pills. Marder was telling Kaplan to put me in the hospital. Kaplan was telling me that without meds, the hospital was my next stop. "OK," I muttered into the phone. "OK."

I'd failed.

I took the whole dose at once. In minutes, I was limp and sleepy. Ed left, I went to bed, and except for my appointments with Kaplan, I stayed at home for the next several days.

I could no longer deny the truth and I could not change it. The wall that kept Elyn and Professor Saks separated from the Lady of the Charts was smashed and lay in ruins around my feet. The Lady of the Charts was real. *That* was the truth.

For days afterward, I felt like the survivor of an automobile accident: sore and spent, as if the slightest breeze would knock me to the ground. I tried my best to avoid the mirror in the bathroom, but there she was again, the wild-eyed woman I'd first seen in the mirror at the Warneford: hair matted and dirty; skeletal face, body mostly bones. Anyone guessing my age might have added twenty years to the real number. *Failed, failed.* Hope was dead, and I was in mourning. I wanted to rage, to storm through the apartment, but I was too tired to do much more than pick up the toothbrush and, eventually, the hairbrush.

Psychosis sucks up energy like a black hole in the universe, and I'd really outdone myself this time. When I walked, haltingly, down the sidewalk—one careful foot at a time, testing the pavement as though any minute I'd fall through and be swallowed whole—all I could think of was old ladies who walked like this, and how I'd pitied them.

The idea of shopping—making lists, getting into the car, actually going someplace and accomplishing something as simple as butter, eggs, bread, and coffee—was overwhelming. Thank God for good friends.

After a loss, people naturally gravitate toward the familiar for comfort. Like a wounded animal, I burrowed into my cave and surrounded myself with familiar objects and voices. I talked on the phone with Steve for hours, replaying every decision I'd made, picking through the mess, second-guessing what I'd done, how I'd done it, and trying to get the ending to come out different each time. I had sessions with Kaplan, where "I told you so" hung in the air but was never spoken. I spent time with my friends who had seen me sick, hadn't been repelled, and oddly seemed to still care about me.

And, eventually, I went back to my office at the law school, where I tried to work on an article and prepare for my fall classes. But mostly, I listened to classical music and took long naps on my couch. After all, the couch was still mine; the walls were mine, the books and papers were mine, and the office door had my name on it. When you're worried about falling, you grab hold of whatever you can.

By the time classes began that fall, I was somewhat back on my feet, able to concentrate and genuinely looking forward to greeting students and colleagues who'd been away for the summer. The easiest way to explain things, I guess, is that it was as though I'd had a very bad flu; it took a while to get over, but each day, I felt a little better. Even in sunny two-season California, September always feels especially promising.

In spite of my ugly misadventures with medication, I'd been able to stick to my original plan for tenure—to write and publish enough papers that I could "stockpile" in case I had to take time off for illness. I'd already published several law journal articles on competency to refuse treatment, and the paper I'd written in George Mahl's Freud class at Yale came out in a psychoanalytic journal. I'd also completed my first paper on the criminal responsibility of individuals with multiple personality disorder, and had begun to sketch out several more exploring MPD and the law. For obvious reasons, psychoanalysis and the law had become my main area of interest and academic research.

Certain faculty members at USC's medical school had noticed my published work, and I was gratified and flattered when I was offered an academic appointment there. I happily accepted, but felt that I needed to leave my MDDA support group—the med school appointment was in the psychiatry department, and I couldn't risk my illness being somehow exposed, certainly not before I'd achieved tenure. I called Steve Wizner at Yale and told him that I'd risen above my life-long status as patient and become a colleague to an entire medical school. "I've infiltrated the enemy!" I said. The sound of his laughter was gratifying.

chapter twenty-one

THINGS WITH KAPLAN were not going well. No matter what I did or said, I tested his patience. For example, I'd had a physical, during which the physician found a thyroid nodule which needed to be biopsied. Subsequently, an endocrinologist examined me and said I probably had Marfan syndrome, a genetic connective-tissue disease with a life expectancy in women of about forty-five (in recent years, that's been revised upward, to mid-sixties). At the time, I was thirty-seven. I was devastated, and wild with anxiety.

So I did what I always do—found articles referencing Marfan, frantically read them all, and saw myself on every page. I certainly had a lot of the physical characteristics: tall and thin, highly flexible in my joints, with a fast heartbeat and a brain bleed. I was doomed, I just knew it. My demise was imminent.

"Lincoln had Marfan," I wailed to Steve.

"But that's not what he died of, Elyn. Come on, get a grip. Just don't go to the theater."

Kaplan wasted no time in letting me know that he thought the whole thing was baloney, and dismissed it out of hand. "The doctor's hearing zebras when he should be hearing horses," he said.

"He's an expert," I protested. "A full professor at UCLA. And he said he'd be 'surprised' if I didn't have Marfan. Why aren't you taking this more seriously?"

The results of the intensive medical workup showed that I did not, in fact, have Marfan syndrome. That didn't stop my psychosis from bleeding in around the edges of my life for the next several days. I had to admit it: I was a full-fledged hypochondriac. My body had betrayed me so many times in the past, why did Kaplan expect me to behave as though it would never do so again?

And then one day soon after, I retreated to a familiar theme: "I've been thinking," I said. "Maybe if I were on an antianxiety medicine, I could get off the antipsychotic medication."

Kaplan blew a gasket. "I've repeatedly told you that you'll need to stay on meds the rest of your life, that trying to get off them keeps you stuck in the same place—going from well to symptomatic to well again." He was practically shouting. "I'm just not going to put up with this anymore! If you reduce your meds again, you cannot stay in treatment with me. In fact, you can't even *talk* about reducing your meds and stay in treatment with me. This stops now."

The look on his face registered as pure anger. That was it. There'd be no more discussion of medication with Kaplan. The issue was off the table.

Steve agreed with him. As far as he was concerned, after the last episode, the data were in. "When you lower your meds, your judgment is compromised," he said. "Every time, you go into the downward spiral, one bad decision after another, none of them in your best interests. It's . . . tiring. Aren't you tired of it, too?"

Oh, God, yes, I was tired—tired of being alone, tired of flailing away, tired of beating my head against the wall. For so many years, I'd resisted the "crutch" of the meds—to use them meant I was weak of will, weak of character. But now I began to question my own absoluteness. For instance, if I'd had a broken leg and a crutch was required, I'd have used it without ever thinking twice. Was my brain not worth tending to at least as much as my leg? The fact was, I had a condition that required medicine. If I didn't use it, I got sick; if I used it, I got better. I don't know why I had to keep learning that the hard way, but I did.

A friend used the riptide analogy: You get sucked in, and your first instinct is to fight it. The harder you fight, the more energy you spend. But the simple truth is, a riptide is stronger than you; you cannot outmuscle it, and if you continue to try (if you exercise, as I continually did, "maladaptive stubbornness"), you drown. The simple lesson (as California surfers learn over and over every year) is to stop fighting and go with it. Save your strength, stop fighting, and the riptide itself will quickly propel you out of harm's way, into calmer waters. At that point, if you've preserved your energy, you can make it back to shore on your own. But first, you have to give in.

As exasperating and frightening as my years-long process of tinkering with my meds was for my friends and physicians, I understand now that it was hugely important for me to do it; it was a necessary stage of development that I needed to go through to become my full-fledged self. It was the only way I could come to terms with the illness.

So I vowed I'd take my Navane and do no more experimenting. What happened next was a pleasant surprise: Almost immediately, I actually felt quite good. Once again, I'd learned that it wasn't my stubbornness or discipline that kept the demons at bay; it was the medicine. I knew the demons were there; every single day, they found ways to remind me, however subtle those reminders were. But nevertheless, they were *behind the door*, and it was firmly closed, at least for now. And besides, I decided that there were other, better, more interesting parts of my life worth tending.

I'd met someone, a nice someone. His name was David and he was a microbiologist—and he seemed to like me. He asked me out on an actual date, my first since law school. The first date went well. The second date went OK. Soon, though, he was beginning to press me to be sexual. I wasn't ready for that with him, or with anyone, and things continued, but not easily. After a while, instead of being fun, being with David was tense, and tension was the last thing I wanted.

We stopped dating, but remain good friends to this day. He is kind and smart and funny, and someone whose friendship I cherish. Ending the relationship was right, but it made me sad. Not because I was no longer romantic with David, but because of a bigger question: Was there anyone out there for me? Many of my female colleagues had put their personal lives on hold while they pursued educations and careers, but lately, it seemed, many of them were finding partners, falling in love, having children—living the kind of life I could only imagine. I watched movies in which people met and fell in love, and sat there feeling as though I'd come from another planet. *Damn it, I want that.* Intimacy, and love, and trust, and the touch of someone's arm around my shoulders, someone's hand in mine. The Lady of the Charts was quiet these days, and Professor Saks was humming along just fine. So what were we going to do about Elyn?

The more I explored multiple personality disorder, the more intrigued with it I became, and since the MPD article had been well received, I thought I'd try my hand at writing a book about it. As part of the preparation, I needed to get up to speed on the clinical presentation of the disorder. So I went to a local hospital once a week for several months, and there I met with people actually diagnosed with and being treated for MPD.

The first young woman I spoke with was completely lovely—high-spirited, charming, and committed to therapy and to getting better. She'd recently married, she told me, but only after a two-year engagement, during which her then-fiancé, at his insistence, proposed to and got the consent of each of her alternate personalities!

I also watched a hundred hours of videos of patients being administered a diagnostic instrument called the *Structured Clinical Interview for Dissociative Disorders (SCID-D)*. Even though a good case can be made that MPD is overdiagnosed—and sometimes created by the treaters themselves—it seemed utterly clear to me from the evidence on those tapes that MPD was a genuine phenomenon.

Oddly (but happily), being in the hospital and watching patients being interviewed on the *SCID-D* did not get me all stirred up, nor did it awaken any of my demons. I didn't have much in common with these patients, although I observed a few who obviously had MPD and completely denied it (now *that* behavior I was intimately familiar with). Watching the process really opened my eyes to some commonalities shared by most mental illnesses; it turns out that we all overlap with one another a little bit.

I did have a very funny telephone conversation with one of my nephews while I was working on the MPD book. He was about ten at the time, and asked what I was doing in my office that day.

"Writing a book about multiple personalities," I told him.

"What is that?" he asked.

Oh dear, I thought; *how do I get out of this one?* "Well, some people think they have lots of other people inside themselves," I said. "And if one of those other people does something wrong, should all of the people have to go to jail?"

He mulled that over a bit, we chatted a little more, and then we said good-bye.

A few days later, my brother called. "What have you been telling this kid?" he asked, and he didn't sound very happy with me. "He was misbehaving the other day, and his mom told him to stop it. He just wouldn't settle down, and finally she asked, 'What on earth is wrong with you today!' And he told her, 'I didn't do anything, it was someone else inside of me!' "

In the fall of my fifth year at USC, I submitted my tenure packet: five long articles, four shorter articles, and a lengthy book proposal. Ed and Michael were both very encouraging. A subcommittee of three would read my work and send it out to a dozen or so reviewers; when the reviews came back, the subcommittee would meet and then vote; then it would go before the entire tenured faculty of the law school. The faculty would be given a ballot and a week to return the ballot to the dean's office. The ballot would decide whether I would be made professor.

The year went by quietly, even smoothly. I taught class and I wrote. I spent time with friends. I visited Steve in Ann Arbor, where he was finishing up his doctorate in clinical psychology. I stayed on my medication, on a dose Kaplan found acceptable. Although there were no more dates, someone else did catch my eye, a librarian in the law library. He was blond and attractive, in an open, unprepossessing way—flannel shirts, a ponytail. He wasn't as intense as many students; he wasn't as businesslike as many faculty. He was someplace in between, and seemed calmly at home there. His name was Will, I discovered. He'd been around awhile. He made furniture and gardened in his spare time, somebody told me. After a time or two, he smiled when he saw me. It was a very nice smile. *Well*, I thought. I might have blushed. I'm pretty sure I blushed.

.   .   .

I'd once complained to Kaplan that at lunch earlier that day, I'd been the most senior person at the table and I didn't much like it.

"Oh," he said. "You mean you're a duckling who doesn't want to become a duck!" I told some of my friends this story. Getting tenure around USC then became known as "becoming a duck."

The tenure ballots went out from the dean's office on a Friday in February, four-and-a-half years after I had arrived at USC Law School. A full week passed. The following Friday I sat in my office—*somebody knock, please*. Or call me. Or e-mail me. Or send a carrier pigeon through the window. Something, anything. Midway through that afternoon, the phone finally rang. Shaking, I answered it.

"Congratulations, Professor Saks," replied our dean.

Professor Saks. I'd made it; I was a tenured professor at the University of Southern California Gould School of Law. I'd become a duck at last. A colleague gave me a Mighty Ducks T-shirt to show for it.

At which point, I did what by now had become predictable: I became psychotic. Change, good or bad, is never my best thing. "A jumbo jet can sail smoothly through strong and gusty currents," says Steve. "But a small plane bounces in a small breeze." Mine was a very small plane; getting tenure was a big, albeit pleasant, wind, and for a few weeks, it threatened to blow me right over.

That night, my colleagues took me out to dinner to celebrate. I didn't want to disturb them with the news that beings in the sky were using my brain to spread death and destruction across the earth— that would have put a damper on the evening (not to mention making them second-guess their votes). I talked to Kaplan, willingly went up on my meds, and bounced around for a while, while the demons danced at the edge of every room I was in. Then everything settled back down again. The Lady of the Charts withdrew; Professor Saks had tenure. Time to turn my attention back to the most needy member of the trio, Elyn.

"With tenure," Kaplan told me, "the central issue in one's life moves from survival to desire."

OK, I'd survived. Now, then—what did I desire?

It had taken five years to learn how to use my time with Kaplan well. At first, I'd brought my psychosis into our sessions, as I'd done with Mrs. Jones and White. In the meantime, I worked to keep my symptoms out of view from all but a few of my LA friends—even with them, I shared my psychotic thoughts sparingly, or when I was at my worst and simply couldn't help myself. But with Kaplan, I could let my guard down, much the way one would rest on a shady bench during a long, uphill walk.

But as he'd stated over and over, Kaplan had come to believe that I'd grown too comfortable on that bench, and he finally issued an ultimatum: I couldn't sit there any longer. Filling our hours with nothing other than my psychotic ramblings was no longer an option. Instead, we'd talk about the life I wanted, and how my illness had so often gotten in the way of my having it.

It was a hard line for Kaplan to take, and at first I was frightened. If I couldn't bring my psychosis into that room, where could I bring it? But he helped me through it; he'd interrupt the ramblings, stop them, and then redirect my thoughts—to my teaching, my students, my writing, my friends. Less and less, our sessions revolved around psychosis; more and more, they were about my "real" life. By our sixth year together—the year following my tenure—the Lady of the Charts made only sporadic cameo appearances and no longer held center stage. It was time to take care of other things.

For the most part, schizophrenia is an illness that strikes young people, in their late teens and early- to mid-twenties—a time when we're supposed to be learning to make friends, keep them, and navigate our way through the world. But schizophrenia can knock you out of the loop for as long as three or four years—and for some, forever. In fact, as far as we've progressed in research and treatment, recent statistics indicate that only one in five people with schizophrenia can ever be expected to live independently and hold a job.

Dropping in and out of your own life (for psychotic breaks, or treatment in a hospital) isn't like getting off a train at one stop and later getting back on at another. Even if you can get back on (and the odds are not in your favor), you're lonely there. The people you boarded with originally are far, far ahead of you, and now you're stuck playing catch-up.

A key part of forming a friendship is sharing personal histories, which can be a precarious rite when you're schizophrenic. The gaps in your life—how do you explain them? You can always make up stories, but beginning a friendship with a lie about your life doesn't feel very good. Or you can say nothing about how you've spent the last few years, which strikes people as odd. Or you can choose to tell them about your illness, and find out the hard way that most people aren't ready to hear about it. Mental illness comes with stigma attached to it, and that stigma can set off a negative reaction, even from the nicest people, with good intentions and kind hearts. Even for many of these people, those with mental illness are *other;* they're not like "us."

Sometime late in my fifth year at USC, I was on my way to dinner with an administrator at the law school and telling her about an article I was writing, on the right to refuse psychiatric medication.

"I'm afraid of mentally ill people," Leslie said. "They can be violent and end up hurting lots of people."

Somewhat taken aback, I patiently explained what the research told us. "The vast majority of mentally ill people are no more dangerous than anyone else," I said, "and less prone to violence than many."

"I don't know," Leslie said. "I can't help believing that they're capable of who knows what. Maybe I'm prejudiced. I mean, I've never known anyone who had a mental illness."

I smiled mischievously and said, "You mean you've never known anyone you *knew* had a mental illness."

Leslie returned a mock look of nervousness and shot back, "Could you please take me to my own car now?" We both laughed.

"Crazy people" don't make the evening news for successfully managing their lives; we only hear about them when something horrible happens. The woman who drowned her kids; the man who parked his car on the train track in order to kill himself, but jumped out and watched people on the oncoming train die in the collision instead. The man who shot John Lennon; the man who shot President Reagan. John Nash, the Nobel Prize–winning mathematician whose life was told in the film *A Beautiful Mind,* is the exception that proves the rule.

There's a powerful urge in each of us to talk about our traumas. "A psychotic episode is like experiencing trauma," Steve says. I think Steve's right when he talks about psychosis as being like a trauma. Psychosis does traumatize you, in much the same way that ducking gunfire in a war zone or having a terrible car crash traumatizes you. And the best way to take away the power of trauma is to talk about what happened.

If and when they can, people who have been traumatized will tell what happened to them, over and over. The telling and retelling may become tedious for friends, but it's healthy and important, and good friends encourage it. With psychosis, however, you must carefully balance the urge to tell with the inevitable consequences of telling. Revealing your truth, even to someone you've come to know and trust, brings its own complications. People with schizophrenia—people like me—read the papers and watch the evening news. We see how the

illness is portrayed and how a friend-in-the making is likely to per-
ceive us, once they hear the truth. We move forward with great caution because we must. We'd have to be . . . well, crazy to do
otherwise.

To bring this point home, fast-forward to September 11, 2001.
Steve called me early in the morning from Washington, D.C., to tell
me about the horrific attacks on New York City and the Pentagon. It
was three hours earlier in Los Angeles. He knew I'd still be in bed,
and he wanted me to hear the news as gently as possible, rather than
be blindsided by a blaring clock radio or someone in the school parking lot.

That day, I had an early morning appointment with Kaplan; it
was still too early for him to have heard the news. I started the session in a high emotional state, talking about how the nation was under siege by terrorists and thousands of people were dead or dying.
Carefully, Kaplan began to steer the conversation in another
direction—at which point it was announced on the loudspeaker system that we needed to evacuate the building. Until that moment, I
am convinced Kaplan believed I was in the middle of a psychotic
episode.

Aside from those two years of isolation in Oxford, I'd managed
against the odds to make and hang onto some good friends, who'd
stayed in touch, loyal and loving. But my romantic life, such as it was,
wasn't. I could count on the fingers of one hand the number of dates
I'd had since freshman year at Vanderbilt. I had no clue about getting
someone's attention. I didn't know how to flirt; I didn't know how to
show someone that I was interested; I didn't know how to figure out if
he was interested in me. It was as though I'd been absent from class
when they were teaching "how to be a girl."

For instance, there was Will, the nice librarian. His smile when he saw me was genuine, but I wasn't sure how to respond to it. So, tentatively, I smiled back. The next time I came into the library, I swallowed, took a breath, and said, "Hi."

He said, "Hi" back.

OK, now what do I do? What's supposed to happen next? A few days pass. I go back to the library. I smile, he smiles. "Hi," I say. "Hi," he says.

"I, er, I heard you build furniture," I managed to stutter one day. "I'd really like to see it sometime. I barely have any furniture in my apartment at all; maybe that's because I mostly live in my office." *Shut up, Elyn. Just shut up.*

"Sure," he said. "I'd be happy to show you. It's not much, but I like doing it."

I nodded. "Oh, well, fine," I said. "Maybe we can have lunch sometime."

"OK, great," he said. "Let's do that."

I left the law school library as though the building were on fire.

Time went by, and eventually Will left his position at the law library. But we occasionally ran into each other, and one day my office phone rang.

"Hi," said a man's voice on the other end. "This is Will. From the library? I was wondering if you had a day free for lunch this week."

We went to a small Italian restaurant near campus, and I actually managed to swallow some food. He told me about the furniture, how much he loved working on it, how he used the best woods and stains, and took days and days to design and finish a piece. And he had a parrot that he'd trained and loved. And then there was gardening, too, a source of great pleasure to him. Entranced, I think I mostly nodded.

The next day, Will unexpectedly dropped by my office. In his hand, he held a beautiful multicolored bird feather. He walked over to my desk, took a piece of tape, and placed the feather on my computer. "It's from my parrot," he said, and then he left.

I sat there for a good fifteen minutes, transfixed by the feather. It was the only decoration in the office—I had no pictures, no drawings, no attempts at ambience or personal aesthetic; the walls were bare. I'd never had any decoration in any office I'd ever occupied; I didn't think I deserved it, it seemed fitting that there be nothing. And now here was the little feather. It practically glowed.

That night, I was talking on the phone to Kenny, my friend from Vanderbilt. "Kenny, I have a question. Do you think a guy who plucks a feather from his bird and gives it to me might actually like me?"

He laughed. "I don't know, Elyn, but one thing for sure—he likes you better than he likes his bird!"

A week or so later, I received a letter from Will—an actual letter, handwritten, and illustrated with hand-drawn flowers. He asked if I'd like to take a day to drive to the Antelope Valley Poppy Reserve near Lancaster, California. The poppies were in their spring bloom, and it was really beautiful there now. Would I like to go?

"Yes," I said when I called him. "I'd like that very much."

It was beautiful there, and it was wonderful to be off campus for a day. The flowers were glorious—acres and acres of poppies, in shades of deep blazing orange, and ivory, and butter yellow. But in spite of the sunshine overhead, it was chilly; spring was having a slow time getting started that year. Astonished at myself, I kept dropping hints that I was cold. I wanted this man's arm around me. I *really* wanted his arm around me. But it didn't happen.

At the end of the day, as he was dropping me off, Will hesitated a moment as we were saying good-bye. Then he leaned in and kissed me. It was a long, lingering kiss. It was great. It was fantastic. It was even better than getting an article published.

chapter twenty-two

ONCE, BACK IN New Haven, White had told me that achieving tenure frees up academics to do their best work. I hoped he was right, because there was so much out there I wanted to do, and now I had the freedom to do it. For the first time in years, I could take a breath, survey my landscape, and be excited about the future. In fact, I'd anticipated tenure in the way a teenager looks forward to a twenty-first birthday: Congratulations, it's official, you're now a grown-up! So—what's next?

When it came to my personal life, I was nurturing a fragile but growing hope for a relationship with Will. Our early times together were tentative and sweet; he was gentle and kind, and more than anything else, he was fun. In spite of having what I think is a pretty good sense of humor, I hadn't had much fun since I became ill. Whenever I was out someplace and heard people laughing together, I'd turn toward the sound in much the same way a flower turns to the sun. To laugh, to tease; not to be afraid of saying or doing something stupid or clumsy, because even if you did, you'd be loved anyway, and you'd always know it. What might it be like, to be completely at home in one's life, and not be alone? To walk across campus and see the one I love coming toward me, and to think, *There he is—that's my person?*

I wanted that, and slowly I began to believe that it actually might happen. I hadn't told Will about myself yet, although I knew I would have to; in fact, I wanted to. It would be a relief, but I wanted to be sure of myself when I did it. The question of intimacy was scary to me; the question of commitment possibly even scarier. I vowed to be realistic and patient, with both of us. This wasn't going to be simple, I knew that, but there was no hurry. We agreed to take our time and figure things out as we went along.

In the meanwhile, Will brought flowers to me at work, and he made me a cake for my birthday. I'd barely figured out which buttons to punch on the microwave in my apartment (let alone how the oven worked), but Will not only knew how to cook, he loved to do it—and actually produced a homemade coconut cake to celebrate the day I was born! It was delicious, and I was amazed—how did I luck into this? I wondered.

And, once again, Will added something sweet to the décor in my formerly bare office—a snapshot of me from our Lancaster trip, looking out over a wide field of brilliant orange poppies. He'd even given it a caption: "Persephone calls forth the flowers of spring to brighten a winter weary world."

If Steve's friendship had made me feel human, Will was making me feel like a woman.

The direction of my professional life was changing as well. Everything up until now had been carefully calculated toward tenure. Most of my published work concerned the legal status of people with severely compromised mental states, as I examined the relationship between mental illness and law in the context of important medical decisions, like con-

senting to surgery or refusing psychiatric medications. I was interested
in the ethical dimensions of psychiatric research, and initially focused
on the issue of capacity in that context. In fact, in collaboration with
colleagues at University of California, San Diego, School of Medicine,
I developed an instrument to measure such capacity, which we then
used to study patients with psychosis. (I was touched and honored when
I was offered an adjunct professor of psychiatry position at the UCSD
School of Medicine.) Maybe an objective critic could have criticized
me for tackling subjects too close to home. On the other hand, who better? I'd been drugged against my will, I'd been held in restraints,
screaming and pleading to be released. This wasn't an academic exercise for me; it was about my life.

However, once tenure was safely accomplished, I wondered if
maybe it was time to explore something a little different. I wondered—
if the Career Fairy were to grant me one perfect wish, what might that
be? The answer was immediate and obvious: I wanted psychoanalytic
training.

Freud and his teachings had always fascinated me, even in high
school. For a while in college, I'd even thought of getting psychoanalytic training. But that was before I got sick. Afterward, I didn't give it
much thought. My yearlong Freud class at Yale resulted in my article
on the Schreber case, so I didn't feel like a complete novice. I knew I
didn't want to change careers—I loved my job at USC (and I still do,
every single day). But when I reflected on the work I'd already done
professionally (and the simultaneous personal journey I'd been on), it
just seemed obvious to me what my next step should be.

Law is based on a theory of personhood; that is, the concept of
someone who can make choices and suffer consequences, and who
understands the threat of sanction. The doctrine of informed consent (indeed, most of American political theory) presumes that we are
not just subjects to be directed, but rather autonomous beings capable of making independent decisions. And for me, psychoanalysis

provides the most interesting route to understanding what that truly means, because psychoanalysis asks fundamental questions: Why do people do what they do? When can people be held responsible for their actions? Is unconscious motivation relevant to responsibility? And what renders a person *not* capable of making choices?

I wanted to know how and why psychoanalysis had worked for me. I wanted to know what was in my analysts' minds when they treated me. I wanted to experience being on the other side of the couch. And if possible, I wanted to find a way to give back—to use what I'd learned and experienced, combined with professional training, to perhaps help someone else the way I'd been helped.

However, I wasn't certain if my illness (no matter how well controlled) could even allow for such a thing. As time passed, and my life was less tumultuous, and my work (and relationship) with Kaplan became more satisfactory, I carefully lifted the idea out of the little box I'd put it away in so long before, and took another good look at it. After all, I'd managed to accomplish a lot of things I wasn't supposed to. Why couldn't psychoanalytic training be one more challenge to add to that list?

The first time I mentioned the possibility of being admitted to the Los Angeles Psychoanalytic Society and Institute (LAPSI) to Kaplan, his response was negative. Out of the question. Perhaps even inappropriate. Besides, my own history might be cause for rejection, and we both knew what my emotional response to that rejection might be. Nevertheless, we just kept talking about it, and slowly Kaplan's position softened. Maybe . . . maybe, just maybe, it might work.

Encouraged by his change of attitude, I called LAPSI's director of admissions, asking if I might meet with him. Fortunately, my professional credentials kept him on the phone, and he agreed to meet with me for lunch, where we talked about my prospects for admission to the program. He asked about my reasons for seeking psychoanalytic training, about my academic work to date, and about my experiences with psychoanalytic treatment. He did not, however, specifically ask about my psychiatric history. Needless to say, in the absence of the question, I didn't volunteer the information. As we finished our coffee, he encouraged me to apply and hinted that if I did, I would likely be admitted.

Up until now, the decision to either disclose or withhold information about my illness had always been primarily about me protecting me—that is, not allowing anything to get in the way of completing my education, doing serious work, and belonging to a respected profession. I knew full well that the stigma that travels with mental illness could trip me up one of these days, but I certainly wasn't going to collaborate in my own "demise" if I could help it. Even Congress recognized the potential for the damage, when it passed the Americans with Disabilities Act, which prohibits employers (and schools) from even asking about a psychiatric history.

Now, however, the issue was more complicated than my own goals and ambitions. If I had the opportunity to treat patients, would my illness put them at risk? Would my delusional periods, however brief, make it difficult for me to know what (and who) was real? Kaplan suggested that the more important questions were: Did I have the capacity to know when I was in trouble? Did I have the judgment to know when I was impaired? And did I have the integrity to take protective steps? Both Kaplan and I believed that I did.

So, on the application for admission, I dutifully sent up a red flag that I had psychological problems—referring to a "turbulent period" in my earlier life that "spurred my interest in issues of mental health." I decided I would not say anything more unless someone asked. In other words, although I didn't straight-out lie, I did deliberately withhold information that someone else might have thought was vitally important.

Through years of trial and error, I'd learned to manage myself and the way I appeared to others, as anyone with a chronic illness or disability attempts to do in order to be out in the world. In any case, I knew there would probably never be a time when I would not be in treatment myself, which in and of itself would be an effective fail-safe. That's not to say the ethical issue was clear-cut; it wasn't. And it isn't. It's complex, perhaps even controversial, and always will be. But I have never come to these decisions—to teach, to go to the Institute, to treat clients—in a vacuum. I discussed the issues involved in my training extensively with both White and Kaplan.

Happily, LAPSI seemed much more interested in my talents and training than in my "turbulent period," and in my sixth year in California, I became a first-year candidate at the Los Angeles Psychoanalytic Society and Institute. As I prepared to begin training to become a psychoanalyst, I marveled at the confluence of events that had brought me here: While medication had kept me alive, it had been psychoanalysis that had helped me find a life worth living.

We met as a class the night before our classes actually began—a small group of five people who knew they'd see one another every week for the next four years (six, for those of us who decided to pursue doctorates).

Unlike most other big changes in my life, this one came accompanied by very little stress; I was excited, and completely certain that it was the right place to be. Happily, I had the support of my law school colleagues and dean; a few colleagues had even offered the opinion that what I was doing was "cool." In many ways, I felt like my whole journey had led me here—between the Institute and USC, I felt like I now had the best of at least two worlds. In fact, I felt so at home in that first gathering that I made a quip about how we'd all be staunch rivals, then quickly said, "Just kidding!"

"Oh, no, you're not!" someone retorted with a laugh, and that was my introduction to Alicia. (When I relayed this to Kaplan the next day, he said, "There should be a sign on that door: 'No Smoking and No Interpretations!'") Now in her seventies, Alicia looks like she's barely in her fifties—fit, energetic, completely engaged in her life. I love to hear the story of how her dad gave her boxing gloves when she was just three, telling her, "Never let anyone take you down!" The word "feisty" is probably overused these days, but in this case, it fits.

Alicia lost her husband to cancer some months before I met her. She managed to turn that sorrow into a kind of wisdom about the human condition—it's no accident that both of her daughters are physicians and that she's a gifted clinician herself.

Janet's some years older than I; she's bright and funny, married (with children and grandchildren) to a man who has his own private practice, too. She specializes in addiction and eating disorders, and it was easy, early on, for me to talk to her about my own illness. I was amazed to learn that she'd been in analysis with someone who actually knew my Mrs. Jones; I like small-world coincidences like that.

For much of my life, I'd thought of myself as a shy, ungainly person, turned in on myself by my illness and with my books. I knew that time and circumstance had changed my outer life, but I wasn't truly aware that my inner life had changed as well—that instant friendships were not only possible for me, but could become precious and lifelong. Alicia brought that lesson home, and right beside her in that same class was Janet. As many gifts as LAPSI has given me in the past few years, these two women were the most unexpected and ultimately the most precious.

Our group met on Wednesday mornings, for two classes, two hours apiece. The building, attractive and ivy-covered, has four seminar rooms in a row; in an interesting exercise in "concreteness," you move up the row for each year you complete—first room for first year, second for second year, etc. On the very first day, I suggested we have lunch together after class, and thereafter we always did, at a casual Japanese restaurant right across the street. We all quickly became close enough that we often saw one another on weekends for dinner or a movie as well.

Our classes ranged from historical to theoretical to clinical; there was an "early Freud" class, one on "object relations," some on technique, and presentations of continuing cases. All the psychoanalytic schools were represented—classical, self-psychological, Kleinian. As in all teaching/learning situations, some of the teachers were terrific; others couldn't have gotten the lesson across if their very lives had depended on it. Since I'd incurred more than a few bruises discovering how hard it is to teach, I withheld judgment; it's not as though there was ever a shortage of knowledge in the place.

Because these classes were small and often quite intense due to the subject matter, it was conventional wisdom that inevitable conflicts might arise among classmates. One evening at a dinner, the dean made some comment to this effect.

"Our group's never had to go through that," I said. "It's amazing how well we all get along!"

"I know," said the dean drolly, "and we're all very suspicious about that!"

After I was far enough into my training to actually begin treating people—in the late part of my first year of classes—I saw patients for several years while under close supervision. I found the work challenging yet rewarding. It is hard to understand analysis fully without the experience of being on the "other side of the couch." I do not intend to continue with clinical work, since analysts are supposed to be "anonymous" to their patients and this book will complicate that.

The longer I was working with everyone at the Institute, the more I came to believe that it was important (to all of us) that I tell them about my illness; I eventually went to Jean, the head of the Institute's "progression committee" (which monitors your progress and allows you to pass from grade to grade and case to case) and started to give her the details.

"Wait, wait," she said, and my heart sank for a split second. *I'm out, I'm out.* But that wasn't it at all. "Do you mind if I take notes?" she asked. "Because this is surprising!" She became my advisor that day, and both she and the committee have remained supportive and positive about my work. Although my clinical work may have to stay in abeyance for now, I've already made significant progress on my Ph.D. dissertation—the subject is "informed consent to psychoanalysis." LAPSI recently merged with the Southern California Psychoanalytic Institute, and we're now called the New Center for Psychoanalysis.

Kaplan, of course, followed my progress very closely; obviously, it provided much grist for our psychoanalytic mill. Psychoanalytic candidates usually have plenty of beefs with their institutes, he told me, "but you seem like a happy camper there."

"That's exactly what I am," I said. "A very happy camper."

It's worth noting that Steve and I did far more than talk about my crises in our frequent phone calls; we often worked, and very hard. He'd been an adept, creative, and endlessly patient coach on my restraints article, and also collaborated with me on *Jekyll on Trial: Multiple Personality Disorder and Criminal Law,* published by New York University Press in 1997 to positive reviews.

From Michigan, Steve had moved on to Harvard, where he took a position as chief psychologist at the day hospital unit of the Massachusetts Mental Health Center, working with patients much like those who'd lived at the halfway house in New Haven. Increasingly, his primary interest had turned to ethics, and he was named a faculty fellow at Harvard's Center for Ethics and the Professions. He also took a position at Harvard Medical School, in the Division of Medical Ethics, and would eventually become the Director of Ethics at the American Psychological Association, in Washington, D.C. In spite of being on different coasts, our friendship had only grown stronger. We talked often, wrote papers together, saw each other at professional meetings or whenever I traveled east to visit my family.

It is interesting that (and in spite of his collaboration) Steve disagreed with the key tenet of my MPD book—that someone with multiple personality disorder whose alter commits a crime should be found not guilty by reason of insanity because innocent alter personalities should not be punished. ("Better to let ten guilty people go free . . .") Steve believed that the "total person" should not be absolved of responsibility. He asked if I minded if he wrote an article in which he'd essentially debate my argument. Laughing, I said, "Go ahead!" Once his paper was published, we appeared on *Dateline NBC* together to argue our opposing legal positions.

Steve's friendship, support, and intellectual companionship have taken me on some interesting journeys over the years, but this was a first. It was high-intensity, somewhat stressful, and on some level a little surreal. They interviewed us for four or five hours, but ultimately used about three minutes. *Crossfire* it wasn't. We were credibly professional, reasonably lucid, and didn't exchange personal barbs, although at a couple of points, Steve did say, "There you go again." I guess I could have commented on his need for a haircut, but then he might have teased me for buying a new blue suit for the occasion. It's a tricky business, debating an old friend who knows you as well as Steve knows me—and in fact, it belatedly occurs to me now that Steve was entirely capable of arguing *both* sides of the question, and I could have comfortably stayed home with Will.

Like every medication, Navane (which I'd been taking for a dozen years) has side effects. Some are dangerous, such as neuroleptic malignant syndrome, a potentially lethal condition in which the medication literally becomes toxic to your system; others are extremely unsightly and uncomfortable, such as TD. And then there's the sedative effect, the grogginess, which I combated with ample vats of black coffee.

In women, one common side effect of Navane is an elevated level of prolactin, the hormone that induces milk production for newborns. Thirteen is a normal prolactin level. Most women on antipsychotic medication go up to 30 or 40. I was consistently running 130 to 140. There's reason to believe (although the research is not without controversy) that breast cancer is associated with an elevated level of prolactin. My gynecologist agreed that elevated prolactin was a risk factor for me, at which point I told Kaplan I wanted to consider other medications.

He suggested Zyprexa, one of a new class of antipsychotic medications that showed great promise and had come on the market only recently. Despite the good things I'd heard, I was wary of new drugs and would have liked to wait awhile, to see whether Zyprexa and its cousins would continue to be safe and effective. But a prolactin level of 130–140 convinced me that now was the time to make the change, and I began to take Zyprexa in place of Navane.

The change was fast and dramatic. First, the side effects were much less than with Navane. Instead of being groggy or feeling tired, I felt alert and rested, energetic in a way I hadn't felt in a long time—so long, in fact, that I'd almost forgotten what those good feelings were like. On the other hand, I quickly gained a lot of weight—thirty pounds. However, in recent years I'd been quite thin, so aside from the dismay I felt at suddenly tight waistbands, I just decided I'd have to find a way to exercise more and get that number down a little.

The clinical result was, not to overstate it, like daylight dawning after a long night—I could see the world in a way I'd never seen it before. While Navane had helped keep my psychosis "tamed," I'd always had to remain vigilant. The psychotic thoughts were always present, and I often experienced "breakthrough symptoms"—fleeting psychotic thoughts—many times each day. With Zyprexa, though, I shut that door and, for the first time in years, it stayed shut. I could take a break, go off duty, relax a little. I couldn't deceive myself—the illness was still there—but it wasn't pushing me around as much as it once did. Finally, I could focus on the task at hand, unencumbered by the threat of lurking demons.

The most profound effect of the new drug was to convince me, once and for all, that I actually had a real illness. For twenty years, I'd struggled with that acceptance, coming right up to it on some days, backing away from it on most others. The clarity that Zyprexa gave me knocked down my last remaining argument.

In spite of my intelligence and education, in spite of all the doctors and the psychotic breaks and the hospitalizations and the lessons so searingly learned, I'd nevertheless managed to hold on to the belief that basically, there was nothing unusual about my thoughts. Everyone's mind contained the chaos that mine did, it's just that others were all much better at managing it than I was. All people believed there were malevolent forces controlling them, putting thoughts into their heads, taking thoughts out, and using their brains to kill whole populations—it's just that other people didn't *say* so. My problem, I thought, had less to do with my mind than it had to do with my lack of social graces. I wasn't mentally ill. I was socially maladroit.

Of course, that wasn't true. Most other people did not have thoughts like mine. They weren't more disciplined about hushing their demons, they simply didn't have any (or at least none that might lead to a diagnosis of psychosis). Thanks to the new chemicals coursing through my body, I experienced long periods of time in which I lived as other people did—with no psychotic thinking at all. The Zyprexa did that.

There's no way to overstate what a thunderclap this revelation was to me. And with it, my final and most profound resistance to the idea I was mentally ill began to give way. Ironically, the more I accepted I had a mental illness, the less the illness defined me—at which point the riptide set me free.

Happily, I'd discovered that writing on subjects I knew well and that genuinely interested me—mental illness in various legal contexts—interested other people, too, including publishers and journal editors. *Refusing Care: Forced Treatment and the Rights of the Mentally Ill* was published in 2002 by the University of Chicago Press. The topics were ones close to my heart: civil commitment, right to refuse medication, restraints and seclusion. The book was well received, getting a good review in the *Times Literary Supplement* and an especially good one in the *New England Journal of Medicine*.

While I still found teaching stressful, I was well liked by students and had become particularly close to some, especially those who did research for me. While not "out" about my illness to my classes, the students knew I had a special empathy for the mentally ill. Not surprisingly, some students taking mental health law have personal issues of their own; one young woman brought me a note in the middle of class one day which read, "I'm suicidal," and I quickly got her to the student counseling service. Another student, an undergraduate, revealed to me that she had been incorrectly diagnosed, heavily medicated (with narcotics, not just the usual psychiatric medications), and hospitalized, at which point her therapist had seduced her. She believed that she'd been somehow programmed to commit suicide by a certain date. Being in my class, and being able to talk to me about her terrible experiences, she felt, had kept her from that.

I was able to refer her to another, ethical therapist who'd had a great deal of experience working with patients with her sorts of issues. The student instituted a case for disciplinary action against her earlier therapist. These days, I talk to her from time to time, and watch her progress with great pride. She has recently passed the bar exam. In her refusal to be dismissed or defeated, I can see a little of myself—and I like that.

chapter twenty-three

I WAS NEARLY forty years old, and for the very first time in my life, I was in love.

Even looking at that sentence now gives me a feeling of such astonishment and joy. I knew I cared for Will; I knew he cared for me. But it wasn't until we had a huge fight and made up afterward that I actually said the words. "You're the first person I've ever been in love with," I told him.

"That makes me very sad," he said, and took me in his arms.

As we'd pledged from the beginning, we'd taken our time getting to know each other well enough to relax into closeness, which then led to something deeper and more complex than any relationship I'd ever known. We decided to live together; he moved into my high-rise apartment, where we tried together to decipher the symbols on the fancy European stove that I'd never once tried to use.

And Will was a different kind of man than I'd ever known, too. Far from being "not much," the furniture he built was beautiful, each piece one of a kind, carefully and lovingly crafted by his own hands;

museum pieces, I thought. He'd made a garden lantern of hammered copper, with inset cut glass that reflected a blue green light much as the ocean did. He had a gigantic collection of music, all kinds, and a gigantic sound system as well. Gardening was a creative act; so was baking a chocolate cake, or a meringue or a torte. He had, in short, the curious, insatiable soul of an artist, and something in that soul had made a decision to care for me.

Kaplan had told me that often women feel like they don't have a choice in sex, and in our time together he helped me to understand that I did have choices—about when, and with whom, and under what circumstances. I knew all too well that my illness complicated things—it made certain risks much bigger than they might have been for someone else. Taking off your clothes can feel like taking off armor; revealing vulnerability feels dangerous. And even the sanest person has to admit that the physical experience of orgasm is disorienting, even somewhat hallucinogenic—for me, that letting-go, falling-through-space feeling hadn't always been good. When space looks suspiciously like an abyss, and "losing yourself " can equal psychosis, ceding control can be terrifying.

I'd been disappointed in sex enough over the years to know that the next time I took the risk of a physical relationship, I needed it to be about love. And while like every couple, Will and I had had our ups and downs, he knew intuitively how important this was to me, and when the time came it happened in the most tender and loving way. What happened between us there was everything I'd hoped it would be. I felt safe in his arms, and loved, and fulfilled. (And when I walked into the bathroom the next morning, there was a big toothpaste heart on the mirror, which sealed the deal.)

But still, there was one last truth for me to tell, and many months into our relationship, I still hadn't summoned up the courage to do it. How would he react? Would he be horrified, or disgusted? Would he physically recoil? Would he leave me? Over and over, I rehearsed the scene in my mind: "Will, you know I see an analyst, but actually, my mental health situation is a bit more complicated. I have a pretty serious mental illness . . . ." And then, by happenstance, the man got a little ahead of me.

One day, he handed me a magazine article. "There's something I want you to read," he said. The article was about Asperger's syndrome, a high-functioning form of autism. Will had underlined parts of it. "Some of this sounds like you, don't you think?"

"It does sound something like me," I said. "And that's because it is, sort of. Will, there's something I've wanted to tell you for a long time, but I've been afraid. Afraid of your reaction, afraid that you might leave me. I actually do have a serious mental illness, I've had it for years, and it's not ever going to go away." I carefully watched his face as I delivered the news. So far, I didn't see anything that alarmed me.

"Really?" he asked. "I sort of suspected that it was something like that, but I didn't want to ask. I figured you might get around to telling me at some point. What illness do you have, actually?"

"Schizophrenia," I said. "Do you know what that is? It's not split personality."

"I think I do," he said slowly. "It's when people get out of touch with reality. That's a bit scary to me. But it doesn't change how I feel about you. How often does it happen? Is there medication for it?"

"I still sometimes have episodes," I said. "And yes, there's medication, fairly effective medication. But I have transient symptoms sometimes. Different things can set me off. Stress, stuff like that."

"Will you tell me when it's happening to you?" he asked. "I want to know."

Interestingly, most people I've revealed my mental illness to—and this includes mental health professionals—have been surprised to learn the truth, or perhaps the extent of it. The fact that Will wasn't surprised, and said he'd suspected something all along, was very telling. Either he'd come to know me more intimately than anyone else, or he was more willing to be frank about what he suspected, or he'd read more into my quirkiness. "How did you know?" I asked him.

"Well, you've always been a bit more than minimally eccentric," he said gently. I could tell he was mulling over his words. "And you've got a lot of blank spaces. Culturally, I mean. Almost anything from about 1965 to 1980, if I make a reference to it, you give me a blank look. Almost like you'd been somewhere else during that time. A lot of baby boomer stuff just goes right by you, you know?"

Yes, I did know. He'd paid attention, he'd intuited something, and he was right. It's hard to explain now, but something in the way that he was completely present in the room that night—something in his body language, in his eyes, in his voice—told me that we'd stay together. He didn't flinch, he didn't laugh, and he didn't leave. Of course, he hadn't seen me be "floridly psychotic" yet, but I had a feeling that when that happened, he would stand his ground.

One night, I came home after having had dinner with someone who had presented a paper at our workshop series. "I'm really envious of her," I told Will.

"Why?" he asked.

"Well, she's got a great position at a great law school, is very bright, and has a happy marriage. What more could anyone ask?"

He went out of the room for about ten minutes, then came back in. "So, wait a minute," he said. "You mean being married is something good in your eyes? Something you would want?"

"Yes, absolutely." I thought my heart was going to flip itself right out onto the living room floor.

"So, then—do you want the two of us to get married?"

I didn't have to think about that for one more second. "Yes!"

And then the circus began, the one which is so familiar to engaged couples everywhere: The Arrangements. Months and months of The Arrangements. For a while, I dismissed it—it felt entangling, complicated; it gave me anxiety attacks, it gave me headaches. Where to have the ceremony, what kind of ceremony to have, when to have it, what to eat, what to drink, whom to invite—very quickly, it all seemed overwhelming. And then the air simply cleared. Yes, yes, I wanted *all* of it—the ceremony, the party, the celebration, the family members, the friends and colleagues, the public acknowledgment of our commitment to each other. I wanted the whole damn thing.

I called and told my parents what was going on, and when I asked my mother if she wanted to come west and help out with the preparations, she hesitated for a moment and then haltingly replied that it might be best if I took care of that end of things. I was stung for about a minute, then quickly decided that it was probably better that way. Will and I took over the job of wedding planners—and Will had claimed one job as his. "I'm going to make the cake," he declared.

A funny thing happened when we went to meet Rabbi Julie, who had agreed to perform the wedding ceremony. After driving about an hour deep into the San Fernando Valley, we finally arrived at her house. Ushering us into the foyer, her husband asked if we'd be so kind as to remove our shoes, so as not to dirty the white rug. We then spent about an hour with Rabbi Julie, retrieved our shoes, and drove the hour back home. As we were walking through the lobby of our apartment building, I looked down at my white Reeboks and asked Will, "Didn't I wear black Reeboks to the rabbi's?" I had actually managed to wear our rabbi's husband's shoes home!

Shortly after Will and I became engaged, we received some difficult news: My dear friend Alicia had been diagnosed with breast cancer.

The minute she'd heard about our engagement, Alicia had offered

to have the wedding at her house, in her shady, flower-strewn backyard. Now everything had turned upside down. How could I make all
these happy plans while Alicia was in the fight of her life? We'd find
another place to get married. Or no, wait, maybe we wouldn't get
married right now at all.

"Out of the question," she said. "This will be wonderful, to put together such a beautiful party. Come on, it's going to be fine, and it'll
give me something happy to look forward to!"

I looked at my calendar and realized it was time for me to get my
own mammogram. And there, events took another nasty detour. The
technician took slide after slide, and in between there seemed to be
some discussion going on in the other room. When Dr. Giuliano finally came in to tell me there were "anomalies" that were cause for
concern, I completely fell apart. All my defenses were swept away,
and the room flooded with psychosis.

"Fleeces and geeses and astronomical proportions with the people
growing tumors. It's a growth industry."

"What do you mean, Elyn?" Dr. Giuliano and nurse Becky Crane
said almost in unison.

"The tides have changed. There'll be nothing for it. There's the
drowners and the downers. One will never survive."

"Your friend Alicia is in the other office," said Giuliano. "Would it
help if you talked to her?"

Alicia knew I had a mental illness, but didn't know the details and
had certainly never seen me ill. When I went into the examination
room she was sitting in, I started babbling in a scared and anguished
way. Alicia responded with enormous kindness and comfort. "Oh,
sweetie, what's wrong?" she asked. "Now, now, everything's going to
be OK. No, your head isn't going to explode." She wrapped her arms
around me and held me tight. And I held on to her as well.

I had the biopsy the next day. The day after that, Will, Alicia, and
I went to get the results: I had breast cancer, too. There were some

large in situ regions (so-called DCIS—ductal carcinoma in situ) and a small microinvasive part. That meant that only a small part of the cancer had breached the boundaries of the ducts; the rest of the cancer had been contained. When Guiliano and Becky gave me the news, I lost my grip and started muttering again. Will had never seen me like this; months later, he finally confessed how freaked he'd been by what he'd seen.

Although the cancer was in a fairly early stage, I needed to have surgery, followed by weeks of radiation. The stress of it all overwhelmed me—once again, my little airplane had been swallowed by a gale. I'd learned to expect disaster around every corner—I guess I thought it was my fate—but Will is basically an optimist, and he calmly continued to behave as one.

Kaplan was out of town at the time, and I had been seeing his backup. The backup's daughter, I knew, had died in early adulthood from cancer. When I told him my diagnosis, tears came to his eyes, which touched me. When Kaplan returned, he saw me immediately, and let me know he'd be available whenever I needed him.

The initial intensity of fear and anguish gradually lessened, but for several days after the diagnosis, I could do little other than sit at home and listen to music while I tried to keep a grip on what was real. Will instinctively knew that I couldn't tolerate any other intimacy than being hugged. Later, he also, somehow, knew when I was ready again to be loved.

My parents came as soon as they could. Friends and colleagues rallied around as well. And many people sent flowers. When Steve arrived, he looked over my shoulder past our embrace, to my dining room table, and remarked on the many bouquets of flowers sitting there. When you have cancer, people send flowers; when you lose your mind, they don't.

There's nothing like a cancer diagnosis to focus the mind, even a frayed one. While I was undergoing radiation—five days a week for eight weeks—it was hard to think of anything other than where I was, what I was doing there, and why. I worried that my friends were unnerved to be around me; maybe I reminded them of their own mortality. There wasn't a pill for this—it was all a roll of the dice, and I prayed every day that the luck would swing my way.

I live on top of one of the world's largest earthquake epicenters, but I'm not afraid of earthquakes. I'm not afraid of automobile accidents, and I'm not afraid of being attacked or robbed when I'm on the way from my office back to my car in the dark of evening. But my health, my inconsistent body, scared me to death. How many times, I wondered, would I have to deal with the betrayal of this mass of nerves and blood vessels and muscle and skin? It made me wild with anxiety, even anger.

My dear friend Janet (from LAPSI) had once worked at a Los Angeles chapter of the Wellness Community, a support group for the benefit of cancer survivors that was founded in the mid-eighties (and became notable due to the visibility and participation of one of its earliest members, Gilda Radner). At Janet's strong recommendation, I decided to check it out. I couldn't have said what I needed when I first went there, but whatever it was, I found it.

The empathy between people who are fighting cancer is a powerful thing; there's strength in it, and solidarity, and an innate understanding that "well" people don't have, in spite of their best efforts. I made some very close, very dear friends in the Wellness Community. Inevitably, given the nature of what brought us all together, I also lost friends. Sometimes, I was asked if it wasn't more stressful to spend time with a roomful of people with cancer than it might have been to skip a meeting once in a while. But I needed to see them. There were people there far sicker than I, and people who'd been sicker longer, and they were living their daily lives with equanimity, dignity, and even humor. How could I deny myself the comfort and the teaching they so freely offered? And, as time passed and "new" people came in behind me, how could I not then turn around and share what I'd learned with them?

Battered but unbowed, Alicia and I (and our respective families) made it through our cancer battles. We were tired and shaky and a little ragged around the edges, but by God, we were going to throw a wedding!

For weeks in advance, Will baked cakes and tested recipes, and every few days there was another confection. Remember when you were a kid and said something like "Someday, when I grow up, I'm going to eat all the cake I want!"? Well, that's what we did, every night after work. A French cake, with beaten egg whites and ground nuts. A ginger-flavored one, with fresh raspberries. A creamy lemon one, which Will then switched to orange. Yes, we both agreed—that's the one! Happily, we then hired a caterer to prepare and serve the rest of the food. If Will had tackled anything beyond the cake, both the kitchen and our relationship would have been at risk.

He'd also been taking a computer animation course, and was about halfway through the "advanced editing" section of the class when he came up with an ingenious and very funny form of wedding invitation. It was a video, which opened with the theme music from *I Love Lucy,* the familiar typeface that the show always used, and a black-and-white scene in Lucy and Ricky Ricardo's living room— with Will and me appearing as Ricky and Lucy, complete with scripted dialogue. For the background, he'd done some "screen captures" from Nick at Nite, then matched the video frame by frame, substituting pictures of me and Will into the "portraits" of Lucy and Ricky on the living room wall. When he dropped the driving directions into the video, he used the theme music from the old *Route 66* TV series, and to end the invitation, he closed with the theme to the Jackie Gleason show. We sent out fifty copies all over the country. Not for me the heavy ivory bond paper from Tiffany's; no, this wedding was being announced with a contemporary cultural artifact!

We were married in June, on a beautiful sunny day. Janet and her husband Al, and Michael and Ed, from the law school, were my witnesses; Steve and Alicia were my people of honor. Afterward, Steve gave a loving and hilarious toast.

In spite of the free-form nature of the event, there was just enough tradition to fit my sense of what a proper wedding should be. My family was there. My brother, who had been struggling with a terrible phobia of flying for some time, managed to make the trip. It was the most generous gift he could have given me.

That's not to say the day was without a bump or two: Earlier that morning, after I'd had my hair done, Steve and I were out sitting in my car, talking quietly, away from the din of preparations. A serious question had been troubling me for hours, and finally I just had to ask it. "Will aliens be attending the reception?"

"No," he said calmly, and he reached out to hold my hand. "There won't be any aliens there, Elyn. Don't worry about that."

I needed to hear that reassurance from him, and having heard it, I happily went on with the day. It was as beautiful as I ever could have imagined, and it left me feeling quite fragile, as though a sudden noise or movement would blow the dream wide open. It was true, then: I was married, to the man I loved.

Will and I went on a honeymoon trip to France and England. There, we met up with old friends from my Oxford days—Patrick, Dinah, and Janet—and had great fun reminiscing. Janet was romantically involved with a nice American man, and her lovely daughter, Olivia, was now the age I had been when had I lived in Janet's house. Though many miles away, I had continued to love and value these people who'd stayed my constant friends, and I always believed that they felt the same about me. And now we could add Will to the mix. Will, my husband.

.   .   .

Within a few years, with two dozen articles and three books published, I was deemed deserving by the law school to receive an "endowed chair," one of the highest honors that a university bestows on
a faculty member. On a spring afternoon, with friends and family
gathered, the University of Southern California Law School named
me the Orrin B. Evans Professor of Law and Psychiatry and the
Behavioral Sciences. Ed McCaffery—my "classmate" and dear
friend—was similarly honored with his own chair. It wasn't hard to
remember our first days wandering the law school halls together, trying to figure out what we were supposed to be doing in order to be
successful, and half worried that any minute we'd be "discovered" as
poseurs. I was so happy that Ed and I were honored in this way at the
same time. In my acceptance speech, I even dared to make a small
joke, suggesting that perhaps a couch would've been more appropriate for me than a chair. Afterward, there was a lovely luncheon reception at the Town and Gown (often referred to as the "living room"
of the university), and that was followed by another party that my
family threw for me that night. It was a beautiful day, and a night full
of great fun and strong emotions. It seemed that I had come at last to
a time in my life when there were more good days than bad ones.

chapter twenty-four

THE HUMAN BRAIN comprises about 2 percent of a person's total body weight, but it consumes upward of 20 percent of that body's oxygen intake, and it controls 100 percent of that body's actions. So in terms of how much territory the brain occupies vs. how much power it wields—well, it is mightily powerful indeed. And as much as we've learned about the brain over time (especially in the last two decades), we're nowhere close to knowing everything. Each revelation opens the door to a new set of questions; each mystery solved leads to another mystery. For a research scientist whose primary focus is the brain, it must sometimes feel like the laboratory is more akin to a hall of mirrors; for me and my somewhat ad hoc exploration of the brain, it feels on some days like I'm walking on the edge of the Grand Canyon, constantly at risk of taking that one big wrong step. And always, just before I fall, comes the same question: How did I get here?

. . .

As successful as I'd been on the Zyprexa regimen, I had my usual concerns about side effects; after all, it was still a relatively new drug. And then there was the annoying weight gain, which I was having a hard time reversing. So once again I wondered about lowering the dosage. Could I do it, and, if so, how far could I take it and still be safe? When I discussed it with Kaplan, he agreed to go along with me this time, on one absolute condition: If, in his judgment, I was in trouble and he decided I needed to go back up on my dose, I'd do it, immediately—no bargaining, no equivocation.

"You have to promise me," he said firmly.

"OK," I agreed. "That sounds fair."

As I dropped my levels over the next few weeks, I faintly sensed the fog drifting in, the early signs of disorganization beginning. I gritted my teeth and concentrated on work. *I can adjust to it*, I thought. *It'll get better. Just wait.* I flew east for my tenth law school reunion (accompanied by the familiar horrors on the plane flight), and for most of the evening's program at Yale, I sat next to Steve and struggled with the urge to jump out of my chair and scream at the terrifying creatures hovering in the air around me.

When I returned home and reported in to Kaplan, he quickly invoked our pact: I needed go back to a regular, healthy dose of Zyprexa. We settled on my usual dose of forty milligrams, double the maximum dose recommended by the manufacturer but one that had worked well for me before.

Soon afterward, I went to San Francisco, where I was scheduled to present two papers at a weeklong conference on dissociative disorders. Evidently, the Zyprexa withdrawal had been rougher on my system than I knew, leaving me vulnerable and even a little frail. I began to feel "off" soon after I arrived at my hotel. Once again, I gritted my teeth and narrowed my focus to work and my obligations at the conference, hoping no one would suspect anything was wrong. But the delusions and the disorganization accelerated; I was coming apart at the seams. I called Kaplan.

"If you can, why don't you deliver your Saturday paper, as scheduled," he said, "and come back here. Then you can fly back up early Wednesday morning to deliver that one."

On some level, his suggestion made sense; I was never very good in unfamiliar territory, but maybe I could regain control once back in LA, in my own apartment or in the haven of my office. But as I mulled over Kaplan's suggestion, I decided that having to leave the conference would signal that I was a failure. Of the two scenarios— being sick vs. being a failure—I could more easily accept the first one. So I decided to stay.

At which point my sickness took a new, horrific turn. For some reason, I decided that Kaplan and Steve were imposters. They looked the same, they sounded the same, they were identical in every way to the originals—but they'd been replaced, by someone or something. Was it the work of alien beings? I had no way of knowing, but I was terrified.

Much later, I learned that what I was experiencing was called "Capgras syndrome." The scientific literature about Capgras likens the sensation it produces to the cult film *Invasion of the Body Snatchers*. In my mind, the people I so depended on were simply gone, and the two who remained were not who they said they were. Therefore, I could not trust either of them.

It was a struggle, but I delivered my Wednesday paper and fled back to Los Angeles, shaky and completely paranoid. In nearly ten years of treatment, I had never missed an appointment with Kaplan. Now I didn't go to my next two scheduled sessions, and didn't call him to tell him why. So he called me. "Elyn, you're not at your appointment. What's going on?"

I did not respond. *It's not him. Don't say a word, it's not him.*

"Elyn, what's happening?"

Nothing.

"I think it's important for you to come to your sessions," he said. "I expect you to be here tomorrow. Is there something I can do?"

"I know what's going on and who you are or are not," I said finally.

"That doesn't get us anywhere," he said. "Talk to me straight."

Nothing. No answer. *Because you are not you.*

"Okay, then, I'll see you tomorrow." And he hung up.

I did not attend our next session.

Steve, sensing that something was very wrong, was calling frequently. I didn't return any of his calls.

Will, of course, recognized that I was very agitated, but he didn't know why. "What's going on?" he asked.

"The two who call themselves Kaplan and Steve are imposters," I said. "The real ones are gone, and they've been replaced; the ones who are leaving messages on the answering machine are fake."

To his everlasting credit, Will stayed calm. I'd warned him that this might happen, and now it had. "Maybe I should call Steve," he said.

"I don't see the point, since Steve's not there anymore," I said. "But go ahead, if it will make you feel better." He thought it over for a while, then called Steve in the middle of the night. Steve awoke early to find the message on his machine and called back. As best he could, Will explained what was going on.

Steve began to call and leave messages for me on the machine ten, sometimes twelve times a day. I ignored them—because he wasn't Steve. And I got angry—because he was treating me like a recalcitrant child. In analysis, there's a term for this: infantilizing. How dare he, I thought, looking at the answering machine as though it had been manipulated by aliens as well. But of course, he was in an impossible situation.

I was frightened and isolated. Even though I somehow knew that

Will was the real Will, I found no comfort in that. I couldn't sleep, I couldn't work, and I couldn't make the connection between what was real and what wasn't.

The next day, after my third missed appointment with him, Kaplan called and insisted I go up on my Zyprexa. Although I knew in my soul that he wasn't really Kaplan, I paid attention to him, because I was just that desperate and miserable—and over the next several days, the delusion slowly passed.

If I was still harboring any hope that I would someday be free of the need to take antipsychotic medication, losing both Kaplan and Steve to my psychosis convinced me utterly.

This was Will's first major experience of me as wildly delusional. He didn't get too scared, he didn't go away, and he never treated me with anything less than kindness and tender care. Afterward, he did admit to being shaken to see me so disturbed and unhappy, and being frustrated at not being able to comfort me or calm me down. "But I still want you to tell me when you start to feel like that," he insisted. "I'm not much use if you don't let me know what's going on."

Sometimes, even now, when I'm going into an episode, I don't tell him—not to keep secrets, but so as not to burden him. Nevertheless, he almost always knows. He can tell from my silence—or a certain kind of silence. It's a gift to have someone know me so well.

Dr. Kaplan and I had done years of good work together—thirteen years, to be precise. And I'd accomplished many successful life changes during that time. But he'd often been hard on me, and over time (Kaplan's many strengths and his humanity as an analyst notwithstanding) it had come to feel too hard, even punishing. He'd become more restrictive somehow—for example, he didn't want me moving around the office; he didn't want me to cover my face with my hands during our sessions, something I'd done with all my analysts to help me feel safe and contained. He kept saying that if things didn't change, he'd "terminate" me. "I'm going to terminate you." It was brutal to hear that, brutal for him to keep saying it. Was he doing it to elicit some kind of response from me? I didn't feel safe with him anymore; he was unpredictable, mercurial, even angry. Some days, I'd walk out of session feeling like I'd been beaten up.

"We're not getting anywhere," he'd say. "This isn't even therapy we're doing." It had been going badly for two years, he said—since around the time of my diagnosis with cancer and my engagement to Will. I'd been aware that we were somewhat at odds, but I'd thought it had only been for a couple of months.

And then Kaplan threatened to tell the Institute that I was no longer having analysis. My Institute (like most these days) is "non-reporting": that is, your analyst does not report on your progress (in analysis) to the Institute's Progression Committee. But he does report "analytic hours" to the Institute, so he holds in his hands a round-about way of signaling that you're not quite up to standard. Eventually, I told my advisor at the Institute what Kaplan had threatened to do. A few sessions later, he told me he no longer needed to do what he'd threatened. Still, I wasn't reassured. I couldn't jump through the right hoops for him, and finally, I couldn't handle it anymore. I decided I needed a consultation with someone who might be able to be objective, and scheduled an appointment with Dr. Freed, whom I had seen as Dr. Kaplan's backup once and whom I knew from the Institute.

"You've done years of good work with him, Elyn," Freed said. "Relationships go through transitions; perhaps this is one. You really should try to work it out with Kaplan. It's vital that you do."

I wasn't sure I could; I wasn't sure I wanted to even try. "If we can't—if I can't—would you consent to be my analyst if I can't continue with Dr. Kaplan?"

He shook his head. "It's unethical for me to even discuss that with you, as long as you're in treatment with him. Go back and discuss this with him, Elyn. You need to come to a resolution."

I went to my office to draw up a plan, some kind of negotiation. What had to change, I wondered, in order for me to stay with Kaplan? I made a list: I needed him to stop saying we weren't getting anywhere. I needed him to stop threatening "termination." I needed a lessening of the physical restrictions. None of these seemed onerous. I told Kaplan I would need these things to change in order to keep working with him.

Kaplan flat-out refused to change a thing.

I was stunned. "I'm sorry," I said. "I guess that means we'll have to end our work together."

For the rest of that session, it was as though there were an EXIT sign hanging just over the door. Once we'd finished and I prepared to walk through that door, I turned back and looked at him. "Goodbye," I said. "Thanks for everything. I'll see you around." And then I saw Kaplan flinch.

I then called Dr. Freed and told him that I'd left Kaplan. I don't know what I might have done if Freed hadn't agreed to become my analyst, but he did.

A few days later, Kaplan called. "Where have you been?" he asked. "You've missed two scheduled appointments."

I took a deep breath. "I told you that I was terminating with you, and I meant it," I said. "I've transferred myself to Freed."

There as a moment of silence at the other end of the line. Of surprise? Of anger? "I think you need to come and speak with me about this," Kaplan said.

"No, I don't," I said, but I already felt myself starting to shake. I'd never been very good at confrontation. Maybe I'd moved too fast. Maybe I was wrong.

"We can negotiate the changes you asked for," Kaplan said. "In any case, this is too abrupt. If we're going to end our time, it should be with some resolution, some agreement."

I agreed to meet with him twice a week while we wrapped up; simultaneously, I met with Freed. Maybe it was overload, or the pain of the transition, but for the next four weeks, I spent every session with Kaplan weeping—which, in spite of being a fairly emotional person, I don't do. I'm just not a crier. But something about being in that room with him tore me up, every single session. I felt sad, and vulnerable; I was leaving someone important, some*thing* important, and what I felt was grief.

To his credit, Kaplan didn't use the time to try to coerce me into coming back, and when I told him I was indeed going to continue to see Freed, he told me Freed was a wonderful clinician and he wished me well. And then it was over.

Dr. Kaplan probably helped me more than anyone else in my life, and I love him today as much as I have ever loved anyone. For a long time, I carried inside me a palpable sense of loss. The decision to leave him was so awful, but I couldn't see any way around it; besides, it always felt like he'd made that decision first. By refusing to negotiate with me, by threatening me and pushing me, he had in fact fired me. He'd rejected me, he'd betrayed me. And why I didn't end up hospitalized as a result of the upheaval, I don't know to this day.

Yet even now, when I am in a bad way, the first thing I think of is to call Kaplan. In fact, I often call his answering machine still, just to hear his voice. But I don't leave a message. That time is over.

Dr. Freed is about sixty, I would guess, and kind-looking. Unlike Kaplan (who, like my father, has a very strong personality), Freed has a certain softness and gentleness about him. At the same time, he stands his ground. He doesn't pull his punches with me; he homes right in on what I'm feeling, and helps me to understand how I sometimes use my psychotic thoughts to avoid the ordinary bad feelings that everyone experiences—sadness, rage, garden-variety disappointment.

Freed also has more faith in the analytic process than I do; he even thinks I might be able to get off meds entirely someday. In addition, he tries to understand my psychotic thoughts as unconsciously motivated and meaningful (which of course they are). Sometimes, interpreting them, he refuses to discuss a diagnosis. "Schizophrenia is just a label," he says, "and it isn't helpful."

Both of these views stir me up quite profoundly. I spent years fighting the idea that I was schizophrenic and needed medication. Now that I acknowledge that I am and I do, he raises the possibility that things may not be so clear. I believe that Freed is, in part, trying to give me hope and, in part, not appreciating the very real biological component to my illness. His primary area of concern is the psychoanalytical side; because of this, he referred me to a psychopharmacologist, Dr. Gitlin—internationally known in his field—to manage the medicine-cabinet aspect of it. Gitlin believes that I will need to be on medication the rest of my life.

Recently I've had to change drugs again. Zyprexa became somewhat less reliable, and I started having a lot of "breakthrough" symptoms. Raising the dose wasn't an option; as it was, I was on twice the highest recommended dose. So Gitlin suggested clozapine, a drug usually prescribed to those who are, to some degree or another, treatment-resistant, and he put me on a hefty dose, six hundred milligrams. Clozapine's a cumbersome drug to use; at the beginning, it requires a weekly blood test to monitor side effects and watch for signs of agranulocytosis, a precipitous drop in one's white blood count that can be fatal. However, it works, and it works well; there are days now I feel almost guilty for feeling so good.

But that did not happen overnight. Indeed, transitions from one

drug to another can be difficult, as happened when I first started seeing Gitlin and we tried to switch meds. In short order I was very psychotic.

"Elyn, what's going on?"

"Are you the real Dr. Gitlin or the marionette Dr. Gitlin?"

"Why, I'm the real Dr. Gitlin," he said.

"That's just what the marionette would say."

Dr. Gitlin later told me he seriously considered hospitalizing me as
a result of this episode. Thankfully, instead of doing the easy thing,
he did the hard one, and waited me out.

So: Medication changes can set off psychosis, because the biochemical transition in my body from one drug to another can take
time. Abrupt change can set it off as well; that's why familiarity is my
touchstone. And stress—from outside sources, pressure, or events I
can't control—can have the effect of someone hitting the evil "start"
button that reignites my symptoms.

As had happened with the breast cancer diagnosis, a routine
checkup indicated there was a possibility that I had ovarian cancer.
And once again, quickly, reality receded and the devils came in.
There was a two-week wait before surgery; after surgery, I'd have to
wait another two weeks for final results. I'd heard that there was only
a 20 percent survival rate after three years with this kind of cancer. I
was desperately afraid, even sad; had I come this far, fought this hard,
only to be defeated again by my unreliable body?

Once again, the apartment filled with flowers; once again, Will
never wavered in his tenderness and his steadfast belief that all would
be well. My friends rallied around me; Steve came from Washington;
even someone I'd dated briefly at Yale—a psychiatrist and lawyer
who continues to be a good friend—came to see me and offer support. But my parents were among the missing.

Well, not technically; they were on the phone. My father did not
want to come and would not explain why. My mother said, with a no-

table lack of enthusiasm, "Maybe I can come for couple of days. And Dad will come if the diagnosis is a bad one."

My parents not coming to see me was a major blow. All my life, I'd idealized them, even though there were many complexities to our relationship. When I felt at death's door, and their first and last impulse was to stay where they were, I was crushed. I could no longer deny they're flawed (as are we all), and that sometimes they've deliberately chosen to be unavailable to me. Maybe that's part of their own coping mechanism; maybe it's that the disease itself is just too enormous for them. Or maybe it's a result of the signals I send them: I'm fine, I'm strong; I don't need you. I'm not sure; we've never really had that conversation.

It occurs to me that there are often two sets of trickery going on in my life. The illness—the entity—is always just off to the side, just barely out of my sight. But I know it's there. And it tries to trick me into believing this isn't the real Will, this isn't the real Steve, that reality isn't reality, that I can kill thousands of people with my thoughts, or that I'm profoundly evil and unworthy.

At the same time, I'm trying to trick the people around me. I'm OK, I'm functional, I'm fine. And maybe, sometimes, this determined effort to trick them tricks the illness itself. It's like one big con. Steve says he's never seen anyone who fights as I do. I don't consider myself a fighter (and I certainly don't come across as ferocious). But if he's right, then perhaps in my childhood, and in this push-pull with my parents, one can see not only the beginnings of my illness, but the seeds of my health and strength as well. If I'm a fighter, perhaps it's because that's who they taught me to be.

"Never mind," I said to my mother. "Don't come. We'll call you when it's over."

The final results were very good, although all the warning signs were there; as a result, I had a complete hysterectomy and oophorectomy (removal of ovaries). Unlike the sadness and loss that many women might feel after such an overwhelming procedure, what I felt was almost relief. The danger was gone. And since I'd long since come to terms with the reality that I—and Will and I—would never have children, I was at peace with it.

What is schizophrenia? In the United States, diagnoses are mostly made according to categories established by the American Psychiatric Association's *Diagnostic and Statistical Manual of Mental Disorders*. The *DSM* makes a rough distinction between disorders of *thought* and disorders of *mood*. Schizophrenia is an example of a disorder that affects thinking, and so it is referred to as a thought disorder. Bipolar disorder (what used to be called manic depression) is an example of a mood or "affective" disorder—a disorder that rests primarily in how one feels.

The *DSM* places schizophrenia among the thought disorders characterized by psychosis. Psychosis is broadly defined as being out of touch with reality—what one of my professors at Yale once referred to as "nuts."

Schizophrenia, the most severe of the psychotic disorders, seems to affect about one out of every hundred people. Some researchers think that it may actually be a whole set of diseases, not just a single disease, which would explain why people with the same diagnosis can seem so different from each other. In any case, whatever schizophrenia is, it's not "split personality," although the two are often confused by the public; the schizophrenic mind is not split, but shattered.

A common misunderstanding is that people with schizophrenia are wildly psychotic all the time. Most, like myself, are not. When I am symptomatic, I suffer from delusions and hallucinations, and my thinking becomes confused and disorganized. Though I do not hallucinate much—sometimes I see things, sometimes I hear things—I often become frankly delusional. The disorganized thinking I suffer is also a core feature of schizophrenia.

These symptoms are examples of "positive" symptoms of schizophrenia, i.e., things you have but don't want. Many people with schizophrenia also have "negative" symptoms, some sort of deficiency or lack, such as apathy and withdrawal, a profound "not caring," or perhaps more to the point, not caring about not caring. Save for my first few years at Oxford, I've been fortunate largely to escape the negative symptoms.

What's important in all of this is that I have a thought disorder. I am not someone whose illness consists primarily of having high and low moods. And that aspect of my illness—its cognitive nature—was central in my decision to write this book.

Many people who suffer from manic depression and depression lead full and rich lives: Journalists Mike Wallace and Jane Pauley, the writer William Styron, and the psychologist and writer Kay Redfield Jamison are just a few prominent examples. Famous historical figures may have suffered from mood disorders as well—Abraham Lincoln, Vincent Van Gogh, Virginia Woolf, and Samuel Johnson. Go to any support group of people with mood disorders and, with some understandable sense of pride, they will name their famous forebears and their contemporary heroes.

However, people with thought disorders do not keep a list of famous and successful people who share their problem. They can't, because there *is* no such list. Comparatively few schizophrenics lead happy and productive lives; those who do aren't in any hurry to tell the world about themselves.

That said, some people with a thought disorder accomplish great things before they become incapacitated by illness. John Nash, for example, received the Nobel Prize for discoveries he made early in his career. He then spent much of his ensuing adult life delusional, wandering the Princeton campus, drifting aimlessly in and out of the university library. In time, Nash (and his family and his doctors) built a support system sufficient for him to largely manage his disease and even "recover" from it, which was movingly captured in *A Beautiful Mind*.

However, a more typical example of the way people with a thought disorder find their way into the media is the tragic example of Michael Laudor. Like me, Laudor attended Yale Law School. In 1995, shortly after his graduation, the *New York Times* ran a story about Laudor, focusing on how someone with schizoaffective disorder managed to make it through arguably the finest law school in the country. Yale Law School, Laudor told the *Times*, was "the most supportive mental-health-care facility that exists in America." After graduation, he contracted to write a book about his life, his travails and his successes.

And then, in 1998, for some reason—no one is quite sure what set him off—Laudor went off his medication. When his pregnant fiancée tried to convince him that he needed both the meds and possibly even hospitalization, he stabbed her to death at their kitchen table.

I had been thinking for a long time about writing a book about my life when Laudor's story became public. I already had mixed feelings about putting everything down on paper. The heartbreaking story happening on the other side of the country only increased my ambivalence. Maybe coming out about my illness would change the way friends, colleagues, and students perceived me. Maybe, once they knew the truth, they'd see me as too fragile or too scary to trust as a professional colleague or an intimate. Maybe they'd believe that a tragic, violent breakdown was inevitable.

In the end, though, it was Laudor's story that convinced me to go ahead. The media frenzy that surrounded it only added to the mythology that fuels the stigma: that schizophrenics are violent and threatening. In truth, the large majority of schizophrenics never harm anyone; in fact, if and when they do, they're far more likely to harm themselves than anyone else.

Another reason I was compelled to write about my life was to give people hope: A mental illness diagnosis does not automatically sentence you to a bleak and painful life, devoid of pleasure or joy or accomplishment. I also wanted to dispel the myths held by many mental-health professionals themselves—that people with a significant thought disorder cannot live independently, cannot work at challenging jobs, cannot have true friendships, cannot be in meaningful, sexually satisfying love relationships, cannot lead lives of intellectual, spiritual, or emotional richness.

Medication has no doubt played a central role in helping me manage my psychosis, but what has allowed me to see the meaning in my struggles—to make sense of everything that happened before and during the course of my illness, and to mobilize what strengths I may possess into a rich and productive life—is talk therapy. People like me with a thought disorder are not supposed to benefit much from this kind of treatment, a talk therapy oriented toward insight and based upon a relationship. But I have. There may be a substitute for the human connection—for two people sitting together in a room, one of them with the freedom to speak her mind, knowing the other is paying careful and thoughtful attention—but I don't know what that substitute might be. It is, at the heart of things, a *relationship*, and for me it has been the key to every other relationship I hold precious. Often, I'm navigating my life through uncertain, even threatening, waters—I need the people in my life to tell me what's safe, what's real, and what's worth holding on to.

I write, then, because I know what it's like to be psychotic. And I know, better than most, how the law treats mental patients, the degradation of being tied to a bed against your will and force-fed medicine you didn't ask for and do not understand. I want to see that change, and now I actively write and speak out about the crying need for that change. I want to bring hope to those who suffer from schizophrenia, and understanding to those who do not.

I now have almost everything in life I could have wished for, but my illness took an enormous toll. I lost years of my life. I missed countless relationships—intimate friends, cherished lovers. I never had children. I never enjoyed the excitement of working in a high-powered law firm, with challenging cases and extremely hardworking and bright colleagues. Even now I can't travel the way I'd like to—spontaneously, for weeks at a time in a strange and new place. I can speak Spanish, but I can't go to Spain. My comfort limit for out-of-town trips, even with Will, is about four days. He threatens to make me a "virtual office" computer program so we can go away and yet I'll feel like I'm safely in my office at USC. Work is both my solace and my mirror—when I lose track of who I am, it is there on the page, to remind me; when I'm away from it, I lose my bearings.

For years, I'd seen my body as the place that I lived, and the real me was in my mind; the body was just the carrying case, and not a very dependable one—kind of dirty, animal-like, unreliable. Will has changed much of that for me, and so has surviving cancer. I'm more comfortable with my body lately, maybe even more possessive of it—but I'm wary at the same time. It has, after all, let me down more than a few times.

So I fight the lethargy that comes from being buried in books while on sedating drugs. Exercise has always provided a challenge—I've never taken to treadmills, or stationary exercise bikes; they bore me. And unlike most of California, I was certainly never a runner. So I roller skate. My parents started skating in Central Park years ago, and one time they asked me to come along; I thought they were maybe losing their grip a bit, but I went with them, and loved it, immediately. So now I roller skate and I take lessons—artistic skating, dancing, plus the basic steps and forms. For a while, I did it twice a week; now I can manage to protect the time for only one session a week, with a professional coach. It's focused, and disciplined, and predictable and invigorating. And most of the time, it's just plain fun.

Writing this book meant that I needed (and wanted) to start telling people I hadn't told already the truth about my illness. Some of these were quite close friends, but friends whom, for some reason or other, I'd been hesitant to disclose to before. For instance, one of my friends used to joke around about the mentally ill a lot; I thought he would look down on me when he heard the truth. Other friends were professional colleagues of fairly recent vintage, and I didn't want them to lose faith in my academic abilities.

My experience of revealing my illness to all these people has been eye-opening. Most people have been very accepting; many said they had no idea and were shocked. Did this happen long ago and was it not an issue now? One person, a law professor, revealed in turn that he struggled with bipolar disorder; with that revelation—together with our mutual support over the years—we have become close friends. Another friend, a psychiatrist, urged me to use a nom de plume when writing this book, but I thought that that would send the wrong message—that all of this was too awful to say out loud. She then said something that made me think: "But, Elyn, do you really want to become known as the schizophrenic with a job?" I was taken aback by her question. Is that who I am? Is that *only* who I am?

Ultimately, I decided that writing about myself could do more good than any academic article I'd ever pen. Why do it under a pseudonym if what I intended was to tell the truth? I don't want to be marginalized; I've fought against that all my life.

I needed to put two critical ideas together: that I could both be mentally ill and lead a rich and satisfying life. I needed to make peace with my demons, so I could stop spending all my energy fighting them. I needed to learn how to navigate my way through a career and relationships with a sometimes tenuous hold on what was real. I needed to understand what lay behind my terrible thoughts and feelings and how my psychosis served to protect me. Through years of hard and intense work, Mrs. Jones, White, Kaplan, and Freed had helped me find my way to a life worth living. My last two hospitalizations left me with "very poor" and "grave" prognoses. Those are the prognoses I would have lived out had I not had very skilled, very dedicated talk therapists—psychoanalysts—by my side.

I believe (at least I have no reason not to believe) that skills and talents are distributed among the mentally ill more or less as they are among the general population. Everyone has a niche. Of course, resources are heavily skewed against the mentally ill, and the majority never have a chance to realize anywhere near their potential. That said, I'd feel terrible to learn that anyone had read this book and said to a family member or friend, "She did it, so can you." I'm *not* saying that everyone with schizophrenia or a psychotic disorder can become a successful professional or academic; I'm an exception to a lot of rules, and I know that. But much of that is about the ticket I drew in the lottery: parents with resources, access to trained and talented professionals, and a frequently unattractive stubborn streak that's worked in my favor as often as it has against me.

My life today is not without its troubles. I have a major mental illness. I will never fully recover from schizophrenia. I will always need to be on antipsychotic medication and in talk therapy. I will always have good days and bad, and I still get sick.

But the treatment I have received has allowed me a life I consider wonderfully worth living. USC Law School is an ideal place for me to write and teach. I have smart and generous colleagues there who have nurtured me through difficult and trying times. I count the school's dean and associate dean as my good friends, and they have been kind to me. The school has supported me as I've ventured to work with other disciplines, psychiatry and psychology, and have found grants to do empirical research relevant to my legal scholarship. In 2004, I was awarded USC's Associate's Award for Creativity in Research, given to two professors each year—the highest honor the university bestows for scholarship. At the same time, my *Refusing Care* was honored with a USC Phi Kappa Phi Faculty Recognition Award. According to the administration, no one has ever won these two awards in a single year.

Recently my work life has gotten even better. Apart from the first few years teaching criminal law, I have always been a reasonably popular teacher. But over time (and it should have been going in the opposite direction), I began to find teaching more and more stressful. Blessed with a dean who has always tried to be supportive and accommodating, I was offered a new job: Associate Dean for Research. Instead of teaching, I now help colleagues obtain research grants. Of course I love most doing my own research, but given all the responsibilities one might have on a law faculty, helping my colleagues find support for their work is an excellent second best.

My studies to be a research psychoanalyst have also taken place in a rich environment and given me lively and interesting colleagues, many of whom have become my closest friends. I am actively involved in committee life at the psychoanalytic Institute. I still talk often—pretty much every day—with dear Steve, and I enjoy our work together. I am in love with and married to a kind and funny man who understands and accepts me and makes me feel like a woman. So—it's a good life, all in all.

Recently, however, a friend posed a question: If there were a pill that would instantly cure me, would I take it? The poet Rainer Maria Rilke was offered psychoanalysis. He declined, saying, "Don't take my devils away because my angels may flee too." I can understand that. Mania in manic depression has been described as a sometimes pleasurable high that brings with it feelings of omnipotence. But that's not the experience of schizophrenia, at least not for me. My psychosis is a waking nightmare, in which my demons are so terrifying that all my angels have already fled. So would I take the pill? In a heartbeat.

That said, I don't wish to be seen as regretting that I missed the life I could have had if I'd not been ill. Nor am I asking anyone for pity. What I rather wish to say is that the humanity we all share is more important than the mental illness we may not. With proper treatment, someone who is mentally ill can lead a full and rich life. What makes life wonderful—good friends, a satisfying job, loving relationships—is just as valuable for those of us who struggle with schizophrenia as for anyone else.

If you are a person with mental illness, the challenge is to find the life that's right for you. But in truth, isn't that the challenge for all of us, mentally ill or not? My good fortune is not that I've recovered from mental illness. I have not, nor will I ever. My good fortune lies in having found my life.

acknowledgments

Like My Life, this book is a collaborative effort, the result of the contributions of my many friends and colleagues.

In terms of the actual writing of the book, two people have played central roles. Through her writing, Larkin Warren helped bring the book to life, in a way that will allow me to "speak" to more people in these pages. Stephen Behnke, a gifted writer and my closest friend, knows me and my psychotic states—"spells," as Steve sometimes calls them when teasing me—better than anyone. Steve suggested many of the metaphors in the book to help convey the experience of my illness.

I wish to thank the publishing people who made this book happen: my agent, Jennifer Joel, and my editor, Leslie Wells. Each is brilliant at her job. It is their efforts that made *The Center Cannot Hold: My Journey Through Madness* possible.

I would also like to thank my publisher, Robert Miller, for coming up with a great title.

Other writers played a part in creating this book: Tristine Rainer, my initial "memoir" teacher; Samantha Dunn, teacher of two memoir writing classes; and Gladys Topkis, an editor friend who read and made comments on the manuscript. Many others have read and made suggestions on the manuscript. I thank especially Scott Altman, Judith Armstrong, Gregg Bloche, Catherine Broger, Dinah Cannell, Kenny Collins, Gerald Davison, Susan Estrich, Esther Fine, Susan Garet, Michael Gitlin, Janet Hall, James High, Lissy Jarvik, Dilip Jeste, Shannon Kelly, Stephanie Losi, Edward McCaffery, Alexander Meiklejohn, Thomas Morawetz, Stephen Morse, Michael Shapiro, David Shore, Larry Simon, Janet Smith, Matthew Spitzer, Philip Stimac, Nomi Stolzenberg, Randy Sturman, Carmelo Valone, Marlene Wagner, and June Wolf.

I would also like to thank those at USC who have helped me administratively, so I could devote myself to writing: my assistant, Keith Stevenson, and reference librarians Brian Raphael and Jessica Wimer.

Over the course of my university studies, certain people opened my mind. In retrospect, it was they who started me on the journey of using my mind to heal my mind. John Lachs, my philosophy professor at Vanderbilt, awakened me to the joys of thinking and learning. Joseph Goldstein and Jay Katz of Yale Law School underscored that lesson in the context of my interest in mental health. Stephen Wizner helped me put my ability to think in the service of helping underserved people, a lesson Steve has taught to generations of Yale law students, not just through his words but in how Steve lives his life. George Mahl gave me a course in Freud that was among the best classes I have ever taken and helped spur my interest in psychoanalytic training.

Friends are a group of people who make life worth living, and I have been blessed with many. Among my closest are: Russ Abbott, Scott Altman, Judith Armstrong, Meiram Bendat, Gregg Bloche, Catherine Broger, Dinah Cannell, Joel Chesler, Maria Chvirko, Kenny and Margie Collins, Paul Davis, Patrick Dennis, Esther Fine, Paul Forbath, Ronald and Susan Garet, Elizabeth Garrett, Thomas

Griffith, Janet Hall, Norah Heenan, Carrie Hempel, Joshua and Tamar Hoffs, Lissy Jarvik, Ehud Kamar, Ken Kress, Martin LeVay, Andrei Marmor, Edward McCaffery, Alexander Meiklejohn, Thomas Morawetz, Craig Parrish, Allan Rabinowitz, Noel Ragsdale, Daria Roithmayr, Catherine Sabatini, Sam Scheer, Jean Scott, Michael Shapiro, Larry Simon, David Slawson, Janet Smith, Edward Sokolnicki, Matthew Spitzer, Nomi Stolzenberg, Christopher and Ann Stone, Randy Sturman, Jennifer Urban, Robert Von Bargen, Catharine Wells, Richard Wittenborn, Stephen Wizner, John Young, and Mark and Martha Youngblood.

More generally, I wish to thank all of my colleagues on the USC Law faculty. You know who you are, and I deeply appreciate your friendship and support.

I have also developed good friends at the Wellness Community, a group for cancer survivors. Our group leader, Carla, has helped me and many others in our struggles, and I have forged close bonds with many in the group, including Alex, Ann, Bracha, Carl, Christina, Hiam, Janet, Julia, Margie, Mira, Sarah, Tracey, and Trudy. No one understands cancer better than other cancer patients, and my groupmates have often been inspirational to me.

My most important mentors at the New Center for Psychoanalysis have been Gerald Aronson, Helen Desmond, Maimon Leavitt, and Heiman Van Dam. They have helped me appreciate what psychoanalytic thinking tells us about the complexities in every human interaction.

My psychiatrists and therapists saved my life. I am enormously grateful to the psychiatrists who focused on the biological aspects of my illness, including Michael Gitlin and Stephen Marder. They have helped me manage in the face of horrible symptoms and have brought me to a place where I can most benefit from psychoanalysis. I do not name my four analysts (I use pseudonyms in the text), because doing so could complicate their relationships with past and current patients. I owe my success and well-being—a debt I can never truly repay—to the work in psychoanalysis we have done together.

I want to say a final word about those dearest to me. My parents and brothers gave me the love and support that allowed my life to proceed. I have kept things from them, for complicated reasons that have served all of our needs, but I couldn't love them more. Steve has been my colleague, my confidant, and my closest friend, the true witness of my struggles. Steve understands me as well as anyone and has given me the strength to go on many times. Will—well, what can I say about Will? He is my true love—he gives my life a meaning that I never thought possible. I go to bed every night and wake up every morning thinking how lucky I am to have found him.

From all of these people, and others too numerous to mention, I have gotten what I need to lead a life worth living. I hope that by writing this book I help others to take some of what they need to make their own lives a little better, too.